BEATING DIABETES

The First Complete Program Clinically

Proven to Dramatically Improve

Your Glucose Tolerance

David M. Nathan, M.D.

Linda M. Delahanty, M.S., R.D.

McGraw·Hill

New York   Chicago   San Francisco   Lisbon   London   Madrid   Mexico City
Milan   New Delhi   San Juan   Seoul   Singapore   Sydney   Toronto

Library of Congress Cataloging-in-Publication Data

Nathan, David M.
    Beating diabetes : the first complete program clinically proven to dramatically improve your glucose tolerance / by David M. Nathan and Linda M. Delahanty.—1st ed.
        p.   cm.
    ISBN 0-07-143831-9
     1. Diabetes—Popular works.   I. Delahanty, Linda M., RD, MS.   II. Title.
    RC660.4.N378   2005
    616.4′62—dc22   2005000997

1 2 3 4 5 6 7 8 9 0   DOC/DOC   0 9 8 7 6 5

ISBN 0-07-143831-9

Illustrations by Scott Leighton and Ed Wiederer

McGraw-Hill books are available at special quantity discounts to use as premiums and sales promotions, or for use in corporate training programs. For more information, please write to the Director of Special Sales, Professional Publishing, McGraw-Hill, Two Penn Plaza, New York, NY 10121-2298. Or contact your local bookstore.

The information contained in this book is intended to provide helpful and informative material on the subject addressed. It is not intended to serve as a replacement for professional medical advice. Any use of the information in this book is at the reader's discretion. The authors, publisher, and the President and Fellows of Harvard College specifically disclaim any and all liability arising directly or indirectly from the use or application of any information contained in this book. A health-care professional should be consulted regarding your specific situation.

This book is printed on acid-free paper.

To my brothers, Ed and Dan

David Nathan

For my husband, Paul, who supports me;

my sister Joanne who inspires me;

and my parents, John and Helen,

who would be so proud.

Linda Delahanty

Contents

Acknowledgments

We are grateful to Laurie Bissett, M.S., R.D., and Terry Michel, D.P.T., D.Sc., for sharing their expertise in preparing the chapters on popular weight loss programs and physical activity.

Anthony L. Komaroff, M.D., and Nancy Ferrari of Harvard Health Publications provided important guidance to make certain that our message was clear. Raquel Schott organized the editorial process, and Judith McCarthy, senior editor at McGraw-Hill, helped greatly in shaping the manuscript.

The clinical research that forms the basis of this book is the result of the collaborative effort of many investigators around the world. In particular, our colleagues in the Diabetes Prevention Program, the Look: AHEAD study, and the Diabetes Control and Complications Trial have not only advanced the cause of medical science, they have taught us. Finally, the heroes of this story are the research volunteers. Their selfless dedication to answering important medical questions reminds us of the very best qualities that distinguish us from other species.

Introduction

Like many diseases, diabetes is caused by our genes and our personal environment, which is created by our lifestyle. We cannot yet modify our genes, but we can modify our lifestyle. Here at Harvard and in medical centers around the world, we and many colleagues have conducted studies involving thousands of people who were at risk for developing diabetes or who had diabetes. That research proved that changes in lifestyle—changes that anyone can make—have enormous power both to prevent and to help treat diabetes.

That is why we wrote this book. We want to share the information from scientific studies with you so that you can make the best choices for your health, whether you have already been diagnosed with diabetes, have been told that you are at risk for it, or simply want to be as healthy as you can be. You are probably bombarded on a daily basis with advertisements, infomercials, and other advice regarding your health. Our message is based on the most up-to-date scientific data available.

Enormous changes in lifestyles have occurred in the past century. For much of the world's population, subsistence lifestyles, characterized by farming, hunting, and other occupations in which substantial energy had to be expended to obtain food— or the currency to obtain food—have given way to lifestyles in which little physical effort is needed to obtain nutrition. Farming, hunting, and fishing have been replaced by efficient mass production of food with near unlimited quantities available in most places in the world for little effort or expenditure of energy.

As machines and automation have improved, physical labor in factories and trades has been progressively replaced by white-collar jobs. Travel has been made increasingly effortless, threatening to make our feet vestigial organs, except for the need to operate the gas pedals of our cars.

Obviously, the industrial revolution and the technological-computer revolution that followed it have had spectacular benefits for much of the world. However, the changes in lifestyle accompanying these revolutions have a dark side that has spawned epidemics of obesity and diabetes. The consequences of these conditions, including the increasing occurrence of hypertension, abnormal lipid metabolism, and cardiovascular disease, have become the major health problems for much of the world's population in the twenty-first century. These chronic, degenerative diseases have replaced, to a great extent, the infectious diseases of the past two thousand years—such as tuberculosis, cholera, malaria, and the plague—as the major causes of illness and death in North America and Europe and, increasingly, in Asia, Africa, and South America. The pandemic of obesity, diabetes, and heart disease, based on changes in lifestyle, poses the greatest threat to our survival for the foreseeable future.

The major goals of this book are to provide you with a practical understanding of how today's typical lifestyle has led to these problems and to give you strategies that have been proved in clinical studies to improve health for people with diabetes or at risk for it. We will focus on practical changes you can make in how you shop for food, how you plan your meals and snacks, how you cook your food, and even how you look at eating, as well as changes in physical activity that have been shown to decrease weight and make a real difference in diabetes, obesity, and cardiovascular disease. In addition, we will discuss the complex interactions between lifestyle and diabetes, and the adjustments of lifestyle and medical treatment that should be made if you or someone you care about has type 1 or type 2 diabetes.

We have both spent our careers developing, studying, and teaching the lifestyle changes that are discussed here. We believe fervently that the program we offer works and can be one of the best things you can do to preserve and even improve your health. All of our recommendations are based on scientific evidence and practical experience and are the choices that are most likely to improve your prospects for long-term health.

The battle against the damaging effects of our current lifestyle is often framed as a cultural war against the manufacturers and sellers of processed foods, drive-through nutrition, all-you-can-eat buffets, supersized meals, and processed meals that are high in fat and calories. Similarly, television and computer games are often blamed for our lack of exercise.

There is a measure of truth to this. Marketing can be quite powerful. However, in the end, we are responsible for the lifestyle choices we make. In this book, we will provide you with proven strategies that you can use to prevent and help treat diabetes—specific approaches to shopping, cooking, eating, and activity and exercise. The strategies do not require superhuman willpower, an unreasonable amount of time, or more money. They require only that you make a conscious commitment to your health and to the health of your family.

CHAPTER 1

The Basics: Diabetes and Prediabetes and Why They Are on the Rise

The number of people suffering from type 2 diabetes and related conditions has skyrocketed over the past fifty years. And more and more people have blood-sugar levels that, while not high enough to qualify as diabetes, are too high for good health. This condition goes by the name glucose intolerance, or prediabetes.

If you have normal blood sugars or prediabetes, the program in this book will help you protect your health and perhaps stave off diabetes and its serious long-term complications completely. And if you already have type 2 diabetes, this program can help you take control of your condition, improve your blood-sugar levels, and perhaps enable you to cut back on some of your medications. What you're about to learn is a program for living. It isn't based on drastic changes or extreme recommendations for diet and exercise. It is about reversing lifestyle history.

This chapter will begin by explaining what diabetes is, how we normally handle the nutrients in our food, and how disturbances in metabolism can affect your overall health. Then we'll discuss why we're facing an epidemic of obesity, prediabetes and diabetes, and heart disease. When you understand how pivotal lifestyle is to these conditions, you'll understand how and why this program can make a difference.

Blood Sugar and Insulin: The Basics

You need to know a little about normal metabolism to understand how so many of us are developing prediabetes and then diabetes. Metabolism represents the body's processes that direct energy into storage, such as in fat, or into fueling normal growth, development, and physical activity. Carbohydrates (including complex starches and simple sugars), fat, and protein are the three nutrient groups in our diet that provide the energy and building blocks for metabolism and growth. Carbohydrates and fat provide most of the energy to keep our body's machinery working, including our muscles for locomotion and our vital organs such as brain, liver, heart, lungs, and kidneys.

Carbohydrates are broken down in the intestine into smaller sugars that can be absorbed into the circulation. (See Figure 1.1.) Sugar or glucose is then transported from the blood across the cell wall and into the cell where it is broken down further, providing a major source of energy. Alternatively, sugar may be stored in the liver or muscle as glycogen, which is a complex carbohydrate that serves as an energy reservoir in times of energy need. Fatty acids, a breakdown product of dietary fat, are the other major sources of energy. Like glucose, they may provide instant energy for cells or may be stored as fat for later energy release.

For sugar to gain entry to most cells, it must be carried across the cell wall by glucose transporters. This is where insulin first comes into play.

Insulin is a hormone, which means it is a protein that is made and secreted by specialized cells and then circulates in the bloodstream and affects other organs and their function. Insulin is made

FIGURE 1.1 Digestion

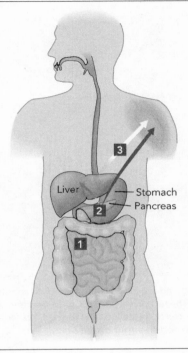

Food is broken into its building blocks, simple sugars from carbohydrates, fatty acids from fat, and amino acids from proteins, and then absorbed into the blood from the small intestine (1). The breakdown of the food groups is aided by chemicals secreted by the pancreas (2). The pancreas also releases insulin, which helps transport sugar, fatty acids, and amino acids into muscle, fat, and the liver (3).

in the pancreas, an organ located in the back of the abdomen. Most of the pancreas makes digestive chemicals that help break down nutrients from your food so that they can be absorbed in the intestine. The pancreas also contains small clusters of cells called "islets." Although different types of specialized cells are in the islets, the most important are the beta cells that make insulin.

These beta cells can sense the level of sugar in the blood, for example after a meal. When blood-sugar level starts to rise, the beta cells make and secrete insulin, which increases the transport of sugar into the cells and keeps the blood-sugar level from rising too high. But the work of insulin has only just started at that

FIGURE 1.2 Normal Glucose Absorption

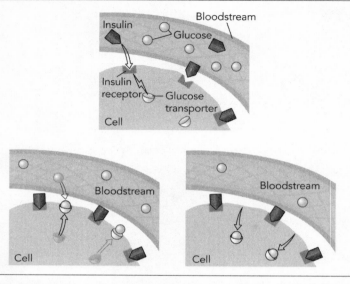

When insulin is present in adequate amounts, it binds to specialized receptors (like a key fitting into a lock). The receptor-insulin complex results in glucose transporters moving from inside the cell to the cell surface where it attaches to a glucose molecule and moves it from the bloodstream inside the cell.

point. Insulin also stimulates the processes in the cells that direct the storage of sugar as glycogen, the storage of fatty acids as fat, and the use of amino acids, the building blocks of proteins. In addition, insulin prevents protein breakdown, fat breakdown, and glycogen breakdown. Therefore, insulin directs the storage of energy and stimulates the building of tissue and growth. (See Figure 1.2.)

When blood-sugar levels fall, insulin production and secretion shut down and all of the processes are reversed: sugar is released from the storage depot instead of stored in muscle and liver; fat is broken down and fatty acids released; and proteins are broken down rather than synthesized. Insulin is like a traffic cop, directing nutrients into storage and growth. When insulin levels are low, the traffic moves in the opposite direction with energy released from its storage sites.

This is what happens in a healthy person. When something disrupts any part of this finely tuned system, there is trouble. Diabetes is by far the most common disease of abnormal metabolism.

Type 1 and Type 2 Diabetes

The two main forms of diabetes are called type 1 and type 2 diabetes. Although they have different causes and, to a great extent, affect different categories of people, they share three main features.

First, type 1 and type 2 diabetes are both characterized by metabolic abnormalities that include high levels of blood sugar in the circulation, as well as increased levels of other nutrient breakdown products that are released from their storage sites. See Table 1.1. Second, decreased insulin secretion or a decreased sensitivity to insulin action is the reason for these metabolic abnormalities. In the case of type 1 diabetes, the body makes no or very little insulin because the insulin-secreting islets have been harmed or destroyed. In type 2 diabetes, the body cannot meet the increased insulin demands brought on by a condition called insulin resistance.

TABLE 1.1 How We Diagnose Diabetes

Test	Diabetes* level	Prediabetes level
Fasting plasma glucose Plasma glucose (sugar) is measured after an overnight (8-hour) fast.	≥126 mg/dL	100–125 mg/dL
Oral glucose tolerance test After fasting overnight, the patient drinks a solution with 75 grams of glucose. Plasma glucose is measured 2 hours later.	≥200 mg/dL	140–199 mg/dL
Random plasma glucose** Plasma sugar is measured at any time of day	≥ 200 mg/dL	

*To make a diagnosis of diabetes, abnormal results should be confirmed with repeat testing.
**Diabetes can be diagnosed in the presence of typical symptoms.

Third, both types of diabetes can result in long-term complications that affect the small vessels of the eyes, kidneys, and nervous system. These complications are related to the high levels of blood sugar that are sustained over time and can result in serious damage such as blindness, kidney failure, foot ulcers and amputations, and the dysfunction of other organs. Both types of diabetes also substantially increase the risk of developing heart disease and stroke. In the short term, very high blood sugars, if not treated, can lead to severe dehydration and can cause confusion, coma, and even death.

Even with their shared features, the two types of diabetes are quite different in many respects. Type 1 diabetes characteristically occurs in children and young adults (it was once called *juvenile-onset* diabetes) and requires treatment with insulin for survival (type 1 also used to be called *insulin-dependent* diabetes). In type 1 diabetes, the body's immune system attacks the pancreas. This autoimmune attack destroys the beta cells, leaving them unable to make insulin.

The causes of type 1 diabetes are not fully understood. We don't know what triggers the immune system to start attacking the pancreas, although certain inherited genes can make you more vulnerable. However we do know that type 1 diabetes is not primarily caused by lifestyle, being overweight, or obesity; however, controlling body weight and exercising regularly are important parts of the treatment. Maintaining blood-sugar levels as close to the nondiabetic range as possible is critical to avoid long-term complications.

Type 2 Diabetes: The Twentieth- and Twenty-First-Century Epidemic

For years, type 2 diabetes was called *adult-onset* diabetes because it usually begins later in life. In recent years, however, as more children have become heavier at earlier ages, type 2 diabetes has increasingly been seen in teenagers and young adults. Of all people with diabetes, more than 90 percent have type 2 diabetes.

Unlike type 1 diabetes, the development of type 2 diabetes is strongly influenced by lifestyle.

There are two underlying causes of type 2 diabetes. One is the development of insulin resistance. This condition causes the tissues of the body to become less sensitive to the effects of insulin. As a result, sugar circulating in the blood does not leave the blood and enter the body's cells as easily. For the blood sugar to be lowered effectively and for the other "jobs" of insulin to be carried out, more insulin is required. The second cause of type 2 diabetes is the inability to increase insulin to cope with increased demand. Insulin resistance, decreased insulin secretion, or both can result in the development of type 2 diabetes.

Various factors contribute to insulin resistance: being over-weight, advancing age, a sedentary lifestyle, an inherited suscep-tibility, and certain hormonal conditions such as polycystic ovary syndrome. We don't completely understand why insulin resistance develops, and there is probably more than one explanation, but recent research suggests that fat cells produce chemicals that cause tissues to resist the effects of insulin. More fat cells, as in obesity, make more of these chemicals. As a result, sugar can't move into cells and begins to accumulate in the blood, especially after meals. The rising blood-sugar levels drive the beta cells to produce more and more insulin to help push the sugar into the cells where it is needed. And since rising blood-sugar levels also worsen insulin resistance, a vicious cycle begins.

An estimated forty million people in the United States have insulin resistance or prediabetes. They have minimally elevated sugar levels because the pancreas is able to keep making enough insulin. However, in 25 to 50 percent, the pancreas, after many years of overwork, slowly loses the ability to maintain these high levels of insulin. It can still make insulin, but not enough to keep blood-sugar levels in the normal range. Over time, blood-sugar levels drift up, resulting in diabetes.

Sometimes, the elevated blood-sugar levels lead to the usual symptoms of diabetes that patients with type 1 diabetes develop: frequent and excessive urination, increased thirst, fatigue, and weight loss. However, in many people who progress from prediabetes to type 2 diabetes, the rise in blood-sugar levels is insidious and may not cause any symptoms. This helps explain why as many as one-third of the people who have type 2 diabetes don't even know that they have it and why the diagnosis is often delayed by as much as nine to twelve years. It is important to identify blood-sugar problems early on so that you can begin a program to prevent diabetes or if you already have it so you can begin to take care of it and prevent its complications. As with type 1 diabetes, tight control of blood-sugar levels is required to prevent serious and even life-threatening complications.

Metabolic Syndrome: Diabetes Plus

Metabolic syndrome is a constellation of problems that often includes diabetes or prediabetes. What are the other conditions? Being overweight, especially when extra pounds accumulate around the midsection; having high or borderline-high blood pressure; having high triglyceride levels; and having low HDL (good) cholesterol. Specifically, you have metabolic syndrome if you have diabetes or prediabetes and two or more of the following:

- A large waist (forty inches or more for men and thirty-four inches or more for women)
- Borderline or high blood pressure (greater than or equal to 130/85 mmHg)
- A high level of triglycerides (greater than or equal to 150 mg/dL)
- Low HDL (under 40 mg/dL for men or under 50 mg/dL for women)

It's easy to overlook or brush aside the health implications of a few extra pounds. Or of blood pressure creeping toward the high end of the normal range. Or of slowly rising levels of blood fats. Ignoring the cluster, though, is a big mistake. Doctors and researchers think that the impact of the metabolic syndrome on health is more than the sum of its parts. Over the years, this collection of health risks has gone by many names. Besides the "deadly quartet," it has also been called syndrome X, insulin-resistance syndrome, diabesity, and the dysmetabolic syndrome.

Metabolic syndrome, although not as flashy or memorable as some of the other names, is the term used by most clinicians and researchers today.

Why Diabetes and Metabolic Syndrome Matter

The ultimate impact on health of type 2 diabetes and metabolic syndrome is through cardiovascular disease. The cluster of features associated with type 2 diabetes or the metabolic syndrome is a highly potent recipe for heart disease and stroke. People with type 2 diabetes or the metabolic syndrome have at least a two- to fivefold increased risk of cardiovascular disease. The relative risks are even higher in women with diabetes compared with their counterparts who are nondiabetic. In addition, in the United States, type 2 diabetes is the major cause of blindness, kidney failure, amputations, and neurological complications, such as impotence. Type 2 diabetes decreases life span by an average of seven to twelve years.

Why Type 2 Diabetes Is Becoming More Common

If all of human history was represented by a twenty-four-hour day, the nineteenth and twentieth centuries would be the last twelve minutes of that day. Yet in that blink of a geological eye, our lifestyle has changed more than in the previous hundred thousand years. The implications of our current environment are still playing out, but we are already seeing adaptations to our new industrialized lifestyle that aren't necessarily good. Simply put, we're moving our bodies less, eating more, and eating more of the wrong foods.

We're Moving Less: From Farm Worker to Couch Potato

The industrial revolution changed the type and amount of work we perform. Before the industrial revolution, most of us did labor-intensive, physically taxing work. Increasingly, machines have reduced the hard physical work we have to do. "I'm going to work" has a very different meaning now from the meaning it had one hundred years ago. Fewer and fewer of us perform physical labor, and more and more of us sit at desks for most of the day.

The clearest example of this shift in the work we do is in agriculture. In the 1700s, more than 90 percent of the U.S. workforce farmed to grow their own food. Two hundred years later, automated, mechanized manufacturing has reduced the number of people working on farms to about 1 percent of the workforce. Instead of farming, more people became factory workers, building the tractors and other farm equipment that would streamline farming, making it more efficient and a less physically taxing way of life. Not only was a smaller fraction of the population engaged in farming, but farming had changed. The hard-featured, gaunt farmer of the Grant Wood painting was replaced, at least to some extent, by an overweight farmer driving an air-conditioned combine and single-handedly harvesting many acres of corn or wheat in a day. Although the fraction of the population working as farmers in the United States has decreased by more than 90 percent since the founding of the nation, these farmers now raise enough food to feed much of the world.

Labor-saving devices—tractors, forklifts, assembly lines, riding mowers, snow blowers, vacuum cleaners, and paint sprayers— have made not only farming but all of our physical activities less demanding. Granted, these advances have left us with more time for leisure activity. But the vast majority of us are not playing more tag football, planting more tulip bulbs, or taking more walks around the block after dinner. Instead, we're watching television, playing video games, and surfing the Internet. Sedentary activities occupy far more hours of the day for most people than physical ones do.

A recent analysis of the National Human Activity Pattern Survey (NHAPS) paints a clear but startling picture of our culture. The NHAPS surveyed 7,515 adults between October 1992 and September 1994. Study volunteers were asked to record everything they did and for how long. Not surprisingly, people spent the most hours sleeping or napping (about eight hours per day on average). But during waking hours, the top six activities (based on the number of hours people spent doing them and energy burned) were driving a car, doing office work (filing, typing), watching TV or movies (at home or in a theater), taking care of children (feeding, bathing, dressing), doing activities while sitting quietly, and eating. On any given day, only 14 percent of the population spent any time performing leisure-time physical activity (for example, swimming or planned "exercise").

While activity levels vary from person to person, it's clear that our world discourages movement. In addition to changes in the workplace and at home, schools have scaled back physical education programs (daily participation in high school physical education classes dropped from 42 percent in 1991 to 29 percent in 1999). Americans spend more time at work, albeit in sedentary jobs, when compared to other developed countries, which puts the squeeze on time that could be spent in physical endeavors. And between 1990 and 2000 the number of people who commuted for more than thirty minutes per day increased from roughly 20 percent to nearly 34 percent. Even when we do have free time, we tend to use it passively. According to NHAPS, adults spend nearly three hours per day watching TV or a movie, and nearly an hour and a half each day on "activities performed by sitting quietly." As a culture, we're growing roots to the sofa.

We're Eating More than We Need to: From Famine to Buffets

Because of the mechanization of farming, food is more plentiful and more affordable than ever before. For example, fish production and the available supply of vegetables per capita have dou-

What Is a Calorie?

The terms *no carb*, *low carb*, *low fat*, and *high protein* have all but elbowed the word *calorie* out of our vocabulary. In fact, few people even know what it means. A calorie is a measure of heat and reflects energy quantity or expenditure. The amount of energy contained in food is expressed in calories. Similarly, the amount of heat given off by your body is expressed as calories expended or "burned." Using this common term for heat, or energy, allows us to calculate the balance between the amount of energy contained in food we eat and the amount of energy that we expend doing specific activities—or just lying around.

bled in the past thirty years, exceeding population growth. Despite the abundance of fresh produce, the fraction of total calories people derive from dietary fat and the consumption of saturated fat, both of which are associated with heart disease, remain highest in North America and Europe.

While the availability of large quantities of food is obviously not in itself a bad thing, it has set the stage—or the table—for overnutrition. That is, most of us take in more calories than we burn. Not only is there plenty to eat, but we don't have to expend much energy to obtain a meal. The farmer's lifestyle, where every calorie consumed was balanced by a similar expenditure of energy to grow the food, has all but disappeared.

In other words, it isn't just the fast-food burger joint that's the problem. Most of the inconvenience and much of the work required to obtain and prepare food have been reduced. Very few of us hunt or farm for our next meal. Even fewer have to build and maintain a fire to cook, pump water by hand, or even wash dishes by hand. Supermarkets have made grocery shopping easier. One-stop shopping often includes conveyor belts that deliver the food into the trunks of our cars (or home-delivery services that bring food right to our doors). Freezers with large storage capacity decrease the frequency of shopping, microwave cooking makes food preparation faster and easier, and dishwashers make cleaning up nearly effortless. Vending machines and convenience stores also make access to food incredibly easy and require virtually no expenditure of calories. We no longer have to work—meaning to perform physical labor—to obtain or prepare our food.

But that's only half of this story. According to the Centers for Disease Control and Prevention, Americans are eating more than ever (see Table 1.2). Where do these excess calories come from? It's not just what we eat but how much. Serving sizes have increased, both in the home and especially when eating out. Prepared foods such as Hungry-Man–sized TV dinners (a dangerous combination if ever there was one) and "single-serving" portions of prepared foods, such as soups, have almost doubled in size. Over the past twenty years, the size and caloric content of the average egg, bagel, muffin, preformed hamburger patty, and doughnut have grown by 20 to 50 percent. We have become accustomed to giant, economy-size packaging and portions.

On average, Americans eat one in three daily meals out of the home, and competition for customers has resulted in a virtual war to provide large quantities of relatively inexpensive food in fast-food and other restaurants. High-calorie meals abound in fast-food restaurants, an American invention of the 1950s. Hamburgers have become cheeseburgers, double cheeseburgers, double-bacon cheeseburgers, and "truck burgers" (with a fried egg on top). Steak restaurants offer sixteen- , twenty-four- , and even thirty-two-ounce steaks and prime ribs. A typical restau-

TABLE 1.2 Changes in Food Intake from 1971 to 2000

	1971	2000
Average daily calorie intake (men)	2,450	2,618
Average daily calorie intake (women)	1,542	1,877
Percentage of calories from carbohydrates (men)	42.4%	49.0%
Percentage of calories from carbohydrates (women)	45.4%	51.6%
Percentage of calories from fat (men)	36.9%	32.8%
Percentage of calories from fat (women)	36.1%	32.8%

rant prime rib provides 3,410 calories—2,200 of them (or 65 percent) from fat. That's nearly all the calories you would need to survive nicely for two days. All-you-can-eat buffets, pizzas with cheese injected into the crust that come with a pastry dessert as a freebie on the side, and ninety-six-ounce sodas (which exceed the volume of the normal human stomach) are but a few other examples. (See Table 1.3)

We're Eating the Wrong Foods

Not only are we eating too much food, but too many meals contain the wrong kinds of food. Processed, high-fat, low-fiber foods with refined sugars are inexpensive and easy to quickly grab almost anywhere. Unfortunately, they make up a large part of the American diet and are loaded with saturated and trans fats, both of which are associated with atherosclerosis and heart disease. Even single-serving packages of potato chips, nuts, and cheese crackers routinely have 250 to 400 calories with 35 to 50 percent derived from fat. On a recent four-hour cross-country flight, I was given a snack box that contained a 0.5-ounce bag of potato chips, 1.35 ounces of cheese crackers, a 0.5-ounce box of raisins, a 0.7-ounce package of cookies, and a

TABLE 1.3 What's in a Fast-Food Meal?

Fast-Food Meal	Calories	Fat (g)	Protein (g)	Carbs (g)
McDonald's hamburger, small fries, and 16-ounce Coke	690	24	18	103
2 slices Domino's pepperoni hand-tossed classic pizza and 2 Cinna Stix	824	32	28	106
Kentucky Fried Chicken Original Recipe chicken breast, side of potato salad, and 20-ounce Pepsi	860	28	42	119
Subway 6-inch turkey, roast beef, and ham sub, and 1-ounce bag of potato chips	470	16	26	62
Starbucks whole milk grande cappuccino (16 ounces) and blueberry muffin	530	27	13	62

chocolate bar. This totaled 500 calories—45 percent from fat (twenty-five grams of fat, six grams of which were saturated) and 48 percent (sixty grams) from carbohydrate. My total energy expenditure during the flight amounted to approximately 350 calories (I sat in my seat with no physical activity other than the "work" of changing the movie).

Many of us eat fast food at least several times a week. Table 1.3 gives you a hint of what you're really getting for your dollar.

How Our Lifestyle Has Made Us Vulnerable to Diabetes

In 1985, an estimated 30 million cases of diabetes existed world-wide. This number increased to 177 million in 2000 and is esti-mated to rise to at least 370 million by 2030, almost all from type 2 diabetes associated with aging, obesity, and inactivity. In the United States, the numbers of cases of diabetes and obesity have risen in parallel. Diabetes and prediabetes affect 18 million and almost 40 million persons, respectively, and the metabolic syn-drome affects almost 25 percent of the U.S. population.

It is all too easy to ascribe these alarming statistics to the increased numbers of the very obese and the very old. But only about 2.3 percent of the population is severely obese and only 3.3 percent of the population is older than eighty—small percentages. The major public health problem is not caused by very large or very old people. Most cases of diabetes and prediabetes are caused by the ever-increasing population that is overweight or only mod-estly obese. The fraction of the U.S. population in 2000 that was overweight (defined as a body mass index, or BMI, between 25 and 30) increased to almost 35 percent, and the fraction that was obese (BMI of 30 or greater) increased from 13 percent in 1960 to almost 31 percent in 2000. (See sidebar on measuring your BMI.) Thus, the fraction of the U.S. population that is either overweight or obese has risen to an astounding 65 percent.

Are You a Healthy Weight? Measuring Your BMI

Body mass index, or BMI, is a convenient measure of whether your weight is appropriate for your height. Because taller people will weigh more than shorter people, the calculation takes your weight (in kilograms), divides it by your height (in meters squared), and comes up with a measure in kg/m^2. The calculation can also be performed if you know your weight and height only in pounds and feet and inches, respectively (see Table 1.4).

The BMI provides a measure of weight for height; it does not provide a direct measure of obesity, meaning who has excess body fat. Nevertheless, for the vast majority of people, a high BMI (between 25 and 30 is defined as being overweight, and 30 or above is considered obese) is synonymous with having too much body fat. Rarely, bodybuilders and other trained athletes may have "excess" weight and a high BMI that is composed not of fat but of muscle. For most of us, this is not the case.

Estimating Your Body Mass Index (BMI)

You can use Table 1.4 to estimate your body mass index. First, select your weight (to the nearest ten pounds) in one of the

Industrialized Society Disease in the "Third World"

The changes in lifestyle in North America and Europe have occurred slowly over centuries, but today we can see those changes as in time-lapse "photography." Take for example the island of Nauru, in the Central Pacific. Until the 1950s, Nauru island lifestyle consisted of very limited subsistence farming as well as fishing. Diets were largely composed of fish, island vegetables, and plantains. The people were largely cut off from the outside world, and there was little in the way of industry.

Around 1960, investors recognized that Nauru's phosphate-rich soil held great financial potential as fertilizer. By 1976, the columns across the top. Then move your finger down the column until you come to the row that represents your height. Inside the square where your weight and height meet is a number that is an estimate of your BMI. For example, if you weigh 160 pounds and are five feet seven inches, your BMI is 25.

TABLE 1.4 Estimating Your BMI

Height	Weight (In Pounds)														
	100	110	120	130	140	150	160	170	180	190	200	210	220	230	240	250
5'0"	20	21	23	25	27	29	31	33	35	37	39	41	43	45	47	49
5'1"	19	21	23	25	26	28	30	32	34	36	38	40	42	43	45	47
5'2"	18	20	22	24	26	27	29	31	33	35	37	38	40	42	44	46
5'3"	18	19	21	23	25	27	28	30	32	34	35	37	39	41	43	44
5'4"	17	19	21	22	24	26	27	29	31	33	34	36	38	39	41	43
5'5"	17	18	20	22	23	25	27	28	30	32	33	35	37	38	40	42
5'6"	16	18	19	21	23	24	26	27	29	31	32	34	36	37	39	40
5'7"	16	17	19	20	22	23	25	27	28	30	31	33	34	36	38	39
5'8"	15	17	18	20	21	23	24	26	27	29	30	32	33	35	36	38
5'9"	15	16	18	19	21	22	24	25	27	28	30	31	32	34	35	37
5'10"	14	16	17	19	20	22	23	24	26	27	29	30	32	33	34	36
5'11"	14	15	17	18	20	21	22	24	25	26	27	28	30	32	33	35
6'0"	14	15	16	18	19	20	22	23	24	26	27	28	30	31	33	34
6'1"	13	15	16	17	18	20	21	22	24	25	26	28	29	30	32	33
6'2"	13	14	15	17	18	19	21	22	23	24	26	27	28	30	31	32
6'3"	12	14	15	16	17	19	20	21	22	24	25	26	27	29	30	31
6'4"	12	13	15	16	17	18	19	21	22	23	24	26	27	28	29	30

small population of Nauru was one of the wealthiest in the world. The toil of farming and fishing disappeared in a single generation. Motorbikes and cars replaced walking as the common mode of transportation, imported food was sold in the grocery stores, and electric appliances and televisions became commonplace.

The impact of this sudden and dramatic change in the lifestyle of the citizens of Nauru was profound. Before industrialization, obesity and diabetes were virtually unknown; however, by 1976, the average Nauruan was obese. The obesity and inactivity were a potent combination: 34.4 percent of the population had developed diabetes.

Lifestyle and Type 2 Diabetes

You can see now why lifestyle is so important in causing (and potentially preventing) type 2 diabetes. During the same time that our lifestyle has changed, type 2 diabetes has transformed from a disease that was barely recognized to one that affects 8 percent of the entire adult population, 13 percent of those older than forty, and 20 percent of those older than sixty-five. Being obese substantially increases the risk of developing diabetes, but even being a little bit overweight increases the chances of developing diabetes.

Similarly, our sedentary lifestyle, independent of obesity, increases the risk of developing type 2 diabetes. Inactivity leads to insulin resistance and prediabetes, both of which lead to type 2 diabetes. Some of the pernicious effects of inactivity are secondary to obesity, but inactivity also makes our muscles less sensitive to the effects of insulin.

In addition to advancing age, being overweight or obese, and inactivity, inheritance plays a large role in diabetes. Although all of the specific genes that underlie obesity, the metabolic syndrome, and diabetes have not been identified, it is clear that the risk of developing these conditions and diseases is inherited. But how can we explain the widespread inheritance of diseases, the effects of which are so devastating? How would Darwin explain the natural selection process that leads to diabetes? The widespread inheritance of risk for obesity, diabetes, and the insulin resistance that underlies much of type 2 diabetes does make sense according to a theory called the "thrifty gene hypothesis." Until just a few centuries ago, human beings lived in peril of famine. During times of famine, "thrifty" genes that decreased energy expenditure were highly advantageous to human survival: because the energy people took in was small, and because of difficulty in finding food, burning less energy protected people against starvation.

However, according to the thrifty gene hypothesis, genes that protect us during famine make us vulnerable when food is plentiful. An adaptive response has become maladaptive. Put another way, genes that protected our primate ancestors for nearly a million years have made our species vulnerable in the past few hundred years because, for most of us, food has become readily available and the need to do hard physical work has been reduced.

The consequences of this maladaptive response are profound. Obesity, diabetes, and metabolic syndrome—and the cardiovascular disease that accompanies them—represent the major public health problems not only in the Western world but increasingly in Asia, Africa, and South America. The inherited propensity to develop type 2 diabetes emerges when unhealthy lifestyle changes and obesity come into play. If a person with a genetic risk for type 2 diabetes doesn't become obese, the disease may never develop.

We cannot change our "thrifty" genes, but we can change our lifestyle. Moreover, there is now hard data—most notably from the multicenter Diabetes Prevention Program study—showing that lifestyle changes really work. You don't need to eat only certain types of foods or train for a marathon. Very simple changes that nearly anyone can make are clinically proven to protect against the metabolic syndrome, prediabetes, and diabetes. The rest of this book will tell you what those changes are and show you how to incorporate them into your life.

CHAPTER 2

Why We Gain Weight: The Arithmetic of Obesity

With more than 60 percent of the population either overweight or obese, weight gain is a problem that apparently affects most of us. The usual explanations for those extra few—or more—pounds range from, "The holidays killed my diet," to, "I couldn't get to the gym this week," to, "My scale must be broken."

However, there is a simple (yet somewhat painful) reason for weight gain: it's the calories!

We take in fuel in the form of food. The energy we extract from food fires our basic biological functions and provides the energy we need to work, play, think, and survive. But what happens when we take in more fuel than we use? In your car, unused gasoline sits in the tank until it's needed. In your body, unused fuel gets stored for future use as fat. Any imbalance between energy in and energy out results in weight gain or loss. This simple equation explains virtually all we need to understand about why we gain or lose weight.

How We Turn Food into Fuel

The tissues in your body don't know a corned beef sandwich from an apple. That's because all foods are digested and converted into their elements: sugars from carbohydrates, triglycerides and fatty acids from dietary fat, and amino acids from protein. These breakdown products travel in the bloodstream until they are either used for energy or growth or are stored. Some of the sugar that is not used immediately for energy can be squirreled away in the liver as a type of carbohydrate called glycogen. When the body needs energy, it reaches into these reservoirs. But liver glycogen stores are small and supply only enough energy to meet energy demands for six to eight hours.

The glycogen stored in muscle is another energy source, but it is available only to supply the exercising muscle and can't be used to provide energy for other organs. Protein, which is found in muscle, the heart, and the diaphragm, can also be used as a fuel source, but it is tapped only during prolonged fasting or starvation. The risk of digesting the body's protein for fuel is that a person cannot live long after losing too much of the muscle that makes up these vital structures. That leaves fat as our main storehouse of energy, accounting for more than 75 percent of all stored energy. Fat is well suited to serve this role because it is such a high-density energy source. Ounce for ounce, fat contains twice the energy of blood sugar or glycogen.

How We Use the Fuel from Food

We use a lot (roughly 75 percent) of the energy we burn on a daily basis just to keep our body functioning "at rest"—that is, to maintain normal body temperature; keep the heart beating; enable the kidneys, liver, brain, peripheral nervous system, and other vital organs to do their jobs; and fuel the processes that allow the replacement and growth of cells. Scientists call this baseline energy requirement the resting energy expenditure (REE) or the basal metabolic rate (BMR). The REE is defined

Energy for Survival

The average-sized person needs roughly two thousand calories per day just to maintain basic bodily functions. Typical fat stores can provide enough fuel to keep a person alive for almost two months without food.

as the energy you need when you are performing no significant physical work (for example, when you're planted on the sofa watching TV or sleeping).

So what else are our energy requirements? We need energy to eat and digest our food. This is called diet-induced thermogenesis and typically requires fifty to one hundred calories expended per day. If you combine the REE and diet-induced thermogenesis, a person of average height and weight (say five feet eight inches and 154 pounds) who is a total couch potato burns nearly sixteen hundred to two thousand calories a day just by living and eating.

The other significant use of energy is physical activity. Each time we move our arms or legs we use energy to power our muscles. Common daily activities such as walking, lifting, and even driving use relatively small amounts of energy. More strenuous physical activities such as jogging, playing basketball, or swimming use more calories. However, even relatively trivial activities add to the energy expenditure side of the equation. Standing instead of sitting, walking to the refrigerator instead of keeping a six-pack in a cooler by the sofa, or climbing the stairs to the bedroom instead of sleeping on the couch—head nestled in potato chips—all contribute to burning calories. Even twitching, fidgeting, or jiggling your leg takes energy, and while none of these activities or small movements burn very many calories, overall, people who fidget, jiggle, or stand much of the day, or who regularly take the stairs rather than riding the elevator, use more calories in their usual daily activities than calm, sitting, elevator riders.

When Energy In Exceeds Energy Out

When we eat more calories than we use up, we gain weight; that is, we store the excess energy in the form of fat. Conversely, when we use more calories than we take in, we lose weight; that is, we tap into energy stores, usually starting with our fat stores.

Considering the large number of calories an average-size (five-feet ten-inch, 175-pound) adult eats in a year to maintain a steady weight—twenty-six hundred calories per day, which translates to nearly one million calories per year—even the slightest imbalance between energy consumed and energy expended could result in substantial changes in weight. Here's an example.

A moderately active adult man who is five feet ten inches tall and weighs 175 pounds expends approximately 2,600 calories per day (about 1,800 calories as REE and 800 calories for physical activity). If he eats two cookies per day (120 calories) on top of what he needs to fuel his energy expenditures, he will be out of balance by almost 44,000 calories over the course of one year. He'll store that unused energy as ten pounds of weight gain.

Now suppose that same man does not eat the extra calories each day. Instead, he decides to drive his car the one mile to the bus stop (he could walk there or ride his bike), or he takes the elevator instead of walking the three flights of stairs to his office. He's not eating more, but he is moving just a little less, and that means he's using about one hundred fewer calories per day. At the end of a year, those extra calories also get stored as ten pounds of fat.

At first glance, you wouldn't think that innocent cookies or a few blocks of walking could have such a big impact on weight gain or loss. But the math shows us that it does.

Weight Gain Myths

Now, with an understanding of the body's energy balance, let's look at some of the most common myths about the causes of weight gain and weight loss and see how much truth is in each.

"I Don't Know How I Gain Weight; I Eat Like a Bird."

Next to "the check is in the mail," this may be one of the most frequent and inaccurate statements out there—unless the bird in question is a giant condor. The only way to gain weight is to eat food with more energy content than the energy that we expend. Remember that our resting energy expenditure translates into average-sized men or women expending approximately sixteen hundred to two thousand calories per day even if they never get out of bed. Bigger people expend more calories at rest and need more calories to maintain their weight. That means that we have to eat at least sixteen hundred to two thousand calories just to maintain our weight. So, "eating like a bird" but gaining weight is not possible. Several studies have demonstrated that overweight or obese persons consistently underestimate how much they eat.

"I Have a Slow Metabolism; That's Why I Can't Lose Weight."

In general, our basal metabolism (how much energy we burn while resting) is affected by age and weight. Larger people have higher, not lower, metabolic rates. It's like heating a home— larger homes need more energy to keep them warm. As we age, metabolism tends to drop as we lose muscle mass and often curtail activity.

That said, some people really do have a sluggish metabolism— although this is quite rare—that may explain why they gain weight or struggle with weight loss. For example, an underactive thyroid decreases energy expenditure. (And an overactive thyroid ramps up energy expenditure, explaining in part why people with this condition lose weight.) But if your thyroid gland is normal and you think that a little extra thyroid hormone will help you lose weight, don't. Not only is it potentially dangerous, but it simply doesn't work.

You might be surprised to learn that weight loss can actually decrease metabolism. But it makes a lot of sense. Smaller economy cars use less gas, and smaller bodies require less food. What's most discouraging about this is that as weight goes down with dieting and basal metabolic rate falls, the diet that helped you lose weight at first may not be enough to help you reach your goal weight. You will need to reduce your calories further or increase your energy expenditure. Many programs recommend increasing activity levels to get over this barrier and to promote further weight loss.

"Develop Washboard Abs with Only Four Minutes of Exercise per Day."

Midriff-revealing clothing has made people more aware of the appearance of their abdominal muscles. "Six-pack" or "washboard" abdominals, or abs, are all the rage, and marketers are taking advantage. Most of us have seen advertisements for gizmos that will sculpt perfect abdominal muscles in "only minutes a day." Or, for the really busy among us, there are passive exercise devices that deliver small electric shocks to the abdominal muscles and guarantee washboard abs with no sweat equity.

The unvarnished truth behind "cut" abs is that no matter how hard you work those muscles (or which device you buy with "four easy payments"), you won't see washboard abs if you have a layer of fat over the muscle. And it takes a very low body-fat percentage before any of us will look like the "after" pictures we see in those ads. Total body fat has to be less than 12 percent and probably less than 10 percent before you can see the abdominal muscles, no matter how toned. There are no proven ways to "spot reduce" abdominal fat, so you can do sit-ups or use a "crunching device" or any manner of abdominal workout machines for forty minutes a day, but unless you lose the fat—which usually means weight loss—your abdominal muscles will remain hidden from view.

Why Weight Is Important to Diabetes Prevention and Treatment

Now you know the immutable math of energy balance. Actually, you probably "knew" it all along. The good news is that you can use this math to your advantage to develop effective ways to achieve and maintain a healthy weight. In Chapter 1, we briefly described how being overweight alters the way the body metabolizes food, which can lead to high blood-sugar levels. So careful attention to weight is a key part of any diabetes prevention or treatment program.

This book will describe a proven program to maintain a healthy weight. How do we know it works? It's based on principles tested and proved in a major clinical trial called the Diabetes Prevention Program (DPP). We will share with you not only what we've learned during the development and conduct of the DPP and other studies but the stories of people who have made the program work for them. Next, we will briefly describe how the science of diabetes prevention and care evolved. Then we'll tell you how to put those principles to work for you.

3

Proof That Lifestyle Matters: The Diabetes Prevention Program

Don't you already know a lot about diets and exercise programs? Unless you've been living in a cave, cut off from all communication, you probably do. You have, like the rest of us, probably been flooded with advertisements and party talk about how to "eat healthy" and lose weight. Weight loss programs abound. In addition to the potential health benefits of weight loss, its cosmetic appeal has spawned a multibillion–dollar weight loss industry that includes diet books and programs, food supplements, over-the-counter and prescription medications, stomach-restriction surgery, and plastic surgery. It also includes exercise books, tapes, videos, television shows, and equipment; Jazzercise; step and bicycle aerobics; yoga exercise; combat yoga; sweat yoga; and Tae Bo. Indeed, health clubs have grown in parallel with the size of our waists.

The enthusiasm for so many approaches to weight loss must be because none of the programs is overwhelmingly effective. The recurring failure of the programs has led an increasingly obese population to search, in desperation, for any answer. And although plenty of "answers" are out there, virtually none of them has been put to the scientific test. We don't have an answer to a very simple question: do the programs work? This question must be answered not just in the short term, when almost any program can work, but in the long term; we don't know whether the programs are effective over a long enough period of time to improve health. In this and subsequent chapters, we summarize what is known scientifically about what works—and what doesn't—for losing weight and improving health. Of the many health goals that weight loss and increased physical activity might achieve, preventing diabetes may be the most important.

As we described in Chapters 1 and 2, the origin of the diabetes epidemic can be clearly traced back to changes in lifestyle. In the absence of our current maladaptive lifestyle, diabetes and its complications would probably be relatively rare. If that is so, would a program to reverse our current maladaptive lifestyle prevent diabetes? If we could restore at least some elements of the "farmer's life," could we reduce the risk of developing diabetes? To know the answers requires a scientific study.

In the past few years, several such studies have proved that you can protect yourself against getting diabetes by changing your lifestyle and that most people can make the changes successfully. As members of the Diabetes Prevention Program Research Group, we helped to organize the largest of those studies. To explain what these studies have shown, we first need to explain the kinds of scientific studies that have led to the program that we describe in this book.

Observational Studies: The First Scientific Studies of Nutrition and Exercise

Until the twentieth century, anyone recommending a particular diet or exercise program did so without any reliable scientific evidence to support it. They might have observed the results of different diet or exercise routines and then drawn conclusions. Sometimes their powers of observation were good, and—when proper scientific studies were eventually performed—they turned out to be right. Other times they were wrong but had no way of knowing it. Without a scientific method of comparing one approach versus another, enthusiasts could conclude pretty much anything they wanted. The English philosopher Roger Bacon noted, "For what a man had rather were true, he more readily believes." Barbers, shamans, gurus, and doctors could become true believers in their ineffective nostrums.

The first scientific studies of nutrition and exercise began in the middle of the twentieth century. The initial studies were called observational studies. In an observational study, a group of people is examined at least once (a cross-sectional study) or, more typically, is followed over time (a longitudinal study). Information—or data—regarding nutrition and exercise is collected with standardized methods and as objectively as possible. In addition, these observational studies collect information about any diseases or conditions that develop over time.

In such observational studies, the investigator can ask whether people who eat certain foods (for example, high-fat and high-calorie diets) or who exercise to a certain degree (for example, for an hour or less a week) have a greater tendency to develop disease than the members of the population who behave differently (for example, eat low-fat, low-calorie diets). If there are certain diet or exercise patterns that are associated with a greater risk of certain diseases, then it is *possible* that those diet and exercise patterns increase the risk of those diseases—possible, but not proved.

Why does an observational study not prove a direct connection between a particular diet or level of activity and disease? The reason is that an association cannot prove causality. For example, if an observational study were to show that people who eat high-fat and high-calorie diets are more likely to develop diabetes, it might not have been the diet that caused the diabetes. There might have been something else about the people who chose such a diet—maybe they thought they were at high risk for diabetes and thought that a high-fat diet would be good for them. Or perhaps people who eat a high-fat and high-calorie diet follow some other behavior, such as smoking or taking a particular medicine, that actually caused the diabetes. Observational studies have proved immensely valuable in pointing out factors (such as particular diet and exercise patterns) that are associated with increased risk of disease. But they cannot prove that those patterns cause disease.

To prove causation requires a different type of study from a purely observational one. It requires an experiment in which the investigator manipulates the factor that he or she thinks causes a specific outcome. The factor might be a low-calorie diet or a medicine or both. These types of experiments are called randomized controlled clinical trials. Observational studies and randomized controlled clinical trials are discussed in more detail in Appendix A.

Why Randomized Controlled Clinical Trials Are So Important

A randomized controlled clinical trial is a true experiment. To perform a controlled clinical trial of a diet and exercise program, the investigator first needs to enlist the participation of research volunteers. The choice of volunteers to be recruited will depend on the goals of the study. For example, in the Diabetes Prevention Program we and our colleagues chose individuals at high risk to develop diabetes.

What distinguishes a randomized controlled clinical trial from an observational study is that the people recruited to participate in the study are assigned at random either to be in the experimental intervention group or to be in the group that receives either standard therapy or sometimes no therapy (the "control group"). All of the study subjects are then followed, sometimes for years, to see whether there is a difference in the development of diseases between the two—or more—groups. The random—by chance—assignment of the groups means that the two groups most likely will be similar at baseline, before the interventions are applied. Therefore, if a particular disease develops less often in the subjects assigned to the experimental intervention program, compared to those assigned to the control program, then researchers can conclude that the experimental intervention almost certainly *caused* the reduced risk of disease.

The Diabetes Prevention Program

With support from the National Institute of Diabetes, Digestive and Kidney Diseases of the National Institutes of Health, a group of clinical investigators from around the United States developed a program with the goal of preventing diabetes and put that program to a scientific test. The Diabetes Prevention Program, or DPP as it was called, involved 3,234 people who did not have diabetes but who were at high risk for developing diabetes. The DPP was the largest study of lifestyle changes to prevent diabetes that has ever been conducted. The study participants were all adults (older than twenty-five) and overweight or obese, and they all had impaired glucose tolerance (IGT). IGT is a condition in which blood-sugar levels are elevated after a standardized test called the oral glucose tolerance test, but not high enough to be considered diabetic. People with this condition are on the road to developing diabetes, which is why IGT is now called prediabetes. The DPP volunteers were ethnically diverse, including approximately 50 percent Caucasians and 50 percent of the ethnic-racial groups at particularly high risk for diabetes such as African-Americans, Hispanic-Americans, Asian-Americans, Pacific Islanders, and American Indians.

The DPP was supported by grants from the government, the American Diabetes Association, and several companies that make products involved in treating diabetes.

The DPP lifestyle program was directed at achieving long-lasting changes in the behaviors that cause weight gain and a sedentary lifestyle. Although the goals of the lifestyle intervention were not intensive, the training to change the ingrained behaviors of a lifetime was intensive. The people assigned to the lifestyle intervention group were asked to lose 7 percent of their

33

initial weight. This amounted to an average of only fifteen pounds per person. In addition, they were asked to be more physically active, with 150 minutes per week of moderate-intensity activity. To achieve these goals, the lifestyle participants were given individual teaching with a core curriculum designed to retrain them in a lifestyle that would lead to weight loss and increased activity.

The DPP program was not a "one-size-fits-all" program. Instead, we worked with the people in the lifestyle intervention group of the study to find specific nutrition and exercise programs that would work for them. We identified and addressed specific barriers to changing behavior—whether it was shopping, cooking, eating, or physical activity. This comprehensive behavioral approach paid off. It resulted in sustained weight loss and increased activity levels that translated into fewer of these people developing diabetes. Some examples of the basic options of the DPP are presented in this book, so that we can provide you with the same information and options given to the people in the study. And we very much hope you'll experience the same success.

The specific lifestyle changes required to achieve the weight and activity goals were as varied as the population being studied; however, the major thrust was to decrease the amount of fat in the diet. This strategy was chosen because fat carries more calories per gram than carbohydrates or protein, and because it is relatively easy for a person to identify fatty foods and limit them. Program participants were taught to shop for, cook with, and eat less fat. The goal of increased physical activity was to help lose weight and maintain weight loss by increasing energy output. Exercise also was expected to prevent diabetes by increasing muscle sensitivity to insulin (as explained in Chapter 2).

The specific lifestyle goal related to activity was to perform moderate-intensity activity for at least thirty minutes per day, five days per week. Some of the DPP volunteers in the lifestyle group chose to participate in competitive sports, ballroom dancing, or swimming, but for most of them, activity consisted of brisk-paced walking. This could be done outside, in malls, at lunch hour, while walking the dog or pushing a stroller, or after dinner.

This program worked: most people reduced fat, and therefore calories in their diet, exercised for an average of thirty minutes per day, lost weight (an average of fifteen pounds), and kept most of it off during the three years of the study. Most important, lifestyle intervention was effective in preventing diabetes. The people in the lifestyle intervention group were 58 percent less likely to develop diabetes over a three-year period than the people in the control group. In the United States, if these results were applied to the population at high risk to develop diabetes (such as those recruited into the DPP), which is more than ten million people, this would reduce the annual occurrence of new diabetes cases from 800,000 to fewer than 400,000 cases per year.

Because the DPP combined both diet and exercise changes, we could not measure the effects of diet alone or exercise alone. However, other analyses of the results of the study indicate that the changes in diet that resulted in weight loss had a dominant role in preventing diabetes, while the exercise program was important in sustaining the weight loss.

So, by addressing the lifestyle changes that have contributed to the development of diabetes, the DPP showed that diabetes can be prevented—it is not inevitable. The results from two smaller but similar studies conducted in China and Finland have shown similar results as the DPP. These studies—conducted in different societies among people with different lifestyles and genetic makeup—emphasize that the DPP's message is universal: lifestyle changes work in preventing diabetes.

We will talk more about the DPP in subsequent chapters.

Lifestyle Changes Work in China and Finland, Too

Before concluding that the results of a study are universal, scientists often wait to see if similar studies come to the same results. Two studies like the DPP have been published in recent years, and they came to similar conclusions.

The DaQing Study in China

The prevalence of type 2 diabetes in China is low, compared to in the United States. However, Chinese society is being "Westernized," and the Chinese population is experiencing changes in lifestyle similar to those that occurred in the United States in the twentieth century. The number of Chinese who have left the physical labor of farming in the past several decades has been estimated to exceed the entire U.S. population. Predictably, the prevalence of diabetes has increased by almost fourfold—from 1.2 percent to 4.5 percent of the population—in fewer than twenty years. With more than a billion people in China, this translates into a huge number of new cases of diabetes.

To deal with the rising problem of diabetes, a randomized controlled clinical trial was performed in China. The DaQing study was unlike the DPP in that it tested diet and exercise strategies separately as well as in combination. Like the DPP, the DaQing study included people who were at increased risk for developing diabetes.

The results of the DaQing study showed that the lifestyle intervention groups were much less likely to develop diabetes over a six-year study period. In the part of the DaQing study that separately examined the impact of dietary change alone and exercise alone, both dietary and exercise change were found to be effective in reducing diabetes development.

The Diabetes Prevention Study in Finland (FDPS)

This study, conducted in a Westernized and developed nation (such as the United States), used a combined diet and exercise program (as did the DPP). The weight loss goal was at least 5 percent of initial weight, achieved with a high-fiber, low-fat diet. The activity goal was thirty minutes per day of moderate-intensity activity. As in the DPP, the study participants had individual counseling to change lifestyle. Again, the participants in the study generally were able to follow the program, lost weight—although not as much as the DPP lifestyle participants—and kept it off. They had exactly the same reduction in the risk of getting diabetes as seen in the DPP: 58 percent.

Together, the DaQing and FDPS studies reinforce the message of the DPP study: if you are at risk for developing diabetes, there is a lifestyle program of diet and exercise that you can follow successfully, and that will cut your risk of developing diabetes by more than half. The program can be shaped to fit your preferences and tastes and the realities of your life. And it works for people all over the world.

Lifestyle Changes Also Work for Other Heart Disease Risk Factors

One of the reasons that preventing diabetes is so important is that people with diabetes have a higher risk of developing heart disease. Observational studies have found various lifestyle factors that are associated with an increase in risk of heart disease, and many overlap with factors that increase the risk of diabetes:

* Low activity levels are associated with increased risk of atherosclerosis and death from heart disease and stroke.
* Higher activity levels are associated with decreased risk of cardiovascular disease and death. In most studies, those who exercise regularly have a 23 to 29 percent reduction in death compared with those who exercise least.
* Better fitness—a more direct measure of physical fitness and ability to perform exercise—is associated with a 46 percent decrease in death, comparing the 25 percent who are most fit with the 25 percent who are least fit.
* Any combination of obesity, sedentary lifestyle, smoking, and high-fat, low-fiber diets increases the apparent risk of developing diabetes and heart disease.
* A "Western" dietary pattern that includes more red meat, french fries, high fat consumption, refined grains, and sweets is associated with increased risk, while a diet with

more fruits, more vegetables, less fat, and more poultry and
fish and fish oils is associated with lower risk for
atherosclerosis.

- Some types of fat, such as polyunsaturated and
monounsaturated fats, decrease risk for atherosclerosis,
while higher dietary intake of saturated fat and trans-fatty
acids (these are created with partial hydrogenation, a
process used to increase the shelf life of polyunsaturated
fatty acids, such as margarine) increases risk.
- Moderate alcohol intake—one to two drinks per day—is
associated with decreased risk for atherosclerosis.
- Smoking increases risk for heart disease, stroke, and
especially vascular disease affecting the lower extremity.

Randomized Controlled Clinical Trials

Based on the results of observational studies, noted previously,
several randomized controlled clinical trials have been conducted
to see if changes in lifestyle can reduce risk factors for heart disease or can reduce the risk of heart disease itself, along with other
diseases caused by atherosclerosis. (See Appendix A for more
information about such types of studies.) Those studies have
shown the following:

- Maintaining a weight loss diet and exercise, reducing salt,
or both over three to four years decreased the development
of hypertension by approximately 20 percent.
- A diet low in salt (less than eighteen hundred milligrams
per day) and two or fewer drinks of alcohol per day, aiming
for weight loss of ten pounds, allowed 39 percent of people
with high blood pressure to discontinue their hypertension
medications (compared to only 5 percent of the control
group).
- A diet that emphasized greater quantities of fruits and
vegetables, low-fat food choices, or both decreased blood
pressure by about as much as a blood pressure pill usually
does (11 mmHg systolic and 6 mmHg diastolic).

- Eating two fish meals a week, or taking fish oil capsules daily, reduces the risk of sudden death in patients with a prior heart attack and is recommended in patients with risk factors for heart disease (such as high blood pressure, elevated total cholesterol and LDL cholesterol, diabetes, or cigarette smoking, or having fathers or brothers who develop heart disease before age fifty-five, or mothers or sisters who develop heart disease before age sixty-five).
- In the United Kingdom Lipid Program, a decrease in body weight of only 2 percent was associated with a 5 to 7 percent decrease in LDL cholesterol levels.

The take-home lesson of these studies, and others, is that for people who have modest elevations in blood pressure or cholesterol, which affects as much as 50 percent of the population, simple modifications of lifestyle work: they can reduce the need for medications and will probably decrease heart disease and stroke. Ongoing studies, such as the Look: AHEAD study, are examining whether a lifestyle program, similar to the one used in DPP, will reduce heart disease and stroke in people with diabetes.

Lifestyle interventions should not be viewed as a substitute for medications. Many controlled clinical trials have established the powerful effects of cholesterol- and blood pressure–lowering drugs to decrease the development, or recurrence, of heart disease. In some people, both lifestyle changes and medications will be needed.

Medication to Prevent Diabetes

The Diabetes Prevention Program study tested not only the impact of lifestyle. It also tested the value of a medicine, metformin, in preventing diabetes. Metformin is a medicine that is commonly used to treat diabetes. It works primarily by decreasing the amount of sugar made by the liver and by reducing insulin resistance.

As reviewed in Chapter 2, type 2 diabetes develops gradually. In the years that it is developing, but before it causes symptoms or blood test abnormalities that lead to its diagnosis, there is slowly increasing insulin resistance. The resistance of the body's tissues to the effects of insulin causes blood-sugar levels to rise, especially after meals. This, in turn, causes the pancreas to make more insulin. Eventually, the pancreas becomes fatigued from overwork, insulin secretion falls, and full-blown type 2 diabetes results.

Because slowly developing insulin resistance underlies type 2 diabetes, it made sense that using a medication that reduces insulin resistance might prevent diabetes. We found that metformin worked. It reduced the risk of developing diabetes by 31 percent, a significant decrease. However, it did not work as well as lifestyle modification, which reduced the risk of diabetes by 58 percent. And, as with any medication, metformin carries some risk of side effects. Lifestyle modification, in contrast, has few side effects. We did not test the combination of lifestyle modification and metformin to see if it might have reduced the risk of diabetes even more than 58 percent.

Future studies may show that a combination of medication and lifestyle modification is the most potent way to prevent diabetes. Indeed, for the treatment (as contrasted to the prevention) of several major chronic diseases, the combination of lifestyle change and medications is often advised. And, sometimes, the lifestyle intervention can eliminate, or at least reduce, the need for medications.

In summary, the DPP study showed that lifestyle changes had a greater power to prevent diabetes than the medicine we tested. The lifestyle program that the people in our study were asked to adopt proved feasible for them. Lifestyle changes should be suitable for you, too. We hope that this book will provide not only the rationale but scientifically proven guidance as to *how* you can change your lifestyle to a healthier one that can prevent diabetes and its complications.

CHAPTER 4

Applying Lifestyle Changes to Treat Diabetes and Associated Diseases

Unlike Superman, who is able to reverse life events by flying really fast, we cannot live life backward. Therefore, if you have already developed type 2 diabetes, you may wonder whether the lifestyle changes that could have prevented diabetes will gain you anything. The answer is yes: the same lifestyle changes that might have prevented your diabetes can help you to treat it.

As important as lifestyle is in causing type 2 diabetes, it may be even more important in treating type 2 diabetes, as well as type 1 diabetes. Diabetes is a unique chronic disease, affected by virtually every aspect of lifestyle, including eating, physical activity, and school, work, and travel schedules. Conversely, all of these activities are affected by diabetes. While many diseases require attention to taking prescribed medications, diabetes demands constant attention and vigilance with regard to timing and content of meals and physical activity, glucose monitoring, administration of numerous medications including insulin, foot care, and a host of other self-care requirements. And diabetes can be a petulant, jealous companion: if you ignore your care, even for a little while, it will make you pay with uncomfortable and potentially dangerous hyperglycemia or hypoglycemia. And if you do not pay attention to the myriad details of care over a long period of time, the penalty can be much more severe with loss of vision, kidney failure, foot ulcers, amputations, and heart disease.

On the bright side, during the past two decades, clinical trials have shown us that persons with diabetes can live long, productive, and complication-free lives. Studies in both type 1 and type 2 diabetes have demonstrated how to achieve near-normal blood-glucose (and hemoglobin A_{1c}—the measure of long-term, average blood glucose) levels. In addition, we have developed effective interventions to lower blood pressure and cholesterol levels in people with diabetes. The consequence of such "tight" glucose, blood pressure, and cholesterol control is improved long-term health. Blood-sugar levels maintained in the near-normal range over time effectively reduce the development and progression of the eye, kidney, and nerve complications that would otherwise rob people of their sight, kidney function, and limbs. In addition, aggressive blood pressure control benefits eye and kidney disease and reduces the risk of heart disease and stroke. Similarly, lowering LDL (bad) cholesterol decreases heart disease.

How does lifestyle enter into the treatment of diabetes? In this chapter, we describe the role of lifestyle in the management of blood-sugar levels in type 1 and type 2 diabetes and the importance of lifestyle in managing the other important risk factors such as hypertension and dyslipidemia (abnormal cholesterol and other fats in the blood). This is often referred to as the lifestyle approach to the ABCs of diabetes management: $\mathbf{A}_{1c}$ (hemoglobin A_{1c}), **b**lood pressure, and **c**holesterol.

Type 1 Diabetes

Traditionally, doctors have viewed type 1 diabetes as harder to treat than type 2 diabetes, because the pancreas can no longer make any insulin (see Chapter 1 for an explanation of type 1 and type 2 diabetes). Several times a day, a person with type 1 diabetes must adjust his or her insulin injections to match the level of blood glucose; the size, content, and timing of meals; and any physical activity that is planned. (This is in contrast with people with type 2 diabetes, who can still make some insulin on their own and don't require the frequent, fine adjustments of insulin dose that are necessary in type 1 diabetes.)

Providing the right level of insulin at the right time has been made easier in recent years by the availability of a variety of insulins with different profiles of activity. Some are very rapid acting and last for a short period of time, while others are very long acting. By using combinations of insulins, or mechanical devices called insulin pumps that deliver insulin continuously through small catheters into the skin, patients with type 1 diabetes can give themselves insulin in a way that approaches what a healthy pancreas would do. However, to do it right—to select the right dose of insulin for the ever-changing events in their lives—it is critically important for people to understand the effects of lifestyle on blood sugar.

In the past, we told individuals to maintain stable insulin doses and to mold their daily diet and activities to match the insulin. For example, if an insulin had its peak effect at 3:00 P.M., a snack at that time was required to prevent low blood sugar ("hypoglycemia"). In other words, the rigidity of the insulin schedule determined the best time of day for a person with diabetes to eat and exercise. The tail wagged the dog.

For the past twenty years, however, the dog has been wagging the tail. The philosophy of diabetes management has changed: self-monitoring of blood glucose, the flexible new types of insulin, and new insulin-delivery systems have made it possible to adjust insulin doses to match lifestyle. Treatment plans are not only more flexible, they are also easier to follow. For example, when school or work schedules change, insulin timing and doses are adjusted to accommodate them. If diet changes on a consistent basis, or even for one meal, insulin is adjusted to compensate—bigger meals with more carbohydrates require larger doses of insulin; smaller meals or more exercise usually requires smaller doses. The availability of self-monitoring of blood glucose provides people with type 1 diabetes the tools necessary to adjust insulin doses to match blood-sugar levels. Of course, these adjustments require those with diabetes to work with their diabetes-care teams so that they can learn how to make these adjustments. They need to learn how a nondiabetic pancreas works so they can do the same.

Lifestyle Behaviors Associated with Normal Blood-Glucose Levels

These are the nutrition lifestyle priorities for achieving blood-glucose levels as close to normal as possible and an HbA_{1c} below 7 percent for people treated with insulin (either type 1 or type 2 diabetes):

- **Eat meals and snacks at consistent times each day, and eat consistent amounts of carbohydrate in meals and snacks day to day.** A common approach to managing blood-sugar levels is called carbohydrate counting, which involves counting the total grams of carbohydrate or servings of carbohydrate (one serving contains about fifteen grams of carbohydrate) at each meal and snack. This is different from counting calories or fat grams, which you would count for the total day to see if you meet your targets. When you count carbohydrates, you need to know the total amount that you typically consume at each meal and snack (not the total for the day) because carbohydrates usually have their peak effect on blood sugar levels 90 to 120 minutes after eating. So each day for breakfast, you would try to eat about the same amount of total carbohydrate if you want to keep your blood-glucose levels in a stable range (not too high and not too low) after breakfast and before lunch. Likewise, you would try to eat your usual amount of carbohydrates each day for lunches, dinners, and snacks.

The more variable your day-to-day carbohydrate intake, the more erratic your blood-glucose levels will be (unless you know how to adjust your insulin doses for variations in your carbohydrate intake). For example, as shown in Table 4.1, if you ate 55 grams of carbohydrate for dinner one night and the next night you had a pasta-based meal with 130 grams of carbohydrate, then your blood glucose at bedtime would be lower after the 55-gram carbohydrate meal and higher after the 130-gram carbohydrate meal. Your diabetes-care team can help you learn how much extra insulin you need to cover the extra carbohydrate in your pasta meal so that you can keep your postmeal blood glucose in the target range (less than 180); however,

TABLE 4.1 How the Carbohydrate Load of Different Meals Can Affect Your Blood Sugar

Dinner 1	Carbohydrate (Grams)	Blood Sugar
5 ounces chicken	0	100 (before eating)
1 medium potato	30	
1 cup broccoli	10	
1 slice bread	15	
1 teaspoon margarine	0	
Diet soda	0	
Total	55	175 (after eating)

Dinner 2	Carbohydrate (Grams)	Blood Sugar
2 cups spaghetti	90	100 (before eating)
1 cup sauce	10	
1 slice bread	15	
1 teaspoon margarine	0	
½ cup fruit	15	
Coffee	0	
Total	130	275 (after eating)

consistency in carbohydrate intake will help smooth your blood-sugar control.

- **Reduce or eliminate sweetened or naturally sweetened beverages.** Avoid regular soda and fruit punch, and limit natural fruit juices to four ounces per day because liquid carbohydrates cause a rapid spike in blood-sugar levels.

- **Match insulin timing to meal timing.** Some fast-acting insulins need to be taken thirty minutes prior to a meal, and very fast-acting insulins can be taken immediately before you eat your meal. Ask your diabetes-care team what the best timing is for you.

- **Manage hypoglycemia appropriately.** Hypoglycemia is a low blood glucose (typically less than 70) that may cause sweating, trembling, weakness, extreme hunger, irritability, confusion, or even loss of consciousness. The recommended treatment of hypoglycemia is to consume about fifteen grams of fast-acting carbohydrate (see Table 4.2), wait fifteen minutes, and retest your blood glucose to see if it is back to normal (greater than 70 mg/dL). This amount of carbohydrate typically raises the blood glucose by at least 50 mg/dL in fifteen to thirty minutes. However, the response

TABLE 4.2 Treatment of Hypoglycemia*

	If Blood Sugar Is:		
	51–70 mg/dL	41–50 mg/dL	<40 mg/dL
Recommended amount of carbohydrate for treatment	15 grams	20 grams	30 grams
Apple or orange fruit juice	4 ounces	6 ounces	8 ounces
Regular soda	4 ounces	6 ounces	8 ounces
Grape or cranberry juice	3 ounces	4 ounces	6 ounces
Lifesavers	5	7	10
Glucose tablets (5 grams carbohydrate each)	3	4	6
Raisins	1 ounce	1.5 ounces	2 ounces

*Adapted from Powers, MA, Handbook of Diabetes Medical Nutrition Therapy, 1996, Aspen Publishers, Gaithersburg, MA.

can vary from person to person and be influenced by how low the blood glucose is and the cause of the hypoglycemia. If your blood glucose is still less than 70 mg/dL after initial treatment, then repeat treatment with fifteen grams of fast-acting carbohydrate and again recheck your blood-glucose level. Using low blood sugars as an excuse to eat everything in sight will result in high blood-glucose levels later in the day and may contribute to weight gain. Table 4.2 shows a plan for what to eat when your blood sugar is low, at different levels of blood sugar.

- **Learn the effects that food, insulin, and activity have on your personal blood-glucose patterns.** A diabetes educator or a registered dietitian who specializes in diabetes can help you learn to interpret how your eating habits, activity level, and insulin doses are affecting your blood-glucose results and help you learn how to adjust your insulin doses for changes in your usual carbohydrate intake.

Lifestyle Behaviors Associated with Lower HbA$_{1c}$ Level

Research from the Diabetes Control and Complications Trial (DCCT), which studied intensive diabetes therapy (three to four insulin injections per day or an insulin pump, testing blood-glucose levels at least four times per day, and trying to achieve blood-glucose levels as close to normal as possible), showed that four lifestyle behaviors were associated with lower hemoglobin A$_{1c}$ level:

- **Follow a consistent eating plan day to day.** Try to eat about the same amount of carbohydrate at meals (within ten grams—for example, between forty and fifty grams of carbohydrate every day at lunch). This makes it easier to match your insulin dose to your food intake and manage your blood-glucose levels.
- **Adjust insulin dose for variations in food intake.** Learning how much insulin you need to take for your usual carbohydrate intake at meals and snacks will help you learn

how to adjust your insulin dose for times when you might eat more or less carbohydrate than usual at your meals and snacks.

- **Respond to high blood-glucose levels with less food or a smaller dose of insulin.** This is called an insulin-correction factor. Work with your diabetes-care team to help you learn how much one unit of insulin will lower your blood-glucose level. For some people, one unit of insulin lowers blood glucose about fifty points, and for others the correction factor is different.
- **Eat a consistent bedtime snack.** Consistency with your bedtime snack routine will stabilize blood-glucose levels overnight and help keep HbA_{1c} levels low. Remember that your eight hours of sleep are one-third of your total day. Elevated blood-sugar levels overnight will raise your average.

In the same DCCT research study, two lifestyle behaviors were associated with a one-point higher hemoglobin A_{1c} result:

- **Overtreating hypoglycemia** (low blood glucose less than 70) by continuing to eat until you feel better will result in higher hemoglobin A_{1c} levels. So be sure to follow the appropriate treatment for hypoglycemia to prevent blood-glucose swings from low to high after treating hypoglycemia.
- **Eating extra bedtime snacks** was associated with higher hemoglobin A_{1c} levels. Be sure to have a consistent routine at bedtime regarding the amount of carbohydrate you eat for a bedtime snack for the reasons already discussed.

How People with Type 1 Diabetes Successfully Manage Their Diabetes

The tricks to successfully managing type 1 diabetes and maintaining the near-normal blood-glucose levels necessary to stay healthy are paying attention to your daily schedule, understanding the effects of your lifestyle on blood sugars, and adjusting your insulin to maintain blood-sugar levels in the range you and your health-care team agree is right for you.

Maintaining some consistency in mealtimes and meal sizes will help during the early stages of adjustment; however, as time goes on you will learn how to adjust even if you have inconsistencies. For example, if you planned to eat a large Sunday breakfast of cereal, eggs, toast, and orange juice, you would check your blood sugar before starting to eat. If you found that your blood-sugar level was on the high side—let's say 150 mg/dL—you would consider giving ten units of rapid-acting insulin, approximately four units more than the usual dose, because of your relatively high blood-sugar level and the greater carbohydrate content of the meal you are about to have.

As another example, if you planned to play tennis at 10:00 A.M., knowing that exercise lowers blood sugar, you would decrease the usual dose by several units. This kind of attention to lifestyle takes place day in and day out. Before twenty years ago, diabetes took command of lifestyle. Now, millions of people with type 1 diabetes have been able to master the lifestyle requirements and command their diabetes.

Lifestyle Changes to Treat Type 2 Diabetes and Associated Diseases

If you have type 2 diabetes, it should come as no surprise that lifestyle has a major impact on your diabetes—especially your blood-sugar control—and that lifestyle changes can have a beneficial effect.

As explained in Chapter 1, type 2 diabetes represents the end of a long and somewhat complicated road on which insulin resistance, or decreased insulin sensitivity, and the inability to make enough insulin contribute to rising blood sugars. At first, blood-sugar levels begin to rise slightly after meals because, in the setting of insulin resistance, the breakdown products of the meal are not normally stored in the muscle and liver. During this prediabetic phase, there are no symptoms and fasting blood-sugar levels remain in the near-normal range. Prediabetes can sometimes be detected with a fasting blood-sugar test, but more often a stress test called a glucose-tolerance test is required. In most persons who are destined to develop diabetes, the next five to ten years are characterized by increasing insulin resistance and decreasing insulin secretion.

Type 2 diabetes is ultimately a problem of supply and demand. The body demands more insulin to do its work, and the pancreas over time fails to supply enough insulin. When diabetes finally develops, it is usually the result of too little insulin being secreted to do the job. Blood-sugar levels rise more dramatically, including the fasting blood-sugar level, and the complications associated with hyperglycemia begin to develop over time.

How does lifestyle play a role here? The most common cause of increasing insulin resistance is being overweight and having decreased physical activity levels. In addition, and as pointed out in Chapter 3, changing the lifestyle factors that lead to overweight and obesity can reverse, to a great extent, their damaging effects. The same benefits can be seen even after diabetes has developed. Therefore, changes in lifestyle that lead to increased activity levels and decreased weight can improve type 2 diabetes even after it is entrenched.

How is it possible to turn back type 2 diabetes after it has started? It is possible because the insulin resistance that has contributed to causing type 2 diabetes can be reversed by lifestyle changes. It is also possible because the exhausted pancreas—which gives out after many years of making large amounts of insulin to compensate for the effects of insulin resistance—can recover if it gets a breather. The insulin-secreting beta cells are fatigued, but they aren't dead, especially early in the course of type 2 diabetes. There are some diseases that are irreversible once they occur. When someone has a heart attack, for example, the affected part of the heart muscle remains dead ever after. With type 2 diabetes, however, there is a window of time when you can reverse the disease with lifestyle changes. The earlier those changes are implemented, the more likely that improvement will occur.

The first treatment strategy that is almost always applied in the 90 percent of people with type 2 diabetes who are overweight or obese is to implement a weight loss program characterized by both changes in diet and increased exercise or activity. These lifestyle changes can have near miraculous results with regard to blood-sugar levels—even before much weight is lost!

Within days of eating fewer calories, blood-sugar levels often plummet, making the use of medications unnecessary. This has been demonstrated in numerous studies. Why a decrease in calories, even before weight loss occurs, improves blood-sugar levels so dramatically is not entirely clear, but the most likely explanation is that there is an improvement in insulin secretion that occurs rather quickly with levels of insulin resistance falling more slowly.

Increased physical activity also can lower blood-sugar levels even before you have had substantial weight loss, because it makes your muscles more sensitive to insulin, which drives sugar from the blood into the muscles. Over time, increased physical activity will contribute to achieving and maintaining weight loss. The more prolonged changes in lifestyle that result in weight loss will also have the effect of decreasing insulin resistance with a further recovery of insulin secretion.

Many health-care practitioners and people with diabetes are skeptical about the value of diet changes in treating type 2 diabetes. That's because they know how hard it can be for people to continue their diets over the long term. However, we found that the diet and exercise programs used in the Diabetes Prevention Program could be maintained by most of the participants over several years. The same should be true for you.

Studies in recent years have clearly shown that weight loss—achieved in a number of different ways—can make type 2 diabetes much less severe and can even make it disappear. A dramatic example is what happens in enormously obese people—who are usually at least 100 pounds overweight—who undergo so-called bariatric or weight loss surgery. In these individuals, weight loss of 80 to 120 pounds often occurs in the first year after surgery, and almost 90 percent have reversal of their diabetes. At a minimum, such persons can stop most of their medications, and many of them are able to stop all diabetes medications and maintain normal blood sugars.

So if weight loss is effective and sustained, diabetes can be reversed. In most people who are not very overweight, bariatric surgery is not indicated because of its risks. For most people, the answer will not be surgery but a lifestyle approach such as the one used in the Diabetes Prevention Program and described in this book. Our early experience is that people with type 2 diabetes can successfully follow this program just as can people who are at risk for diabetes. We think it is possible that treating newly diagnosed type 2 diabetes with an effective lifestyle program will not only prove successful but may be even *better* than conventional treatment with medicines.

Why do we think that? It's because medicines can reduce blood sugar, which is important, but blood-sugar-lowering medicines do not have direct effects on the other major diseases that often travel with diabetes: high blood pressure, high cholesterol, heart disease, stroke, and related diseases. The lifestyle program described in this book, however, *can* reduce the risk of (and can even help treat) most, if not all, of these risk factors at the same time it is helping treat diabetes.

In fact, a lifestyle program similar to that used in the DPP and described in this book is now being tested in the large Look: AHEAD study, sponsored by the National Institutes of Health (NIH). The Look: AHEAD study is testing the theory that, in people who already have developed type 2 diabetes, effective lifestyle intervention will improve diabetes and other cardiovascular disease risk factors and, ultimately, reduce heart disease, compared with standard diabetes therapy. In the absence of the effective lifestyle intervention developed by the DPP, this study would not have been possible.

As with preventing diabetes in people with prediabetes, the successful treatment of diabetes once it has developed does not require unattainable changes in lifestyle. You don't have to lose an enormous amount of weight or become a marathon runner. Many studies have shown that a ten- to twenty-pound weight loss will be sufficient to reduce insulin resistance, increase insulin secretion, and lower blood-sugar levels.

These are the nutrition lifestyle priorities for achieving blood-glucose levels as close to normal as possible and a hemoglobin A_{1c} level below 7 percent for people with type 2 diabetes:

- **Lose at least five to ten pounds to start.** Consider whether you can continue to lose a total of 7 to 10 percent of your initial body weight (as described in Chapter 8). Reducing your calorie intake to lose weight is the most powerful lifestyle change that you can make to lower your blood-sugar levels. The weight loss recommendations that we will discuss to prevent diabetes can also help to manage type 2 diabetes. If you are lean and do not have an extra five to ten pounds that you can afford to lose, then focus on these other suggestions. They will help control your blood-sugar levels by keeping your carbohydrate intake moderate at each meal and snack by minimizing liquid carbohydrates, distributing solid carbohydrates into three meals and two to three snacks, and incorporating more fiber.

- **Reduce or eliminate sweetened or naturally sweetened beverages.** These include regular soda, fruit punch, and natural fruit juices. Carbohydrates in liquid form are more rapidly absorbed than carbohydrates in a solid form (solids usually contain fiber that slows down the digestion of sugars) and can cause your blood sugar to rise to high levels. Instead of regular soda, try sugar-free diet soda, which has no calories. It is best to limit fruit juice to

53

four ounces per day or to eat fresh fruit instead. Fresh fruit has fiber, is more filling than juice, and is more slowly digested and absorbed.

- **Try several small meals at regularly timed intervals rather than infrequent large meals.** It is better to space your meals and snacks throughout the day than to skip meals and eat one or two large meals. Your pancreas has to produce insulin every time you eat in proportion to the amount you eat at each sitting. If you eat large amounts of food containing large amounts of carbohydrate at a given meal, your pancreas has to strain to produce more insulin, and you will notice higher blood sugars afterward. On the other hand, if you distribute your calories into three meals and one to two snacks per day, your pancreas will have an easier time producing enough insulin to cover the smaller amounts of food and carbohydrate at each meal or snack.

- **Include more fiber in your food choices.** Fiber has several beneficial effects. It satisfies hunger, blunts the rise in blood sugar, and lowers cholesterol levels. Choose fresh fruits instead of juice, whole grain breads and cereals instead of refined grains, and increased amounts of fresh or frozen vegetables.

- **Increase your activity level.** Gradually work toward a goal of at least thirty minutes of activity (equivalent to a brisk walk) five to six times per week (discussed in the next chapter). This level of activity can often lower your blood-glucose levels by fifty or more points. When you exercise, you help the insulin that your pancreas produces to work more effectively.

Peter's Story

Peter was a seventy-nine-year-old man who had type 2 diabetes and came for his first dietitian appointment with a fasting blood sugar of 246 and a hemoglobin A_{1c} of 10.5 percent. He had to urinate three to four times per night, disrupting his sleep. His height was five feet four inches, and his weight was 168 pounds (his BMI was 29). His preferred weight was 155 pounds. He kept a record of his meals and snacks for one week prior to his appointment. His food records showed that he was drinking eight ounces of fruit juice one to two times per day and was eating a lot of nuts and fried foods. He was surprised to learn that 50 percent of his calories were from fatty foods. He agreed to avoid fried foods and bake, broil, or steam foods instead; avoid nuts and substitute low-fat popcorn; reduce oil; and limit fruit juice to four ounces per day. After four follow-up visits over four months, Peter had lost six pounds, his fasting blood sugar was 122, and his hemoglobin A_{1c} was 6.9. For years afterward, Peter was able to manage his diabetes and keep his hemoglobin A_{1c} below 7 percent without diabetes medications. Peter's story demonstrates that small weight losses can make dramatic differences in blood-sugar levels.

Lifestyle Treatments for Hypertension

High blood pressure, or hypertension, goes hand in hand with diabetes and obesity, affecting about 75 percent of people with type 2 diabetes. The combination of the two increases your risk of developing eye, kidney, and heart disease and stroke. If you throw in abnormal cholesterol levels, which will be discussed later in this chapter, you have a potentially lethal combination that increases the risk of heart disease and stroke even more.

All three—hypertension, obesity, and abnormal cholesterol and other blood fats—are connected to the prediabetic and diabetic states, and all three can be improved with lifestyle changes. High blood pressure responds to the lifestyle changes that lead to weight loss and increased activity levels, as we have already discussed. For example, a weight loss of five to fifteen pounds, achieved in studies such as the Diabetes Prevention Program and Trials of Hypertension Prevention Study, can lower blood pressure by two to five points (for example, from 135/80 to 130/76).

While this may not seem like a big change, it is sufficient to decrease substantially your risk of getting hypertension and decrease your long-term risk of heart disease or stroke. Remember, at the same time, you are reducing the risk for developing diabetes or reducing your blood-sugar level if you already have diabetes, and you are reducing your risk of getting heart disease through other mechanisms. Weight loss and increased physical activity may also make you feel and look better.

Other lifestyle interventions have proved to decrease blood pressure. Reducing salt in your diet by approximately one teaspoon per day—as done in the Dietary Approaches to Stop Hypertension (DASH) study and the Trial of Nonpharmacologic Interventions in Elderly (TONE) study—will also lower blood pressure by two to five points. Combining weight loss with dietary salt reduction is even more effective and may lower your chances of developing high blood pressure or needing medications by as much as 50 percent.

The DASH diet reduces blood pressure by emphasizing an eating pattern rich in fruits, vegetables, and grains with reduced saturated fat and total fat content. The reductions in blood pressure were achieved with a sodium intake of 3,000 milligrams per day, a stable body weight, and two or fewer alcoholic beverages per day. As summarized in Table 4.3, the DASH diet recommends a certain number of servings per day from each food group.

To keep your sodium intake to fewer than three thousand milligrams per day, avoid table salt, avoid entrées containing seven hundred milligrams or more of sodium, and keep the following high-sodium foods to a minimum:

- Canned or dried soups, bouillon, bouillon cubes
- Foods with salt toppings
- Processed, smoked, dried, or cured meats, poultry, or fish (bacon, cold cuts, frankfurters, ham, salt pork, sausage, anchovies, sardines, salted cod, smoked herring, corned beef, turkey, chicken loaf or roll)

TABLE 4.3   DASH Diet Servings

Food Group	Daily Servings	1 Serving Equals
Grains	7–8	1 slice bread; 1 cup dry cereal; ½ cup cooked rice, cereal, or pasta
Vegetables	4–5	1 cup raw leafy vegetable; ½ cup cooked vegetable
Fruits	4–5	1 medium fruit; ½ cup mixed fruit
Low-fat/nonfat dairy	2–3	8 ounces nonfat/1% milk or yogurt; 1.5 ounces low-fat/nonfat cheese
Meats, poultry, fish	2 or fewer	3 ounces cooked lean meats, poultry, or fish (trim away visible fat)
Nuts	4–5 per week	1.5 ounces or ⅓ cup nuts; 2 tablespoons or ½ ounce seeds; ½ cup cooked legumes
Fats and oils	2–3	1 teaspoon oil, margarine, mayo; 1 tablespoon regular or 2 tablespoons low-fat salad dressing
Sweets	5 per week	1 tablespoon jelly or jam or maple syrup (may want to use sugar-free versions if you have diabetes)

Adapted from "A Clinical Trial of the Effects of Dietary Patterns on Blood Pressure," *New England Journal of Medicine* 336 (1997): 1117.

- Processed cheese, Parmesan, Romano, Roquefort, feta, blue cheese, cheese spreads
- Canned vegetables, sauerkraut, any vegetable prepared in brine, pickles, olives, pickled beets, tomato or vegetable juice
- Salted snack foods, salted popcorn, cheese curls, potato chips, corn chips, salted nuts, pretzels
- Garlic salt, celery salt, onion salt, chili sauce, sea salt, soy sauce, meat tenderizers, monosodium glutamate, steak sauce, stuffing mixes, package mixes for sauces and gravies, some salad dressings

If you increase your activity level and eat the fewest number of servings in each food category, then you will also lose weight and maximize your blood pressure–lowering potential with lifestyle changes.

The reductions in blood pressure with lifestyle changes may seem small compared with the results that are achieved with some of the powerful medications that are available today; however, for many people with only modestly elevated blood pressure, the lifestyle changes will achieve blood pressure reductions that have a demonstrable benefit on long-term health. Making a lifestyle change is also much less expensive than taking pills. In addition, although there may be side effects of lifestyle changes, such as orthopedic injuries associated with increased activity levels, they are generally infrequent, minor, and temporary.

Lifestyle Treatments for High Cholesterol and Other Blood Fats

Several types of fats circulate in the blood and are commonly measured by doctors: total cholesterol, LDL ("bad") cholesterol, HDL ("good") cholesterol, and triglycerides. In people with diabetes, total cholesterol and LDL cholesterol may be high. However, the most characteristic lipid changes in diabetes are increased triglyceride levels (triglycerides are another circulating fat in the blood) and a decreased HDL cholesterol level. Of the specific types of fat that circulate in the blood, both high LDL and low HDL cholesterol appear to be the most important with regard to future heart disease. Although LDL levels in people with diabetes tend to be in a similar range as in people without diabetes, the LDL particles are small and more likely to cause vascular disease. This combination of low HDL levels and small LDL particle size contributes to the increased risk of heart disease in the setting of diabetes.

The availability of powerful new cholesterol-lowering drugs, called "statins," beginning in the late 1980s, has made it possible to reduce cholesterol levels dramatically and to test whether doing so improves a person's health. In fact, studies with statins have demonstrated a remarkable decrease in recurrent heart attacks in people who have already had one in the past as well as a decrease in new heart disease. Although people with diabetes were initially excluded from such studies, more recent studies have shown that these individuals achieve similar reductions of approximately 25 percent in heart disease outcomes when treated with these drugs.

Unfortunately, although the people with diabetes do better when treated with statins to lower cholesterol levels, they continue to have more heart disease than people who do not have diabetes. In fact, in most studies, people with diabetes who are treated with statins still do worse than the subjects without diabetes who are treated with placebo. The conclusion from these studies is that more aggressive treatment of cholesterol is necessary in people with diabetes than in people without diabetes. An LDL-cholesterol level less than 100 mg/dL is recommended for adults with diabetes. The latest recommendation of the National Cholesterol Education Program (NCEP) is that people with diabetes and previous heart disease lower their LDL cholesterol levels to less than 70 mg/dL. Even if your LDL cholesterol level is between 80 and 100—a level that would have been called "normal" until mid-2004—the latest evidence says that you can benefit from lowering the level.

How does lifestyle enter into this story? As with high blood pressure, the medications are more powerful than the usual lifestyle changes that can be implemented for most individuals. However, it is worth pointing out that in populations where vegetarianism is practiced and with relatively low amounts of dairy intake, LDL levels can be as low as the 40 to 60 range—without medications. Realistically, most of us are not ready to give up all sources of animal fat, eggs, and dairy in our diet, but if you are, you might not need statins.

What dietary changes are most important for lowering your LDL cholesterol? Surprisingly to many, lowering your dietary intake of saturated fats and trans fats does more to lower your LDL cholesterol level than lowering your dietary intake of cholesterol itself. That is because most of the cholesterol in your blood is made by your body, not obtained from cholesterol in your food: high dietary intake of saturated fat and trans fat causes your liver to make more cholesterol. Changes in saturated fat intake—reducing the total fat in the diet from 35 to 40 percent to 30 percent or less, and reducing saturated fat to 7 percent of calories—will typically lower cholesterol levels by 5 to 10 percent. Substituting monounsaturated and polyunsaturated fats for saturated fats and trans fats also has a beneficial effect. Finally, lowering your dietary intake of cholesterol will also help: if cholesterol intake in the diet is lowered from the 300 to 600 milligrams per day that are in a typical American diet to less than 300 milligrams, one gets an added benefit.

HDL cholesterol levels are particularly difficult to affect with lifestyle changes or medications. Although there are a few medications that raise HDL modestly, the medication that is most effective, nicotinic acid (or niacin), has side effects that discourage many physicians and patients from using it. In addition, treatment with the large doses of nicotinic acid that are often necessary to improve HDL levels may actually worsen blood-sugar levels, especially in persons who have diabetes. (There are some experimental medications under development that may dramatically raise HDL levels, but it is difficult to tell whether and when they may be approved for general use.)

There are lifestyle changes that can improve (raise) HDL levels. Losing weight increases HDL levels once weight is stabilized. Increased activity also raises HDL levels slightly. Achieving a clinically significant increase in HDL requires *a lot* of physical activity—probably more than most of us can afford to do. On the other hand, a modest alcohol intake, such as one glass of wine per night, will raise HDL. (This is something we may be more ready to embrace than jogging forty miles per week.)

You may wonder how much benefit you would get from adopting lifestyle changes in order to lower your cholesterol. It has been estimated that a 10 percent decrease in LDL cholesterol will result in a 10 percent decrease in heart disease. Because the average effect of a lifestyle program on LDL cholesterol is to

TABLE 4.4 Nutrient Composition of the Therapeutic Lifestyle Changes (TLC) Program

Nutrient	Recommended Intake
Saturated fat	<7% of total calories
Polyunsaturated fat	Up to 10% of total calories
Monounsaturated fat	Up to 20% of total calories
Total fat	25–35% of total calories
Carbohydrate	50–60% of total calories
Fiber	20–30 grams per day
Protein	Approximately 15% of total calories
Cholesterol	<200 mg per day
Total calories	Balance energy intake and expenditure to maintain a desirable body weight and to prevent weight gain

*"Executive Summary of the Third Report of the National Cholesterol Education Program (NCEP) Expert Panel on Detection, Evaluation, and Treatment of High Blood Cholesterol in Adults" (Adult Treatment Panel 111) *JAMA* (2001): 285 (19): 2486–97.

lower it by 5 to 10 percent, lifestyle changes would be predicted to have a beneficial effect on heart disease. And if you are willing to engage in a maximal lifestyle program, a recent study indicates that you can achieve LDL reductions of up to 25 to 30 percent.

In any case, the idea that cholesterol-lowering medications provide the same benefits as lifestyle changes is incorrect. Lifestyle changes have enormous benefits beyond lowering LDL cholesterol, such as raising HDL cholesterol, lowering triglycerides, improving diabetes, and reducing inflammation without the added expense or side effects that come with taking more medications than necessary.

The nutritional goals of the therapeutic lifestyle changes (TLC) program that is recommended by the National Cholesterol Education Program (NCEP) Expert Panel on Detection, Evaluation, and Treatment of High Blood Cholesterol in Adults are shown in Table 4.4. These nutritional recommendations are based on a thorough review of the research evidence in this area and are an important part of cholesterol lowering whether you are taking lipid-lowering medications or not.

These are the important features of the lifestyle approach to reducing lipid levels and risk for heart disease and stroke:

- **Reduce saturated fat intake** to less than 7 percent of calories and cholesterol intake to less than two hundred milligrams per day by making the lifestyle changes that follow.
- **Limit animal protein** (beef, fish, and poultry) to five to six ounces per day or less; choose lean red meats (flank, rump, London broil, pork loin or tenderloin, lamb leg, ground white meat turkey), and limit consumption of lean red meat to one to two times per week.
- **Limit cheese** as much as possible because whole milk cheese has six times the amount of saturated fat as red meat. (If you have cheese, use low-fat alternatives containing zero to three grams of fat per ounce.)
- **Minimize ice cream** and use low-fat or nonfat dairy products (low-fat or nonfat yogurt, ice milk, and 1 percent or skim milk).
- **Try more meatless meals.** Replace three ounces of animal protein with one cup of legumes or beans or six ounces of tofu.
- **Limit eggs to one egg yolk per week.** Use cholesterol-free egg substitutes or egg whites the rest of the week. (Two egg whites equal one whole egg in recipes.)
- **Minimize use of butter, chocolate, coconut oil, and salad dressings made with eggs or cheese.** Substitute small amounts (three to four teaspoons per day) of unsaturated vegetable oils such as corn, olive, canola, safflower, sesame, soybean, or sunflower oil.
- **Minimize commercial baked goods such as pies, cakes, doughnuts, croissants, pastries, muffins, biscuits, high-fat crackers, or cookies.** Substitute homemade baked goods using unsaturated oils and whole grain breads and cereals.

- **Build in more fruit and vegetables.** Eat five or more servings per day.
- **Reduce intake of trans-fatty acids or trans fats (another LDL-raising fat) as much as possible.** This can be accomplished by reading food labels and avoiding foods that contain "hydrogenated" or "partially hydrogenated" fats. Starting in 2006, the Nutrition Facts labels on grocery store food will specifically mention the levels of trans fats. French fries and doughnuts are typically made with hydrogenated fats.
- **Choose high-fiber carbohydrates.** These include whole grain breads and cereals, fruits, and vegetables.

To further enhance your LDL-lowering potential you can do the following:

- **Incorporate plant stanols/sterols (two grams per day) into your daily diet.** This can be accomplished by using two to three tablespoons per day of a margarine made with plant stanols/sterols such as Take Control or Benecol. If you are trying to lose weight, you could try the "light" versions, which are lower in calories (about forty-five calories instead of seventy to eighty calories per tablespoon).
- **Increase the soluble fiber portion of your diet to ten to twenty-five grams per day.** Soluble fibers are found in oats, barley, apples, oranges, dried beans, and peas. Soluble fibers also help lower blood-glucose levels. Water-insoluble fibers are found in whole wheat, rye, and vegetables and tend to help more with constipation.
- **Reduce your weight** toward a desirable body weight. This can be accomplished by following the suggestions from the DPP lifestyle program that we will discuss.
- **Increase your daily activity level** to include moderate physical activity that expends approximately two hundred

calories per day (about thirty minutes per day of brisk walking).

- **Reduce blood-glucose levels.** When your blood-glucose levels are higher than normal, this can cause your cholesterol, LDL cholesterol, and triglyceride levels to be higher than normal as well. As you reduce your blood-glucose levels toward normal, this will usually improve your lipid levels at the same time.

You may want to consider working with a dietitian who can assess the nutritional composition of your current diet in terms of the amount of total calories, percent total fat, and saturated fat, cholesterol, and fiber that you are consuming; show you how it compares with the therapeutic lifestyle changes program goals; and provide you with personalized lifestyle suggestions so that you can maximize your lipid-lowering potential with as little extra medication as possible.

From a public health perspective, these changes in lifestyle are necessary if we are to stem the long-term effects of diabetes. Without them, the population will almost certainly require more medications at higher doses and at greater costs with more side effects in order to treat the panoply of conditions and diseases that accompany type 2 diabetes. Lifestyle changes have the advantage of being relatively inexpensive and widely available. They have beneficial effects on numerous risk factors that accompany type 2 diabetes. While a substantial fraction of the population will also need medications to treat blood pressure and abnormal lipids that are not adequately managed with lifestyle alone, the lifestyle changes we have discussed can decrease the number and/or dose of medications necessary. In persons with only modestly elevated blood sugar, blood pressure, or lipids, lifestyle modification may do the job without medications.

CHAPTER 5

Activity and Exercise: Move, Move, Move

We've talked about how easy it is to eat too much. Now let's talk about how easy it is to exercise too little—and what you can do about it.

As we discussed in Chapter 3, changes in physical activity have been incorporated into three of the four major studies that have successfully prevented the development of diabetes in vulnerable populations. Only one of the studies included exercise as an individual component; the other two combined a program of increased physical activity with a lifestyle program to change diet and eating behaviors.

Here's what we know about the impact of increasing physical activity:

- Physical activity almost immediately improves your muscles' sensitivity to insulin, making it easier to store sugar in your muscles rather than have it rise in your circulation.
- The impact of physical activity is greatest when performed frequently—at least three to four (and ideally five to six times) times per week.

- While aerobic exercise probably improves metabolism the most and provides cardiovascular conditioning, adding strengthening exercises also helps.
- In addition to its direct effects, physical activity can help people lose weight; it is especially important in helping them maintain weight loss achieved with diet changes.
- The most successful of the diabetes prevention and treatment programs have incorporated increased physical activity of moderate intensity into everyday life.
- The most sensible way to increase physical activity may be to incorporate it into everyday activities, rather than identify specific exercise periods in which to do exercise.

Fad Exercise Programs

The appeal of fad exercise programs is no less than that of fad diets. An entire exercise industry has developed that includes exercise tapes, books, workout programs, specialized centers to facilitate yoga (combat yoga, sweat yoga), strength training, weight training, jazz exercise, step aerobics, spinning, and almost every type of exercise equipment imaginable for home gyms, bedrooms, and traveling.

The problem is that all of these require a specific time period during which to perform the exercise, and, for many of us, that time is often lost in the midst of a busy schedule. All too often, the three hours per week that you planned to work out and balance your energy expenditure against your energy intake get whittled away. Work and family demands, travel schedules, and the frequent changes in our busy lives interfere with our designated workout time. Therefore, instead of getting in two or three hours of workout per week, we get only one hour or less. Forty percent of our population engages in no leisure physical activity on a weekly basis.

Another problem with vigorous exercise programs is that exercise-related injuries may actually interfere with your exercise time while you heal. A final problem with exercise programs at a gym is that the culture is often frightening or unwelcoming to large segments of the population. How often do you see a fifty-year-old or older person working out in a gym? If you are over fifty, go to the typical gym, and see no one like you there, it can make you feel uncomfortable.

Getting home gym equipment—if you can afford it and have the space for it—can eliminate the problem of feeling you are exercising in an alien environment. But it still requires you to set aside the time to get into sweat clothes, exercise, and shower; finding that time can be difficult.

Activity Versus Exercise

There is a very real and effective alternative to regimented exercise. Every day, by making small changes in your daily activities, you can burn a surprising number of calories—and improve your energy balance—by incorporating more activity into your otherwise sedentary schedule.

How do we change our lifestyle to increase the amount of work we do when everything around us has been developed to be work saving? Although there are many guidelines, TV shows, and tapes that instruct us how to exercise in the home setting, there are few practical guides that will help you burn off small numbers of calories frequently during the day.

However, it is not that hard. Specific activities can be performed seamlessly in your everyday life and not require you to put aside one-half hour every day or one hour three times a week in order to fill your exercise prescription. Although we certainly would never discourage people who can keep to a regular exercise schedule and remain fit and healthy from following that schedule, the guidelines that we provide here can be used by everyone every day and should make a difference.

Remember, most of us are out of caloric balance by only a small amount, explaining the slow but steady rise in weight in the entire population. Adjusting energy intake and energy output, even modestly, would do much to reduce the development of overweight and obesity and decrease their toll of diabetes and perhaps heart disease.

Subtle changes in daily physical activity can have substantial practical advantages over an exercise program. See Table 5.1.

The next two sections are designed to help you improve your activity levels on an hour-to-hour and daily basis, as well as give you an understanding of the exercise strategies that may be used and how many calories you can expect to expend with either (or both) approach(es).

How to Change Lifestyle to Increase Physical Activity Every Day

All of our labor-saving inventions of the past century, the field of ergonomics, and many products advertised in the Sharper Image and other catalogs have been developed to make life easier. The side effect has been to make us less active in everything we do. The single greatest impediment to our expending energy has been in the area of transportation. The invention, refinement, and widespread availability of the automobile and the paving of much of the world has allowed us to drive everywhere and to arrive in such close proximity to our destination that walking has become an unusual part of our day. And, if the car hasn't dis-

TABLE 5.1 Advantages and Disadvantages of Activity vs. Exercise

Activity	Exercise
Can be done as part of usual daily lifestyle schedule	Requires set-aside time to perform
Can improve energy balance, prevent or limit weight gain, and promote weight loss	Can improve energy balance, prevent or limit weight gain, promote weight loss, and improve cardiovascular conditioning
Can be performed while at home, work	Often requires a gym or special court
No special equipment required	Often requires specialized equipment and outfits
Virtually no cost	Gym, court, or course time fees
Burns off small numbers of calories frequently	Burns off larger number of calories, but less frequently
Little or no risk of injury	Can lead to twisted ankles, sprains, and other injuries that may interfere with further exercise

rupted our energy balance enough, elevators, escalators, moving walkways, electric scooters, motorbikes, valet parking, and other forms of personal transportation, such as the new Segway "personal transporter," have finished the job. Logically, the first target to try to improve our energy balance should be to reestablish locomotion by means of walking. This approach is logical and reasonable and has already been adopted by numerous programs.

Except for a relatively small number of people who are housebound because of various medical ailments or for other reasons, we all need to go places during the usual course of our day. We travel to work, to school, to shop, and to visit friends and family. If, during our usual travel schedule, we walked more and drove less, we could subtract a modest number of calories on a daily basis. The number of calories spent for any given period of walking isn't very much; however, remember that this is something you would do frequently every day. Table 5.2 shows the number of calories that are spent doing common activities either for a given distance or for a specific number of minutes per day. A number of programs have recommended trying to increase your walking by two thousand steps per day. On flat terrain, this approximates a mile walk and would burn approximately 100 calories. Even if you were able to walk only an extra thousand steps per day, it would expend 50 extra calories. This doesn't seem like very much, but at the end of one year, you would have burned up approximately 18,000 calories. Even with no change in diet, this converts into five pounds lost per year. Or, you could think of this increased activity as allowing you to eat the equivalent of an extra cookie per day, every day, without gaining weight.

Walk, Walk, Walk: Increasing Your Activity Level Really Does Work

The idea that increasing your activity level can bring many of the benefits of a regular exercise program sounds appealing in theory, but is there any proof that it works? In the Diabetes Prevention Program, the majority of people who were in the intensive lifestyle intervention combined the lifestyle diet changes with

TABLE 5.2 Calories Burned per Minute During Different Activities*

Occupational Activities	Recreational Activities	Calories Burned
Standing instead of sitting		7 per hour
Walking up one flight of stairs instead of taking escalator or elevator		11 per minute
	Getting up to change the channel rather than using the remote	1 calorie
Doing desk work, driving a car, typing, talking	Standing still, walking at a stroll, playing cards, sewing, knitting	2–2.5 per minute
Repairing car, sweeping, dusting	Walking on level ground at 2 mph, biking on level ground at 5 mph, riding lawn mower, bowling, golfing with cart, playing many musical instruments	2.5–4 per minute
Plastering, bricklaying, pushing wheelbarrow with 100-pound load, cleaning windows	Walking 2.5 mph, biking 6 mph, golfing pulling cart, pushing light power mower	4–5 per minute
Painting, doing masonry work, hanging wallpaper, doing light carpentry	Walking 3 mph, cycling 8 mph, golfing carrying clubs, dancing fox-trot, playing doubles tennis, raking leaves, doing many calisthenics	5–6 per minute
Digging in garden, shoveling loose dirt at 10 times a minute	Walking 3½ mph, cycling 10 mph, roller-blading or ice-skating 9 mph	6–7 per minute
Shoveling 10 pounds of dirt per shovelful at 10 times a minute	Walking 4 mph, cycling 11 mph, playing singles tennis, shoveling snow	7–8 per minute
Digging ditches, carrying 80 pounds, sawing hardwood	Walking/jogging 5 mph, cycling 12 mph, playing half-court basketball, mountain climbing, downhill skiing	8–10 per minute
Shoveling 14 pounds of dirt per shovelful at 10 times a minute	Running 5½ mph, cycling 13 mph, playing full-court basketball	10–11 per minute
Shoveling 16 pounds of dirt per shovelful at 10 times a minute	Running at least 6 mph, cross-country skiing	11 or more per minute

*Number of calories burned depends on several factors, including your size.

lifestyle changes that generally increased walking. The volunteers frequently wore pedometers—small, inexpensive devices that measure the number of steps you take on a given day. In the DPP intensive lifestyle program, we asked our volunteers sometimes to try to increase their walking to more than ten thousand steps per day, which is approximately five miles, and many of them did. But any amount of increased walking burns off calories.

On average, doing two thousand steps per day by walking one mile after dinner or after your lunch break at work may be practical for many people, but it sounds a little like the "bouts" of exercise we described previously, requiring a specific time period reserved for the activity. What if you were able to increase fifty or one hundred steps per day ten to twenty times during the day? This would have a similar impact, assuming you weren't using the steps only to go to the refrigerator and microwave. Each step uses energy. Incorporating two thousand extra steps per day would help to balance your energy output and input and prevent weight gain and diabetes.

Table 5.2 summarizes how many calories you can burn with different activities, including many that you can incorporate into your daily routine. By choosing to perform these activities each day, you can change your energy balance. This does not require purchasing special equipment, joining a gym, or incurring any of the risks for physical injury that often accompany exercise.

In concert, all of these small changes may not lead us to "the farmer's life," but they will take us closer to where we need to be in order to improve our energy balance and decrease the risk of becoming overweight. Or, for those who are overweight, they will decrease weight and decrease the risk for diabetes and its complications.

Exercise

Farmers and other manual laborers do not include—nor do they usually need to include—exercise as part of their usual routines. After a day of intensive physical labor, farmers and construction workers will not likely be doing squat thrusts or step aerobics. The introduction of exercise and the multiplication of exercise programs is new in human history. Even though regular exercise is hard for many people to fit into their lives, for those who can exercise regularly there clearly are benefits.

Aerobic Cardiovascular Training Versus Anaerobic Strength Training

Exercise has been divided into two types—cardiovascular conditioning and strength training. Cardiovascular conditioning, or aerobic exercise, uses large groups of muscles (instead of isolated muscles) at a moderate intensity (so that you can talk to someone while exercising), lasts for at least thirty minutes, and is dynamic and free moving. Usual examples include walking, riding a bike, swimming, or rowing. Heavy lifting or heavy pushing or pulling is not aerobic-type exercise. *Aerobic* means "uses oxygen," and thus must involve easy breathing rather than heavy panting or breath holding or straining. Aerobic exercise causes a rise in heart rate and usually a moderate rise in blood pressure, both of which are responses that will improve the efficiency of your heart over time.

In contrast, anaerobic exercise is either very high intensity (like a sprint), which drives your breathing, blood pressure, and heart rate very high, or is breath-holding, isometric exercise, such as lifting heavy weights or holding a strong contraction (as in a tug of war). This type of exercise also burns calories but does not benefit the heart in the ways that aerobic exercise does. It is possible to perform strengthening exercises with moderate weights in a dynamic program. Such programs create an aerobic stimulus while also achieving some of the benefits of muscle strengthening, including muscle toning and shaping, and reducing the development of osteoporosis.

As far as everyday activities go, carrying bags of groceries that are too heavy to carry very far would be more anaerobic, while carrying smaller amounts of groceries more often (three times a week) would be aerobically beneficial.

Aerobic Exercise Prescription

To be sure that you get the appropriate amount of exercise, you may follow an individualized exercise prescription, which should consider these things:

- Exercise mode
- Duration
- Frequency
- Intensity

Intensity of exercise is often measured in units called "METS." However, for most people "light" exercise is performed at a comfortable pace and "feels like I could keep going all day." You can talk while you exercise. Moderate intensity is "comfortable for a while, after an hour, I break into a sweat." Heavy intensity can be sustained for ten to fifteen minutes, always causes sweating, and you can't talk while doing it. Very heavy intensity exercise causes sweating, shortness of breath, and can only be sustained for three to five minutes.

In general, an aerobic exercise prescription looks like this:

- **Mode:** dynamic, free-moving, free-breathing, large muscle mass movements; examples: walking (treadmill or overland), biking (stationary bike or overland), swimming, rowing (on a machine or in a boat), cross-country skiing (on a machine or in snow)
- **Duration:** thirty minutes or more at a time
- **Frequency:** at least three days per week, and not consecutive days in beginning
- **Intensity:** fairly light to somewhat heavy, in a heart rate range of 70 to 85 percent of your maximal heart rate, and so that you are able to talk but not sing while exercising

As you become accustomed to performing a certain level of exercise, meaning that it begins to feel too easy (more like "light" or "very light"), it is time to step up the intensity so that it becomes closer to "somewhat heavy" again. This is a good sign, as it means you are making progress and are experiencing a training effect. To make additional progress, you will need to increase intensity, and you may also increase duration, up to forty-five to fifty minutes per session. After one to two months, you can increase your frequency of exercise to five to six days per week.

Anaerobic Strengthening Program

For most people, and probably for you, regular aerobic exercise will help to control your weight and to reduce your risk of diabetes. However, if you want to add an anaerobic strengthening program to your usual exercise, start with relatively light weights, such as two to four pounds, depending on your size and strength. Use the small weights and increase the number of repetitions of each movement (such as flexing your biceps).

People usually describe anaerobic strengthening programs in terms of repetitions ("reps") and sets. Reps are repetition of exactly the same exercise, such as lifting a three-pound weight above your head. A set involves ten to twenty reps of the same exercise. When you do twenty repetitions and more than five sets, you can increase the weights (for example, from three pounds to four pounds).

Safety Tips for Activity and Exercise

Before initiating any change in activity level or a new exercise program, check with your doctor. People with heart disease or who are at risk for heart disease, including those over the age of fifty or with diabetes, may experience chest pain or even a heart attack with increased exercise or activity. While walking is usually safe for everyone, it's still best to discuss your program with your doctor. (See section called "Your Heart" later in this chapter.)

In general, it is best to begin every exercise session with a five- to ten-minute warm-up, beginning with a low-intensity walk or bike ride (depending on your program) and some maintained stretching of the muscles you will be using (calf, low back, and knee, typically). A cooldown period of at least five minutes at the end of your exercise session will also help your adjustment to exercise. These extra steps will help to prevent joint aches, muscle soreness, and injury.

For walking, always use comfortable, fitted walking shoes or sneakers, and buy new ones frequently to protect your feet and joints. This is your only equipment, unless you use a treadmill. Try to avoid high-impact exercise for your joints' sake.

For biking, try to ride on the flat in order to keep your intensity constant. Uphill can be anaerobic, and downhill can be coasting. A stationary bike is much more consistent.

Step up your program gradually: even trained athletes adjust the intensity and duration of their workouts slowly. Reassess how you feel every four weeks during your exercise, and adjust the prescription if you have made noticeable progress.

Special Issues for People with Diabetes

If you have diabetes you need to be careful of certain things.

Your Feet

All people with diabetes need to take extra-special care of their feet. Neuropathy (one of the long-term complications of diabetes that affects the nerves in your feet) may affect your ability to sense minor trauma. This can be compounded by decreased circulation and structural changes of the foot. Even minor repetitive trauma from weight bearing and poorly fitting shoes can lead to abrasions, blisters, and callus formation. Penetrating infections can spread from the skin to the bones, and this can lead to the need for an amputation.

To protect your feet, you need to inspect them before and after exercise. If you have neuropathy, be aware that you may not be able to feel the rubbing of a poorly fitting shoe or of a pebble in your sneaker. Therefore, visual inspection is critical. Wear seamless "tube" socks, and wear walking shoes with good cushioning to absorb the impact. With appropriate foot gear and some caution, most people with diabetes can participate in a wide variety of exercises.

Your Eyes

If you have severe retinopathy (diabetic eye disease), certain high-impact exercises (boxing, football, or diving) may cause bleeding in the back of your eye and should not be done. Although this situation is rare, check with your health-care team (and your mother) before taking up kickboxing or other sports where you might get kicked in the head.

Your Heart

People with diabetes have heart disease, stroke, and peripheral vascular disease (leading to amputations) at more than twice the rate of those who do not have diabetes. The frequency of heart disease in prediabetes is between that of people with diabetes and those without diabetes. Unfortunately, in addition to being at higher risk for having heart disease, people with diabetes have fewer warning symptoms of an impending heart attack. Many people without diabetes who have narrowing of the coronary arteries that supply the heart muscle have chest pain or angina when they exercise, warning them of decreased blood flow. In contrast, people with diabetes often have no warning symptoms. The first time that they become aware of a heart problem may be when they have a heart attack.

How can we encourage exercise—which is meant ultimately to protect the heart—if it may precipitate a heart attack? The answer is that you may need to do an exercise-tolerance test, sometimes called a stress test, to make sure that you can exercise safely without the risk of causing heart damage. The stress test is a treadmill test with monitoring of your electrocardiogram. Sometimes an exercise stress test also includes another technique for taking a picture of the heart, such as an ultrasound or what is called a "nuclear medicine test." These additional ways of measuring heart function or blood supply to the heart can reveal problems that are not picked up by the electrocardiogram.

With the results of the stress test, your doctor can reassure you of the safety of exercise and can give you a target heart rate that you shouldn't exceed during exercise. Stress tests are often recommended in older adults and in many adults with diabetes before they begin a new exercise program or intensify their current program.

The intensity part of your exercise prescription is very important, both for protecting your heart and for improving its function.

For protection do the following:

- Warm up and cool down.
- Do not exceed your intensity prescription.
- Use a pulse monitor if necessary, but do not go above "somewhat heavy" effort. Remember, you should be able to carry on a conversation while you exercise.
- Increase intensity of your workouts slowly, and do not try anything too hard suddenly.

Hypoglycemia

If you take insulin or one of the oral sulfonylureas, exercise or increased activity may lower your need for medications. This is a good thing. However, unless you and your health-care team adjust your medications—or add an appropriately timed snack— you may have a hypoglycemic episode (low blood sugar) either during exercise or even four to eight hours after the exercise. Always carry a sugar-containing snack with you, just in case. And discuss any change in your routine with your physician before starting it.

Intensifying Your Workouts

When you feel more and more comfortable with your exercise routine—less breathless, less than "somewhat heavy" or "fairly light" work—and you notice that your heart rate is lower both during exercise and at rest, it is time to step up your exercise intensity or duration or frequency. Whichever you decide to adjust, do it gradually. Use your warm-up to help you determine how much more intensively you want to exercise. Start with the usual level of exercise, add increments of intensity bit by bit until you exceed your old level, and then maintain the new level while you check how it feels.

Pay attention to your body. It will usually tell you when you are going too fast or too long or too hard. One common signal is more shortness of breath than you usually have. Slow down. If it doesn't go away, or if you have chest pain, consider this an emergency. Other warning symptoms that should be treated as an emergency include chest tightness; discomfort in the jaw, arms, or neck that lasts more than five minutes; light-headedness; or an irregular heartbeat. Stop exercising and seek emergency care.

Increasing activity and exercise is critical if we hope to reverse the pernicious effects of our current sedentary lifestyle. These lifestyle changes will contribute to weight loss and maintenance and have independent beneficial effects on insulin sensitivity and cardiovascular conditioning. Increased activity levels can be incorporated easily into our daily lives, helping to balance our energy intake and output. Similarly, exercise can be safely and enjoyably performed.

6

How to Get Ready to Change Your Lifestyle

Are you really ready to lose weight? If asked, most people who are overweight will say, "I really want to lose weight." Most overweight people can also list several reasons *why* they want to lose weight. But the more difficult questions to answer are: Are you *ready* to do what it takes to lose weight? Are you really ready and willing to change your eating and exercise habits? Examining your readiness to change and your "motivators" and "demotivators" for losing weight are critical first steps in the process of lasting lifestyle change.

What It Means to "Be Ready"

Scientists who study behavior change have identified five stages that people go through when trying to change their habits: precontemplation, contemplation, preparation, action, and maintenance.

People in the precontemplation stage are either not interested in or not thinking about making changes in lifestyle in the next six months. They may not see their weight as a threat to their health, or they may have too many other competing priorities and may just not be ready to focus on lifestyle changes.

If you have moved on to the contemplation stage, then you are thinking about making lifestyle changes within the next six months. You are likely weighing the advantages and disadvantages of changing your exercise and eating habits. People in the contemplation stage are usually looking for motivation and typically say, "I know I should want to lose weight," or, "I need a program to motivate me." They are usually waiting for the magic moment to start, or hoping for a magic pill—the newest fad diet or gimmick that promises quick results with little effort. When they examine the way they talk about losing weight or making lifestyle changes, they find themselves saying, "I know I should, but . . ." or, "It takes too much effort."

The next stage is preparation. People in the preparation stage are planning to make lifestyle changes within the next month. They may have started to make small changes in exercise and eating habits and are interested in doing more. They may be ready to sign up for an exercise class or keep a record of food intake. They usually express an inner motivation to make changes and do not look for (or rely on) external motivators, such as a program or someone else to inspire them.

The action stage is where desire and planning become manifest as distinctive changes in behavior. If you are in the action stage, you have made changes in your exercise and eating behaviors within the past six months and are trying to become more consistent with your new lifestyle habits. People in the action stage will say, "It's getting easier for me to manage my food choices and fit exercise into my routine." Or, "I'm making good progress with weight loss, but sometimes I get off track."

Being in the maintenance stage means that you have maintained your new exercise and eating habits for longer than six months. These lifestyle changes have become part of your daily routine. While you actively try to avoid slipping back into old habits, you're also becoming increasingly confident about your ability to maintain your new ways. You might say things such as, "I just do it now." Or, "My new lifestyle is just a part of me."

So where are you right now? What is your stage of change? How can you become someone whose lifestyle remains in the

TABLE 6.1 The Five Stages of Change

Stage	Characteristics	Typical Statements
Stage 1: Precontemplation Precontemplators have no intention of changing behavior during the next six months.	May be unaware a problem exists. See no reason to change. Not interested in discussing change.	It is not a problem. Not right now. I have other priorities.
Stage 2: Contemplation Contemplators are thinking about making changes within the next six months.	Have limited knowledge of the problem. Weighing the pros/cons of change. No sense of urgency. Waiting to get motivated. Wishing for the magic diet or pill.	I will change someday. I know I should but _____. ____ will motivate me. How about the ____ diet?
Stage 3: Preparation People in the preparation stage are planning to change within the next thirty days.	Motivated and ready to change. Not sure how to get started. May have tried small changes Could slip back to ambivalence.	I am ready to ____. I want to____. How do I start? It is a lot of work.
Stage 4: Action People in the action stage have made changes within the past six months.	Efforts to change are noticeable. Believe change is possible. Have modified environment for success. Want feedback and reinforcements.	I can _____. It's getting easier to __. I'm doing it , but ___. I think I am doing well.
Stage 5: Maintenance People in the maintenance stage of change have made established changes for at least six months.	Change has become part of routine. Trying not to slip back into old habits. Confident about maintaining change. Dealing with high-risk situations, such as vacations and social events.	I just do it now. It's not hard to _____. I feel good about _____. I can manage _____.

Adapted from E. Gehling, "The Next Step: Changing Us or Changing Them?" *Diabetes Care Educ Newsflash* 20 (1999):31–33.

maintenance stage for weight loss, eating habits, and physical activity? Table 6.1 describes these stages and the statements characteristic of the thinking that takes place during each stage. See where you are at this point. The next section will help you determine which stage you are in.

How You Can Gauge Readiness to Change

First of all, it is important for you to know that people do not simply progress through the stages of change in order; they can enter or exit the stages at any point, and they can recycle through the stages by relapsing and repeating stages. For example, life stresses can sometimes cause you to slip and lose focus on your exercise/activity and eating habits, and you may move from the action stage for weight loss, eating habits, and exercise back to the contemplation stage for a period of time. Vacations, social gatherings, or retirement can also cause you to get off track because they disrupt your usual routine. It is also possible to be at one stage of change for reducing calorie intake and at a different stage of change for increasing activity.

To understand how you're moving through the stages of change, it's helpful to examine your motivations. There are several ways to do this, and it is absolutely worth the effort to carefully examine the various aspects of what motivates you.

First ask yourself the following questions that have been adapted from a book called *Health Behavior Change: A Guide for Practitioners*, by S. Rollnick, P. Matson, and C. Butler, and published by Churchill Livingstone in 1999:

On a scale of 0 to 10, with 0 being "not important at all" and 10 being "the highest importance," how important is it for you right now to lose weight?

0   1   2   3   4   5   6   7   8   9   10

If you decided to lose weight right now, on a scale of 0 to 10, with 0 being "not confident at all" and 10 being "very confident," how confident are you that you could lose weight?

0   1   2   3   4   5   6   7   8   9   10

To lose weight, it is necessary to reduce food portions and calorie intake and to increase your activity level. So it is also necessary to rate the importance and your confidence for changing these behaviors. People often have different importance and confidence ratings when rating changing eating and exercise habits. So be honest with yourself about the next questions:

On an importance scale of 0 to 10 (as in the previous questions), how important is it for you right now to reduce your food portions and calorie intake?

0   1   2   3   4   5   6   7   8   9   10

If you decided to lose weight right now, on a confidence scale of 0 to 10 (as in the previous questions), how confident are you that you could reduce your food portions and calorie intake?

0   1   2   3   4   5   6   7   8   9   10

On an importance scale of 0 to 10, how important is it for you right now to increase your activity level?

0   1   2   3   4   5   6   7   8   9   10

If you decided to increase your activity level right now, on a confidence scale of 0 to 10, how confident are you that you could increase your activity level?

0   1   2   3   4   5   6   7   8   9   10

Now let's see what your answers mean.

Importance Ratings

Importance ratings of 7 or higher imply that it is pretty important for you to lose weight, reduce calories, and exercise more. If you gave importance ratings of 5s or 6s, then you may be somewhat ambivalent about these lifestyle changes. If your importance ratings are 4s or lower, making these changes is of fairly low to very low importance to you right now. You are likely in the precontemplation or contemplation stage of change.

Confidence Ratings

Confidence ratings of 7s or higher suggest that you're pretty confident to very confident that you can lose weight, change your eating habits, or exercise more. If your confidence ratings were 5s or 6s, you may be uncertain about your ability to lose weight and make the necessary changes in your eating and exercise habits. If your ratings are 4s or lower, you don't have a lot of confidence that you can lose weight, cut calories, and exercise more.

What to Tackle First

If your importance ratings are lower than 3s, you'll want to focus on importance first. If both importance and confidence ratings are the same, you'll still want to focus on importance first. However, if one rating is distinctly lower that the other, start with the lower rating first. If both your importance and confidence ratings are below 3s, then this may not be the ideal time for you to try to lose weight. On the other hand, if both importance and confidence are high, then you're probably ready to take steps toward long-term lifestyle changes. Let's look at some real-life examples.

Bob

Bob is forty-eight years old with a twin brother who has had diabetes for three years. He has just found out that he has impaired glucose tolerance or prediabetes. His doctor has told Bob that he's very likely to develop type 2 diabetes within five years of his twin brother. When Bob joined the Diabetes Prevention Program (DPP) study, he was five feet ten inches tall and weighed two hundred pounds. His motivation score was 9 out of 10; however, his confidence score was only 5 out of 10.

Bob had never been on a weight loss program before, perhaps explaining his low sense of confidence. However, he was excited to learn that he had been assigned to the lifestyle intervention group. Bob's wife attended each of Bob's individual coaching sessions to learn how she could support his efforts. At first they found that keeping food records and learning about sources of fat and extra calories in their diet was time-consuming. They also found it difficult to adjust the traditional Italian recipes that the family enjoyed. With practice, feedback, and support Bob found out that he could change his eating and lose weight and that over time it got easier. Difficult changes started to become habit. As he saw progress and experienced success, he became increasingly confident that he could maintain his lifestyle changes over time and keep the weight off. Bob's weight loss goal for the study was to reach 186 pounds (a 7 percent weight loss), and after six months, he had lost 15.5 pounds and weighed 184.5 pounds. In addition, he kept this weight off for five years, and at the end of the DPP, his blood sugars had returned from impaired to normal.

Mary

Mary is a forty-seven-year-old woman with type 2 diabetes. She was five feet five inches tall and weighed 244 pounds (BMI 41) at the start of her program, and she was taking several diabetes medications, including metformin (Glucophage), glimepiride (Amaryl), and pioglitazone (Actos). Mary's motivation to change her eating and exercise habits to lose weight was a 10 out of 10. Her confidence level was 7. She participated in a group weight loss program with a goal of losing 10 percent of her body weight.

After six months, Mary lost thirty-two pounds (a 13 percent weight loss) and weighed 212 pounds. Her blood sugars improved dramatically, and she was able to stop taking the Amaryl. Although Mary wanted to get below 200 pounds, she found that her weight fluctuated between 210 and 215 pounds. When asked to rate her motivation for losing those extra pounds, she was somewhat surprised to hear herself say 2 out of 10. When asked how important it was to reduce her diabetes medications further, she rated her motivation to come off the Actos as 8 out of 10.

Together we decided that Mary would meet with her primary care physician to discuss her goals. She asked her doctor if she could try stopping the Actos because her blood sugars were so good. Mary agreed to continue regular blood-sugar monitoring. She knew that to keep her blood sugars well controlled she would need to be especially careful with her food choices and that losing more weight would make it more likely that she could remain off the medication. Now, her motivation to lose weight was 8 out of 10, and she dropped to 199 pounds over the next eight weeks! She is still off the Actos and maintaining good blood-sugar control.

How to Analyze Your Importance and Confidence Ratings

Let's look more closely at your situation. Your importance rating for losing weight was ____. Now, list *all* of the reasons why your rating was not one or two points lower.

_____

_____

_____

Next, list what it would take to increase your importance rating by three points.

_____

_____

_____

Your importance rating for reducing calorie intake was____. List all of the reasons why your rating was not one or two points lower.

_____

_____

_____

Next, list what it would take to increase your importance rating by three points.

_____

_____

_____

Your importance rating for increasing your activity level was ____. List all of the reasons why your rating was not one or two points lower.

_____

_____

_____

Next, list what it would take to increase your importance rating by three points.

_____

_____

_____

Are your importance ratings for losing weight, reducing calorie intake, and increasing activity level similar for all three lifestyle changes? If your ratings for weight loss are much higher than your ratings for reducing calories and increasing activity, then you need to think about whether you're truly ready to make lifestyle changes. Wanting to lose weight without recognizing the behavioral changes required to accomplish this goal is unrealistic, magical thinking. Losing weight may be very important to you, *but* is it important enough that you are willing to invest the time and effort to change your eating and exercise habits? For some people, eating and enjoying food, or using food to cope with unpleasant emotions, is more important than losing weight.

Now look at the reasons behind your ratings. This will help you understand how you view the perceived benefits (the "pros") of losing weight and the perceived barriers (the "cons") that get in your way. As you examine what would increase your ratings, you'll start to see what you'll need to do to start to reduce the barriers.

Let's take Kathy, a sixty-two-old woman with prediabetes, as an example. When she reviewed the pros and cons of losing weight, she first listed the ones that were important for her. Then she rated their importance on a scale of 0 to 10 with 10 being "the highest importance" (see Table 6.2). As you look at her responses, you'll see that the number of pros and cons for losing weight is certainly important, but so is their relative importance.

Although Kathy's list included a similar number of cons and pros, the relative importance of losing weight was greater than that of not losing weight. Her highest ratings were not for appearance

TABLE 6.2 Kathy's Pros and Cons of Losing Weight

Losing Weight Pros	Importance	Losing Weight Cons	Importance
Looking better in clothes	2	Time commitment	6
Able to buy more stylish clothes	2	Dislike exercise	5
Being more attractive	2	Dislike record keeping	7
Having more energy	8	Feeling discipline is too hard	3
Better able to exercise	3	Feeling you'll just regain	3
Better mobility	8	Creates too much attention	2
Improve health	9	Rather be heavy than yo-yo	2
Prevent diabetes	10	Love food too much	7
Reduce medications	7	Socializing gets complicated	7
Healthier pregnancy	N/A	Think too much about food	4
Increased self-esteem	6	Need to buy new clothes	4
Freedom from guilt/shame	6	Other important priorities	3
Less nagging from doctor, family, friends	2	Negative feedback from family and friends	3
Better quality of life	10	Weight can't be an excuse	2
Learning to enjoy food without overindulging	3	Food is my companion and calms my emotions	8
Total Importance Score	**78**	**Total Importance Score**	**66**

TABLE 6.3 Motivators and Demotivators for Losing Weight

Losing Weight Pros	Importance	Losing Weight Cons	Importance
Looking better in clothes	____	Time commitment	____
Able to buy more stylish clothes	____	Dislike exercise	____
Being more attractive	____	Dislike record keeping	____
Having more energy	____	Feeling discipline is too hard	____
Better able to exercise	____	Feeling you'll just regain	____
Better mobility	____	Creates too much attention	____
Improve health	____	Rather be heavy than yo-yo	____
Prevent diabetes	____	Love food too much	____
Reduce medications	____	Socializing gets complicated	____
Healthier pregnancy	____	Think too much about food	____
Increased self-esteem	____	Need to buy new clothes	____
Freedom from guilt/shame	____	Other important priorities	____
Less nagging from doctor, family, friends	____	Negative feedback from family and friends	____
Better quality of life	____	Weight can't be an excuse	____
Learning to enjoy food without overindulging	____	Food is my companion and calms my emotions	____
Other	____	Other	____
Total Importance Score	____	**Total Importance Score**	____

but were related to better health and a better quality of life as she gets older. Kathy knows about the long-term complications of diabetes and wants to do all she can to avoid them. Even though she loves to eat and often uses food to calm her "nerves," and even though she dislikes the inconvenience of keeping food records, the importance of her health and quality of life outweigh these factors.

Take some time to identify your own pros (motivators) and cons (demotivators) for losing weight and rate their importance to you using a scale of 0 to 10. Then total the value of your motivators and demotivators (see Table 6.3).

Which way does your scale tip? If the demotivators outweigh the motivators, ask yourself what you can do to tip the balance. How can you reduce the demotivators and increase the motivators?

Ready, Set, Go!

Before you turn to setting your lifestyle goals to lose weight, be sure that you can truly answer "yes" to the following questions.

- Are you willing to commit the time necessary to lose weight? (This means finding time to exercise and increase activity, shop for and prepare healthy foods, and keep track of your food intake.)
- Are you willing to take a closer look at yourself, your eating habits, and your attitudes toward food, weight, and exercise?
- Are you willing to give up looking for the magic pill or quick-fix diet plan?
- Are you willing to weigh yourself at least once per week?
- Are you willing to accept a rate of weight loss in the area of one to two pounds per week?
- Are you willing to accept that some weeks you may not lose as much weight as you will in others (or may even gain weight)?
- Do you have a positive attitude and realistic expectations for success?

7

Preparing Your Environment for Change and Success

Eating is a complex behavior that, in human beings, is influenced by internal and external factors, or cues. Meals are social occasions, and our environment can influence what and how much we eat.

Why do we eat? If we ate only when we were hungry and stopped when we were full, far fewer people would be overweight. In fact, many overweight people have been eating for so many reasons other than hunger that they can't remember the last time they actually felt hungry. It is important to identify the eating "cues" in your physical, emotional, and cognitive environment so that you can manage them and set up your environment for success.

Your Physical Environment

People overeat primarily because food is easily available and all around them. Everywhere you look, you see food. And the sight and smell of food can trigger you to eat whether you are hungry or not. As kids, lots of us were told not to waste food because people were starving in other countries. If you grew up as a member of the "clean-plate club," you probably developed a habit of eating and not stopping until the food was all gone. We have been programmed from an early age to eat the food in front of us so long as it looks good, tastes good, and smells good. Sometimes we eat only because the full-color poster looks so good, even though the actual food is lukewarm, gray, and tasteless. When the food is all gone, we often feel uncomfortably full, but this becomes our normal experience of eating. An important part of creating an environment for success is to survey your immediate surroundings (including your home, office, car, and so forth) to see where, how, and when food is available to you.

Food Choices and Portion Size

Which kinds of foods do you purchase and keep handy? Will these foods help you to achieve a healthy weight, or are they more likely to sabotage your efforts? If you are serious about losing weight, then you must make a commitment to do an "environmental cleanup" of your eating environment.

Here's how to get started at home:

- **Remove tempting and unhealthy foods from your immediate environment.** Banish them from your sight. Replace them with healthy foods, and keep them readily available for meals and snacks. (See Appendix C for shopping list ideas.)
- **Determine the appropriate amount of food to cook and serve yourself and others at meals.** Immediately put extra unnecessary portions in the refrigerator or freezer for another meal. Serve meals using smaller plates, bowls, and glasses.
- **Keep individually wrapped portions of healthy snacks available so that you will not be tempted to overeat.** These might include single servings of popcorn, pretzels, yogurt, or fruit. (See Appendix E for healthy snack suggestions.)

It may not always be easy, but at home you can control the food you buy and how much you serve (and eat). But most of us eat outside the home on a regular basis. (Most surveys show that the average American eats out at least three or four times per week.) So, the next challenge is to develop strategies for eating outside your home.

As we discussed in Chapter 1, we live in a difficult eating environment. Much of our food—and often unhealthy food—is marketed aggressively and is widely available at all times of the day and night, making it extremely challenging to change our habits. All-you-can-eat buffets and all-inclusive menus or vacation packages offer an overabundance of food—and we want to get our money's worth. Unfortunately, while these deals are financial bargains, they result in a calorie glut that contributes to weight gain. Even if you avoid all-you-can-eat setups, there are still plenty of challenges to sensible eating.

In today's society, we have a major portion-distortion problem (see Figure 7.1). Over the years, the plates, bowls, and cups we use have at least doubled in size. If we fill the plate and then empty it by eating everything on it, it's no wonder that we are gaining weight. Let's take a look at a few examples.

- **A four-ounce juice glass with a one-cup bowl of cereal used to be standard serving sizes.** Now it is more likely that you will drink juice from an eight- to twelve-ounce glass, and your bowl probably holds at least two cups of cereal. If you clean those plates, you'll also have doubled or tripled your calories.
- **A standard bagel used to weigh two ounces and contain about 160 calories.** Today's bagels weigh from four to seven ounces and pack 320 to 560 calories—that's before the cream cheese! And of course, it will take more cream cheese to cover a bigger bagel, so you'll pile on even more extra calories.
- **Restaurant meals are now 25 percent larger than they were fifteen years ago.** And even when you choose

well in a restaurant, you can easily consume at least one thousand calories. If you don't choose carefully, that could mean more than two thousand calories in a single restaurant meal.

You'll face the same supersize dilemma when you buy snacks outside the home. When you're at the movies, you might see the following choices for popcorn.

Small	$3.13
Medium	$3.84
Large	$4.44

FIGURE 7.1 Portion Inflation 1955–2002

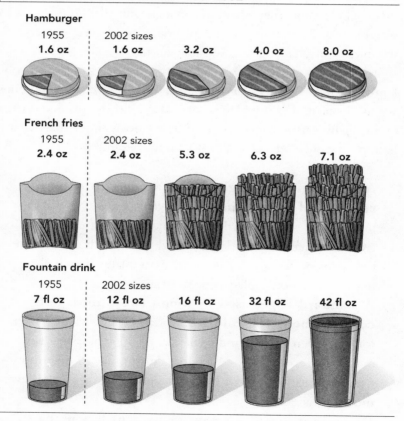

In 1955, the typical hamburger, order of french fries, and a soda were small compared with the order sizes available today.

Certainly the large popcorn is a better deal, and sometimes if you buy the large popcorn, you can get free refills too. Is it really a good bargain? It depends on what you're counting. Let's look at Table 7.1 to see all you get for your money.

For an extra $1.31 (an increase in cost of less than 30 percent), you get an extra 760 calories (an increase of 190 percent) and 50 grams of fat—and that's before adding the butter. As you can see, you'll need all of the facts before you can truly decide if the price and portion are worth the extra calories, fat, and potentially extra weight.

How about those tasty french fries at McDonald's? Table 7.2 illustrates the nutrition information for each of their serving sizes. That sixty-four cents extra (an increase of about 65 percent) buys you an extra 330 calories (an increase of more than 100 percent). Making this choice on a daily basis could contribute to a weight gain of about three-quarters of a pound per week—that's thirty-four pounds in a year.

What if you choose a value meal? Does this really mean "good value" for your money? It all depends on how you define "good value" and "a good bargain." See Table 7.3.

So despite the "better value" in terms of cost per portion (and cost per calorie—forty-four cents per calorie for the Quarter

TABLE 7.1 The Caloric Costs of Supersizing Movie Theater Popcorn

Size	Price	Portion	Calories	Fat (Grams)
Small	$3.13	7 cups	400	27
Medium	$3.84	16 cups	900	60
Large	$4.44	20 cups	1,160	77

Tables 7.1 to 7.5 adapted from National Alliance for Nutrition and Activity (NANA), "Prices, Calories and Fat Intake for Portions of Food," in From Wallet to Waistline: The Hidden Costs of Supersizing, Washington, D.C.: June 2002.

TABLE 7.2 Supersizing the French Fries at McDonald's

Size	Price	Portion	Calories	Fat (Grams)
Small	$1.03	2.4 ounces	210	10
Medium	$1.50	5.2 ounces	450	22
Large	$1.67	6.2 ounces	540	26

TABLE 7.3 The Fat Costs of "Value" Meals

Size	Price	Calories	Fat (Grams)
Quarter Pounder with cheese	$2.33	530	30
Medium value meal (adds medium drink and fries)	$3.74	1,190	52
Large value meal (adds large drink and fries)	$4.32	1,380	56

Pounder vs. thirty-one cents per calorie for the large value meal), if you buy a large value meal instead of the Quarter Pounder, you are also getting an extra 850 calories and 26 grams of extra fat. If you eat 850 extra calories per day beyond what you need once or twice per week, this translates to a weight gain of twelve to twenty-five pounds in one year.

Twenty years ago, having a soda meant drinking 6.5 ounces that contained about 85 calories. Today at 7-Eleven, you can purchase the following Coca-Cola Classic options: a Big Gulp (32 ounces), a Super Big Gulp (44 ounces), a Double Big Gulp (64 ounces), or a Slurp and Gulp (32 ounces of fountain drink and 22 ounces of Slurpee). At McDonald's, you have the choices listed in Table 7.4. So for an extra sixty cents you get an extra 260 calories. If you have diabetes or are trying to prevent it, it is also important to know that the small Coke has almost 54 grams of sugar. That's about fourteen teaspoons. The Supersize has 140 grams of sugar—a whopping thirty-five teaspoons of sugar!

How about a caffe latte from Starbucks? It is true that black coffee has no calories, and a latte is typically made with milk, not cream. Sounds like a decent choice, right? Or is it? (See Table 7.5.) So what happens if you switch from a coffee with one ounce of low-fat milk to a grande caffe latte each day? Well, you get an extra 250 calories and an extra half of a pound of weight

TABLE 7.4 Drink Sizes and Calories at McDonald's

Size	Price	Portion	Calories	Fat (Grams)
Small	$1.04	16 ounces	150	0
Medium	$1.20	21 ounces	210	0
Large	$1.44	32 ounces	310	0
Supersize	$1.64	42 ounces	410	0

TABLE 7.5 Supersizing Caffe Lattes at Starbucks (made with whole milk)

Size	Price	Portion	Calories	Fat (Grams)
Tall	$2.44	12 ounces	210	11
Grande	$2.99	16 ounces	260	14
Venti	$3.29	20 ounces	350	18

per week. The math is bad for your waistline. That's an extra 26 pounds in a year! A tall latte made with skim milk would be 120 calories and 0 grams of fat. On a daily basis, adding this more health conscious drink to your diet would increase your weight by *only* thirteen pounds per year.

So how do you eat well in this potentially toxic food environment with growing portion sizes and marketing strategies that tempt you to eat supersized meals with their "get more for less" messages? You should start with these strategies:

- Don't put yourself in tempting situations with buffets or all-inclusive menus.
- Choose not to buy "value" or "combo" meals. Buy just what you really want.
- Ask for and review nutrition information so that you can make informed choices that support your health and well-being. Most fast-food restaurants do have this information available if you ask.
- Ask for half-size portions or order appetizer portions at restaurants.
- Avoid extra calories from your beverages. You can drink a large amount of calories in a short amount of time, and most research shows that people who drink excess calories don't simultaneously decrease their calories from food to compensate. People with diabetes must also avoid the large sugar content of regular sodas and naturally sweetened juices.
- Remember not to skip meals. "Grazers" who eat frequent, small meals will lose more weight than "bingers" who eat

only one to three larger meals per day, even when the total number of calories per day is the same. Therefore, consider having at least three meals a day; three small meals and two snacks may be even better.

Your Emotional Environment

For many of us, our feelings play a role in when, what, and how much we eat. For example, we may eat to soothe physical or emotional pain or to suppress uncomfortable or painful feelings and temporarily distract ourselves from them. Because eating offers only a temporary solution, many people repeat the process and fall into the habit of using food to cope with painful emotional experiences. Some of us use food as a reward: Had a bad day? Treat yourself to a "special meal." This is a particular problem for people who feel that they are always giving to others and have little time to nurture themselves. Food becomes a quick and convenient reward.

On the other hand, some people have too much extra time on their hands and use food to cope with boredom or to procrastinate. It is common for some people to take breaks from studying, housework, or other projects and use food to fill those breaks even though they may not be hungry. Interesting patterns in eating behavior start to emerge. People who are angry often look for foods with crunch and say that they need to chew. People who are sad, depressed, anxious, or emotionally upset turn to the "comfort foods" that they associate with pleasant feelings and memories stemming from childhood. Let's consider John's situation.

John has been struggling to lose weight. He noticed that whenever he felt stressed he would binge on cookies and milk, which made him feel better, but this sabotaged his weight loss. As we talked with John in detail about this pattern, he realized that he associated eating cookies and milk with happier times. His mother used to set out cookies and milk for him when he returned home from school. Once John realized why he binged on cookies and milk, he found other ways to connect with the nurturing feelings he associated with his mother. John started to look at his mother's pictures and read the letters that he had saved when he needed to feel comforted or wanted to soothe his stress.

As we've seen (and some of us know all too well), eating can help suppress bad feelings. Think about your own situation. Do you eat when you are angry, bored, tired, lonely, anxious, or depressed? What about positive emotions—birthdays, holidays, vacations, parties, and other happy occasions where food is the center of the celebration? When you celebrate, do you overeat?

Instead of suppressing your feelings with food ("jack-in-the-box phenomenon"), try to process and deal with uncomfortable emotions by trying some of the following ideas:

- Keep a journal about your feelings. Write them out instead of stuffing them down with food.
- Talk about your feelings with a trusted family member or friend.
- Discuss your feelings and how they affect your eating with a therapist or counselor.
- Create a list of alternative things to do that do not involve food when you feel angry, lonely, bored, or depressed. For example, you may have a list of necessary tasks or house projects that you have been hoping to accomplish. Next time you feel bored, pull out your list of necessary "to-dos." Next time you feel angry or upset, try putting your feelings down on paper, and then do something distracting like taking a walk, listening to music, or watching a movie. Transforming eating behavior to physical activity would of course be a win–win.
- Have a list of nonfood ways to treat yourself when you feel you deserve a reward. Taking a hot bath, buying a magazine or flowers, calling a long-distance friend, or buying a good book are just a few examples.

Your Cognitive Environment: Changing Your Self-Talk

Not everyone overeats because of easy access to food or because of their emotional state. Some people overeat because their self-talk persuades them to. Self-talk is the narrative that goes on in our heads—our cognitive environment. We don't usually think we control this self-talk, but if we're conscious of it, we can. Do any of these self-talk statements sound familiar?

- That food looks delicious; I bet it tastes good.
- This is delicious. I may not get this again any time soon, so I better eat as much as I can now.
- I am so stressed. I need something sweet to calm my nerves.
- Hmm, what should I do now? Let me just check in the refrigerator and see what there is to eat.
- I paid for this, so I am going to get my money's worth.
- I am so frustrated; let me crunch on some peanuts.
- A nice bowl of ice cream would be soothing right now.
- I don't want to waste this food, so I'll just finish it now. There are starving children in Africa.
- I deserve a treat.
- I don't want to be alone. Those cookies will keep me company for a while.
- I can't sleep. Maybe if I get up and have a snack, it will relax me and pass some time. Then I'll try again to get back to sleep.
- I'm tired of studying; let me take a break and get a snack.

Some of these self-talk "tapes" are so familiar that they're practically background music—we don't even realize that we are saying them to ourselves. It is important for you to pay attention to your self-talk and change your inner dialogue, your cognitive environment.

Let's take Sonia as an example. Food and desserts are always out on the counter at her workplace, and whenever she walked by any of the food, she said to herself, "That looks delicious."

She tasted the food and then thought, "This tastes good. I want some more." She ate more and thought, "That's OK. I'll make up for it later." The next day, the same inner dialogue occurred, and again Sonia overate and found that her weight was up instead of down at the end of the week. She decided to become more conscious of her self-talk and to challenge it. She walked by a tray of cookies and said to herself. "That looks good, but I'm not hungry, and if I start eating those cookies I will have a hard time stopping, and then my progress with losing weight will get stalled." She passed the cookies.

Later she went by, and only half of a cookie was left. She said to herself, "That looks good; there's only a small piece left and that won't do any harm. But I don't want to get started on that today. I've done so well this week." She again passed on the cookie. She lost three pounds that week.

As you start to monitor your self-talk, listen for certain types of negative self-talk patterns.

All-or-Nothing Thinking

Many of us tend to think of ourselves and our personal qualities in the extremes. We are either "good" or "bad," "a success" or "a failure," "on the diet program" or "off the diet program." If you think in these extremes, you might set unrealistic goals; for example, "I will never eat desserts," or, "I will walk every night after dinner." This type of goal setting expects perfection and because it is unrealistic sets you up to feel like a failure. The remedy: beware of thinking that includes words like *good* or *bad*, *always* or *never*. Instead, work toward a balanced view, and remember that one slip isn't the end of the world. In reality, true lifestyle change is a process that is typically two steps forward and one step back. Now, that's a realistic expectation.

Should Statements

Many people try to motivate themselves by saying "I should" do this, or "I have to" do that. "Should" statements often backfire because they can trigger feelings of guilt, shame, resentment, and anger that do not motivate in the least. The remedy: reframe "should" statements as "want" statements. For example, instead of saying to yourself, "I *should* walk every day," try saying, "I *want* to walk four times per week so that I build some stamina and burn some calories to help with my weight loss."

Filtering or Disqualifying the Positive
Many of us have a tendency to magnify the negatives of a situation while at the same time filtering out or diminishing any positive aspects—seeing the glass as half empty rather than half full. For example, let's say you keep focusing on the fact that while you were on vacation you strayed from your healthy eating plans and gained two pounds. You might decide, "Well, there goes the last month of dieting. I may as well eat whatever I want." You've essentially squashed any positives in the situation. The remedy: reframe your view. You could also legitimately say, "I really enjoyed my vacation. I did keep up with my activity goal. Overall I have still lost six pounds. I just need to refocus on my lifestyle goals now that my vacation is over. Next time, I'll plan to set a goal for maintaining my weight over vacation."

Excuses
It's easy to blame someone or something for our problems rather than taking responsibility for choices we make. Many of us say, "I have to buy these cookies and have them available for my children to eat," "I have no willpower," or, "It's too cold to walk." The remedy: change these self-talk statements to ones such as, "I could buy my children healthy treats we all could enjoy so the whole family's eating habits can improve." Or, "It is hard to change long-term eating habits, but I can give it a try and see how it works." Or, "I'll try to dress with layers and start walking. If it gets too cold, I'll stop, although as I walk I may warm up."

Negative Labeling
Some people constantly stick negative labels on themselves and their efforts. Any error or slip becomes a reason to be self-critical.

Instead of noting, "I didn't exercise this week," a negative labeler would think, "I'm fat and lazy," or, "I'm such a failure; I knew I couldn't do it." The remedy: do not translate a slip in behavior into self-criticism or a character flaw. Try saying, "One slip isn't the end of the world. Slips are normal and to be expected. I'll get back on track now."

Doom, Gloom, and Giving Up

A doom-and-gloomer jumps to conclusions well ahead of time without any real evidence, expecting failure and making self-defeating self-talk statements such as, "This program is too hard. I just knew I would regain the weight once I got started." The remedy: mentally rewrite these statements to be one step at a time. Try, "I've learned something about what is hard for me. I'll try a different strategy next time."

Strategies for Improving Your Self-Talk

Carefully monitor your self-talk. Replace your sabotaging self-talk statements with helpful and positive self-talk statements as often as you can.

Write down the negative self-talk statements that you notice, and see whether they really make sense. Are the statements logical, reasonable, or helpful to you and your lifestyle goals for weight loss? Would you talk to a friend that way? If not, reframe the statements to be logical, reasonable, and supportive of your efforts.

Create positive self-talk statements, and repeat them frequently so that they eventually displace your old, negative self-talk statements. Make positive self-talk statements visible in your environment. For example, post a sign on your refrigerator and kitchen cabinets that says, "I am committed to healthy eating and a healthy weight loss."

And remember to ask yourself, "Am I really hungry? If I'm not hungry, then what is it?" Help yourself to identify why you are eating, what your self-talk statements are, and how they affect your eating behavior.

Ditching Old Habits

People commonly overeat out of habit, and old habits die hard. You go to the movies and buy popcorn and eat it all because that is what you always do. The TV is on, so you eat, and commercials may give you ideas for some additional snacks, so you nibble some more. In these situations we are like automatic eating machines, plowing through the food in front of us until it's gone—even though we weren't hungry. And when the food *is* gone, we hardly remember eating it. This is called distracted eating and it is the least satisfying way to eat. Distracted eating is also a high-risk way to eat because we're not giving eating our full attention and it's hard to remember everything we've consumed.

Many of us also eat because we think it's expected—a ritual. For example, stuffing yourself at Thanksgiving dinner is practically a family tradition. Cooking and eating an abundance of food can become a habit. So make sure that your rituals are helpful habits that recognize hunger effectively and not habits that lead to overeating.

You may be uncomfortable saying no to extra food because you do not want to insult the host or hostess. Or maybe you just eat whatever is served because you don't want to be "rude." Some people overeat to avoid getting hungry later. "It is going to be a busy day and I may not get a break, so I better eat extra now even though I'm not hungry." These are more habits, and habits can be broken.

The best way to change an old, unhelpful habit is to replace it with a new, more helpful one. What if you bought a cup of coffee or bottle of water to drink during the movie instead of soda and popcorn?

Are You Hungry or Are You Eating out of Habit?

Evaluate your degree of hunger before eating and your degree of satiety or fullness after eating. Rate your degree of hunger on a scale of 0 to 10 with 0 being "overhungry or starving," and 10 being "stuffed."

0	1	2	3	4	5	6	7	8	9	10

0 = overhungry   5 = satisfied/comfortable   10 = stuffed/

1 = very hungry   6 = a little full   uncomfortable

2–3 = hungry   7 = full

4 = a little hungry   9 = very full

If you are not sure whether you're genuinely hungry, close your eyes and put your hands on your stomach to help you focus on your body rather than your self-talk, emotions, or other eating triggers. If you think that you might be thirsty, try drinking a tall glass of water and see if you feel satisfied. Ask yourself how long it's been since your last meal or snack. If you have eaten within the past two hours, it is unlikely that you would be physiologically hungry again so soon. On the other hand, if it has been more than four hours since your last meal or snack, it is more likely that you could be truly hungry.

Once you decide how hungry you are, then you can decide on how much food you'd need to quell your hunger and bring your satisfaction rating to a 5 or a 6 (being satisfied or a little full). It is important to eat consciously and enjoy your food without other distractions. It takes twenty minutes for the signal to go from your stomach to your brain that you have eaten, so if you eat too quickly (in less than twenty minutes), then you will not be able to accurately evaluate your degree of satisfaction or fullness. In fact, if you eat a lot of food quickly because you are overhungry, then twenty to thirty minutes later when the signal finally reaches your brain, you could feel uncomfortably full at a 9 or a 10. So it is really important to slow down. Sometimes playing slow music in the background may help; if you play a march in the background, research shows that you will eat faster to keep that pace.

By now, you're probably starting to understand that modifying your behavior—making a true lifestyle change—involves more than just changing your diet. It involves evaluating and managing your food environment (where and what you eat), your emotional environment (how you respond to your emotions), your cognitive environment (the way you think), and your habits (the way you eat). Now let's focus on how to start changing what you eat.

CHAPTER 8

Setting Weight, Activity, and Nutrition Goals and Tracking Your Progress

Setting goals provides a target and direction for transformation and is an important component of successful lifestyle change. Let's look at some of the elements of successful goal setting. Consider the following as you set your goals and go about achieving them:

- **Positive phrasing** minimizes the "shoulds" in your vocabulary, thereby fostering a habit of positive self-talk rather than negative self-talk; for example, "I will include fruit for dessert," instead of, "I won't have cake for dessert." We discussed this at length in Chapter 7.
- If your goal is specific enough to be **measurable**, then you can easily evaluate whether or not you've achieved it; for example, "I will walk after dinner for thirty minutes five times per week," or, "I will walk to the corner market," instead of, "I will exercise more."
- Setting a **time frame** for reaching a goal is crucial to establishing accountability with yourself. Doing so will help you stay focused and assess your progress at specified time

points; for example, "I will lose five pounds in one month," instead of, "I will lose five pounds."

- Make your objective **realistic and achievable**. When setting goals, it is important that you be at least 80 percent confident that you can achieve them. If you're not, then it is important to calibrate the goal until you can be confident. Realistic and achievable goals don't include all-or-nothing words like *always* or *never*. If you set realistic, achievable goals, you'll be less likely to expect perfection. When you set realistic goals, you begin to experience "small wins." The path to successful lifestyle change is made up of such small wins—one win at a time. Try, "I will start by walking twenty minutes four times this week," instead of, "I will walk sixty minutes every day."

- **Make lifestyle changes in small steps.** Lifestyle goals often involve preplanning and interim steps. For instance, you need to make sure that you have the appropriate footwear and clothing before you can put your activity goals into action. You'll need to plan meals ahead so that you shop for the foods that you need to prepare. Start with, "I will buy apples, oranges, and carrots and put them in the refrigerator to pack for my lunches this week," instead of, "I will eat fruit and carrots for lunch."

- Lifestyle change is hard work and takes a lot of focus, but **positive reinforcement and nonfood rewards** for achieving your goals can help you stay focused and motivated. Try, "If I bring a healthy lunch from home three times this week, I will use the money I saved for a magazine or music CD," instead of, "I will bring my lunch from home three times this week."

Setting Weight Loss Goals: How Much?

Experts recommend an average initial weight loss goal of 10 percent of body weight because research shows that this degree of weight loss is associated with significant improvements in cardiovascular risk factors and psychological well-being. This doesn't mean that further weight loss may not be beneficial: it may very well be, depending on your initial body mass. In the Diabetes Prevention Program, weight losses of 5 to 7 percent were associated with a 58 percent reduction in the development of diabetes.

But research also shows that obese individuals would find a 17 percent weight loss "disappointing," a 25 percent weight loss would be "acceptable," and a 37 percent weight loss would meet their "dream weight" expectations. Even when participants in a weight loss program were repeatedly counseled that a weight loss of 5 to 15 percent was a reasonable expectation, they still hoped for a weight loss of 25 percent. However, for most overweight or obese people, a 10 percent weight loss is achievable and will make a difference.

To figure out how many pounds you'll need to lose to meet your weight loss goal, multiply your weight by the percent you want to lose. Let's say Joanne, who weighs 250 pounds, wants to lose 5 percent of her body weight; she would multiply 250 by .05, which would be 12.5 pounds. For a 10 percent weight loss, she'd need to lose 25 pounds. For Joanne, a weight loss of 12.5 to 25 pounds would significantly improve her cardiovascular risk factors and reduce her risk of diabetes.

A person's weight loss goals are often based upon other personal considerations, such as appearance. As you set your weight loss expectations, keep in mind that the amount you need to lose to improve your health is probably different from (and likely less than) how much you'd need to lose to bring you to your pre-

Calculate Your Own Weight Loss Goal

My current weight is ___ pounds. To lose 5 percent of my body weight, I'd have to lose ___ pounds. To lose 7 percent, I'd have to lose ___ pounds. To lose 10 percent, I'd have to lose ___ pounds.

ferred weight. But, remember that you don't want to set your goals so high that you become discouraged and give up on a reasonable weight loss that will have important health benefits.

Using the Weight Loss Graph, (see Figure 8.1 on pages 112 and 113), record your current weight at the beginning (at week 0) and mark your 5 percent, 7 percent, and 10 percent weight loss targets at week 26. Draw a line connecting your current weight (before any weight loss) and your target weights so you can follow your rate of weight loss and see whether you're losing at a rate that will yield health improvements.

Setting Weight Loss Goals: How Fast?

What rate of weekly weight loss should you aim for? Most people aren't satisfied with a gradual loss of one to two pounds per week, even though this is the safest and healthiest way to lose weight. It sounds slow, but at a rate of one to two pounds per week most of you will have lost at least 5 to 10 percent of your body weight in about six months. This is an impressive achievement when you consider how long it took you to gain that weight and the number of calories you need to cut to lose it.

One pound of fat carries 3,500 calories of energy. If your weight has been steady and you want to lose one pound per week, you need to reduce your calorie intake by 500 calories per day for seven days (3,500 calories), or expend an extra 500 calories each day by walking briskly five miles per day for seven days, or some combination of decreased energy intake and increased energy output that totals 3,500 calories. To lose two pounds per week, you would need to reduce your calorie intake by 1,000 calories per day for seven days or walk ten miles per day for seven days. If you have been gaining weight, then you would have to reduce your calories even further to create the same weight losses. So, losing one to two pounds per week requires a substantial effort.

Moving More: Activity Goals

As you set goals for activity, it is important to consider your start-ing point. If you are not currently active, you'll want to set goals that are not out of reach. It may be best to start with walking for 10 minutes, five times per week (50 minutes per week). (A vari-ety of practical approaches to increase your activity level were reviewed in Chapter 5.) Once you are walking 50 minutes per week, increase the goal to 15 to 20 minutes, five times per week, for a total of 75 to 100 minutes per week. As you build stamina and establish your new habit, you can continue to increase your activity goal to a minimum of 150 minutes per week. That was the minimum activity goal for participants in the Diabetes Pre-vention Program. In the DPP, lifestyle participants kept a diary of their activity levels and often used pedometers (small, inex-pensive devices that count the number of steps you take) to help measure their level of activity.

Eating Well: Nutrition Goals

To lose weight and prevent or slow the progression of diabetes, your nutrition goals should include targets for calorie and fat intake, based on your starting weight. Table 8.1 shows the calcu-lated calorie and fat goals necessary to achieve weight loss. (We'll talk more about that in Chapter 12.) As part of this effort, you'll need to establish goals for changing your food shopping, prepa-

TABLE 8.1 The DPP Goals for Daily Amounts of Fat and Calories*

Starting Weight (Pounds)	Fat (Grams)	Calories
120–170	33	1,200
175–215	42	1,500
220–245	50	1,800
250–300	55	2,000

*To determine fat and calorie goals, round your starting weight to the nearest starting weight on this table.

FIGURE 8.1 Weight Loss Graph

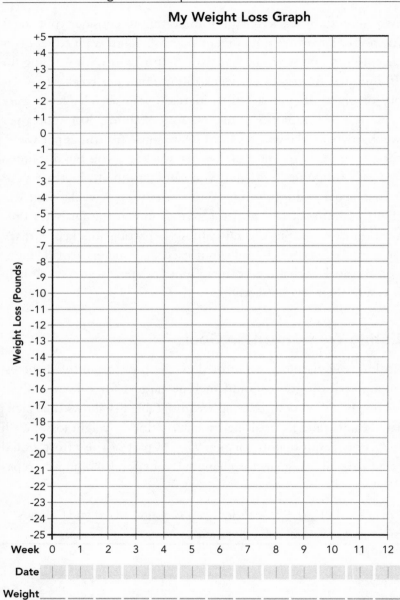

My Weight Loss Graph

My starting weight = _____ pounds

My Weight Loss Graph

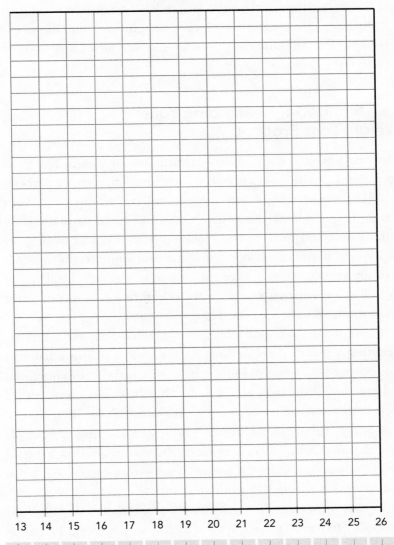

ration, and eating habits and patterns. For instance, you may decide to go no more than four hours between meals and snacks to prevent getting overhungry, which leads to overeating.

Once you have determined your weight loss, nutrition, and activity goals, self-monitoring helps you see how close you are to achieving them.

Self-Monitoring: Recording Your Weight Loss Progress

The first step to self-monitoring is to put your weight loss goals on paper. Identify your current weight and 5 percent, 7 percent, and 10 percent weight loss targets and record them on your weight loss graph. Weigh yourself on a reliable scale at the same time of day and in the same clothing (either naked or in your underwear, if you're self-conscious) because your weight can fluctuate by several pounds over the course of the day. Ideally, you should weigh yourself in the morning before eating to minimize fluctuations in your measurements.

How often should you weigh yourself? You may start by weighing yourself daily to keep focused and get into a habit of monitoring your weight. However, if you find this discouraging and counterproductive, weigh yourself a little less often, either every other day or twice a week. Research shows that people who weigh themselves regularly do best at keeping weight off over the long term, so it is critical that you establish a habit of weighing yourself at least once per week—more often if it helps you focus, but not if it discourages you.

Post your weight loss graph in a place that will help you remember to record your weight at least once per week. Plot your weight on your graph, and draw a line connecting your readings from one week to the next so that you can observe your pattern of weight loss. You will notice that weight loss does not always occur in a straight line. Sometimes weight holds steady for two weeks and then drops several pounds in the next week. As long as you focus on meeting your behavioral and lifestyle goals, weight loss will follow. More consistent lifestyle changes result in more consistent weight loss.

If your weight does not budge for three weeks in a row, then step back and look for what might be getting in your way. For instance, many people underestimate portion sizes and think that they are consuming three ounces of meat when they're really eating five or six ounces. What seems like a teaspoon of butter or salad dressing might be more like a tablespoon.

Self-Monitoring: Recording Your Food Intake and Activity

Research has consistently shown that people who keep a log of their daily food intake tend to underestimate calorie and fat intake by at least 20 percent. So, if you record 1,000 calories of food in one day, it's likely that you've probably eaten closer to 1,200 calories or more. It's not that most people are being dishonest when they keep a food log; rather, individuals often underestimate portion sizes and tend to forget to write down everything—especially if they try to think back and record food at the end of the day or if they engage in "distracted" eating. It is harder to remember how much and what you have eaten when you are combining eating with other activities like reading, watching TV, or socializing. Nibbling a few chips, peanuts, or other snack foods in transit from kitchen to den is often forgotten or not counted, but all calories count and they add up.

It is important to keep a record of your activity and eating habits. Here's how to break it down: most experts recommend that you focus on recording minutes of activity that are similar in intensity to a brisk walk and ten minutes or more in duration. Record specific strength-training and aerobic workouts separately. You'll also want to record when you've done no physical activity on a given day.

Figure 8.2 is a sample lifestyle log for recording your eating habits. Figure 8.3 is a sample activity log for tracking your exercise habits.

FIGURE 8.2 Lifestyle Log

Time	Food	Portion	Calories	Fat (Grams)	Hunger	Location	Comments
Daily Totals							

FIGURE 8.3 Daily Physical Activity Log

Type of Physical Activity	Duration of Activity

Although burning calories with increased activity helps lose weight regardless of the frequency of exercise, the added benefit of exercise in improving the sensitivity of muscle to insulin (either your own or injected) persists for no more than thirty-six hours; therefore, it makes sense to try to do exercise no less frequently than every other day—ideally, five to six days per week.

Your food intake record should go beyond what you've eaten. It should also include the time you eat meals and snacks and the number of calories and fat grams in the portions you consume. The best way to record food intake is to note the details as you go through the day. There are two good reasons for doing it this way. First, you will be less likely to forget what you've eaten (or to write it down). Second, you can tally how many calories and fat grams you have consumed as you go along, which lowers the chances that you'll overshoot your calorie and fat gram targets. Recording your food intake at the end of the day is helpful as a historical record, but it can't help you adjust as you go along.

It's also helpful to note how hungry you are before meals and how satisfied you are after meals. This can help you determine whether or not you're meeting hunger and satiety needs. If you find that you're "starving" before meals, you may have gone too long between meals or snacks. Here's an example: if you notice that you are overhungry before dinner at 7:00 P.M. and that you ate lunch at noon and had no afternoon snack, then you might want to try having a healthy snack at 3:00 or 4:00 P.M. to help manage your hunger—and perhaps more important, to help keep you from overeating at dinner. (You can take some of the calories you planned to have at dinner and have them as a midafternoon snack.) If you are not satisfied (that is, if you still feel hungry) after meals, you may not have eaten enough. On the other hand, if you're too full after a meal, your food log can help you reduce your portions further.

Some people eat very few calories and fat grams during the first half of the day and then eat a large dinner and snack late into the evening. As a result, they tend not to feel hungry the next morning. This eating pattern (when food intake is disproportionately high in the evening hours) can cause high blood-sugar levels in the evening and the next morning. (In addition, concentrating your calories into one or two meals a day, or "gorging," is counterproductive for weight loss. Ideally, calories should be spread out during the day.) To break the pattern of infrequent, large meals, rate hunger and satiety before and after meals and spread out your eating so that you don't go more than four hours between meals and snacks (except when you're sleeping, of course). People who try this find that they can better pace their eating at night and feel satisfied with reasonable portions at dinner and evening snack. As a result, blood glucose levels will be lower at bedtime and when you wake up.

Another important part of your food record is to keep track of how many calories you take in through liquids. Sweetened beverages (such as juices or sodas) add lots of calories, don't help satisfy hunger, and can raise blood-sugar levels quickly and to relatively high levels if you're prone to diabetes or have diabetes. For these reasons, diet soda, water, or flavored (no-calorie) seltzers are better choices than regular soda. It is also much better to eat fresh fruit rather than drink the juice, because the fiber in the fruit provides a greater sense of fullness and helps moderate blood-sugar surges.

The calories in alcohol work against weight loss in several ways. First, it is high in calories (7 calories per gram; see Table 8.2), and the body processes alcohol somewhat as it does fat. Drinking alcohol can also reduce self-control, and you may notice that you eat more calories overall on days when you drink alcohol. Finally, the sodas and juice drinks and bar snacks, such as nuts and chips, add substantial calories. So be very careful about including alcohol in your daily plan, and evaluate how it affects your ability to stick to your plan.

Use the comments section of your log to note observations about your eating, including your physical environment (where you eat—for example, the car, bedroom, restaurants, fast-food places); your self-talk, which is your state of mind or your "cognitive environment"; and your mood (your "emotional environ-

TABLE 8.2 The Calorie Content of Alcohol and Bar Snacks

	Calories	Fat (Grams)
12 ounces beer	150	0
12 ounces light beer	110	0
7 ounces table wine	144	0
4 ounces dessert wine	180	0
1.5 ounces alcohol (1 jigger)	100	0
Bloody Mary (5 ounces)	115	0
Daiquiri (4 ounces)	224	0
Gin and tonic (7.5 ounces)	171	0
Martini (gin and vermouth) (2.5 ounces)	156	0
Rum (1.5 ounces) and Coke (8 ounces)	180	0
Rum and Diet Coke	100	0
Whiskey sour	158	0
White Russian (made with cream) (3 ounces)	225	7
Nuts (1 ounce)	170	14
Trail mix (1/4 cup)	150	8
Pretzels (1 ounce)	108	1
Chips (1 ounce)	152	10

Adapted from Jean A. T. Pennington, *Bowes and Church's Food Values of Portions Commonly Used*, Philadelphia, PA: Lippincott-Raven Publishers, 1998.

ment"). As you do this, you'll start to see patterns in the physical cues that trigger eating as well as the relationships among your feelings, emotions, thoughts, attitudes, and how much (and what) you eat.

Think of self-monitoring as a process of self-discovery about the what, when, where, why, and how much you eat. Once the patterns become clear, you can develop strategies to break the ones that sabotage your goals and reinforce the ones that will lead to good health.

Even the best plans and intentions can get waylaid by circumstances. The next chapter offers you tools to help keep you on track.

CHAPTER 9

Solving Problems

You're ready for change, you've set your goals, and you've been self-monitoring your progress. You're feeling good about your progress. And you should. But before you know it, you notice that certain situations interfere with your plans. You need to recognize, anticipate, and plan for the obstacles that can sabotage your success. Problem solving is a crucial part of your efforts to be more active and eat fewer calories and less fat.

There are five basic steps to effective problem solving:

- Step 1: describe the problem or barrier in detail.
- Step 2: brainstorm possible solutions.
- Step 3: pick one of your solutions to try.
- Step 4: make a positive plan using goal-setting skills.
- Step 5: try your first plan and see how it works. Be ready to try two or three different plans to complete the problem-solving process.

Let's look at Sandra's story. Sandra is a fifty-two-year-old woman who was trying to lose weight to prevent diabetes, which her mother developed at age fifty-five. She has been feeling that her eating is chaotic—she's noticed that she's consuming a lot of unplanned extra calories. Sandra uses her lifestyle log to help her figure out what's going on.

Woke up late and rushed out of the house without breakfast.

Had two doughnuts and coffee with cream at a morning meeting.

Should have gotten up earlier. Shouldn't have had the doughnuts.

Felt upset with self.

Skipped lunch to make up for the doughnuts.

Arrived home overhungry, tired, and frustrated.

Too tired to prepare supper. Munched on chips. Roommate arrived home and suggested ordering pizza. Ate too much pizza.

When Tom reviews his lifestyle log, he notices that he is doing a lot of late-night eating and these extra calories are stalling his progress with weight loss. He sits down and describes the problem in more detail.

Finished dinner and had argument with wife.

Felt upset and ate ice cream to feel better.

Watched TV and saw commercial for favorite snack food.

Went to the kitchen, saw favorite snacks and leftover dessert, and wolfed down some of each. Felt bloated and guilty. Self-talk said, "Why bother trying?"

As you look at the triggers and cues that led to overeating for both Sandra and Tom, you can see how the following contributed to their overeating:

- Things in their environment that made them want to eat (high-calorie foods in the office or at home, TV commercials)
- Self-talk, thoughts, feelings, or emotions that triggered them to eat even when they were not hungry
- People who didn't support their efforts to lose weight

When we respond to these cues by overeating time and again, we develop the habit of eating in response to feelings, emotions, and situations that have nothing to do with our hunger. Before we know it, getting up late or arguing with someone predictably leads to overeating.

Once Sandra and Tom described the details of the problem, then they could brainstorm options to circumvent the chain of events. See Tables 9.1 and 9.2.

The earlier in the sequence that you can interrupt behavior patterns, the more successful you will be in changing your response habit of overeating. It is important to list options that are realistic and likely to work and then to weigh the pros and cons of each option. Also, the more places that you can interrupt the domino sequence, the more success that you will have in changing the outcome.

The next step is to make a positive plan or goal to deal with the barrier.

TABLE 9.1 Sandra's Chain of Overeating

Sandra's Triggers	Other Options
Woke up late	Set alarm earlier
Rushed out of the house without breakfast	Get a piece of fruit to go
Had two doughnuts and coffee with cream at meeting	Have toast/English muffin in the office
"I should have gotten up earlier."	"I was tired. I'll go to bed earlier tonight."
"I shouldn't have had the doughnuts."	"I chose to enjoy the doughnuts, but now I'll eat lighter for lunch."
Felt upset with self	Use positive self-talk to refocus
Skipped lunch to make up for the doughnuts	Have salad and roll for lunch
Arrived home overhungry, tired, and frustrated	Have a snack, then take a nap
Too tired to prepare supper	Heat up a preportioned frozen dinner
Munched on chips	Munch on carrots, celery, or pretzels
Roommate arrived home, suggested pizza	Order salad with the pizza
Too much pizza!	Preplan how tomorrow will be a better day

TABLE 9.2 Tom's Chain of Overeating

Tom's Triggers	Other Options
Had argument with wife	Talk issue through with wife—feel better
Felt upset	Take a walk—feel better
Got ice cream to soothe feelings	Get a hot cup of tea to soothe feelings
Watched TV	Read a book or exercise while watching TV
Saw commercial for favorite food	Read mail during the commercial
Went to the kitchen for more food	Ask self if hungry or not; if not hungry, what is it?
Saw favorite snacks/leftover dessert	Keep snacks/desserts out of sight
Took some of each	Take a small amount
Ate them in a hurry	Eat slowly
Felt bloated and guilty	Focus on what can be learned from this slip/event rather than feeling guilty
"Why bother trying?"	"I'll take this one step at a time. I'll try another option to deal with this next time."

Sandra's goal is to buy fruit, English muffins, and jelly and bring them to the office so that if she wakes up late, she will still be able to eat a healthy breakfast. Her reward will be to buy herself some flowers at the end of the week if she has a healthy breakfast four out of five mornings next week.

Tom's goal is to take a walk after dinner four nights out of five to clear his head after a day at work and transition into a calmer evening with his wife. His reward will be to see a movie on the weekend.

The final step is to try the plan and see if it works. If it doesn't, think about how to adjust your plan so that it does work. Keep trying. Just like lifestyle changes, problem solving is a process.

CHAPTER 10

Maintaining Your
New Lifestyle

Lifestyle change begins with goal setting, self-monitoring, and problem solving. But the key to making those changes stick is your personal plan for follow-up, accountability, and support.

Follow-Up

Each participant in the Diabetes Prevention Program was assigned a lifestyle coach to help him or her with goal setting and problem solving and to provide feedback on weight, activity, and food-intake records. Typically, the lifestyle coach was a registered dietitian. Almost all of the participants said that simply knowing that they had to check in with their coach weekly was important in keeping focused. If you need help finding a registered dietitian to serve as a lifestyle coach, you can check with your physician for a referral or try the website for the American Dietetic Association—eatright.org. This site provides hundreds of quick tips, monthly hot topics, and the Find a Nutrition Professional searchable database.

Research shows that the more frequent the check-ins—the more frequent the accountability—the better the results with weight loss and behavior change. Dietitians and personal trainers are professionals who provide personalized feedback and support and keep you "accountable" for achieving your goals. Some people establish an accountability plan by enrolling in formal group weight loss programs like Weight Watchers that include regular weigh-ins and record keeping. Others may be disciplined enough to be their own "accountants," but as with income tax preparation, it's not so easy.

Developing an Accountability Plan

As you make lifestyle changes and move toward your goals, you'll want to have an accountability plan that identifies *who* you will check in with to review your progress with self-monitoring of weight, activity, and food intake. The accountability plan also specifies *how often* you will check in with your lifestyle coach to set goals and to engage in problem solving.

Once you reach your goals, you can transition to a less frequent follow-up schedule. For instance, you may try a check-in once every other week and see if you can maintain your goals; then you can move to once every three weeks and then once per month. Many participants in the DPP transitioned to a once-per-month schedule to sustain lifestyle changes. Toward the end of the program, contact became more spaced out—first to once per six weeks and then to once every two months. During the transition, each person learned just how often he or she needed to check in to stay on track.

Many folks decided to join Weight Watchers to have a place to weigh in regularly and stay focused. As we discussed earlier, keeping close track of weight helps increase your chances of long-term success. Those who most successfully keep lost pounds off weigh themselves regularly—as often as daily and at least once per week. If their weight starts to sneak up, they immediately increase their self-monitoring by keeping careful track of daily minutes of activity, food portions, and calorie and fat intake until they have returned to their target weight.

If you decide to join a weight loss program for guidance, accountability, and support, then consider the following:

- Decide if you are ready to devote the time, attention, and effort necessary to succeed at weight loss. Ask yourself, "Am I ready to make lifestyle change a priority?"
- Define your short-term and long-term weight loss goals, and find out whether or not the program will help you meet those goals. Ask yourself, "How much weight do I want to lose in the first month, and how much do I want to lose by the end of the program?"
- Ask for the credentials and training of the staff and factual information about the successful results of the program, not just personal stories. Look for programs that are run by experienced registered dietitians, exercise specialists, and/or psychologists.
- Ask if the program includes components that focus on healthy eating, how to increase activity, how to improve self-esteem, and how to maintain weight loss in the long term.
- Look for programs that will help you learn to change your eating habits through information, guidance, and skills train- ing, not programs that just give you menus or provide meals.
- Ask about possible health risks of the program (especially if it includes very-low-calorie diets, medications, or surgery).
- Discuss with your health-care provider how the program will work for you in light of your medical history and weight loss expectations.
- Find out about the costs of the program and whether they are covered by insurance.
- Make plans for regular medical appointments to measure the changes in your health after you begin the program.

Building a Positive Support System

Another key to success is to build a positive support system and surround yourself with people who support you in your weight loss efforts. Take a few minutes to think about your family, friends, and coworkers, and list those on whom you can and can't rely for support. Take some time to think about the attitudes of those around you and how they might affect your weight loss efforts. Make a point of surrounding yourself with people who have a positive attitude about your lifestyle-change efforts. Tell them how they can "help the cause" (including not encouraging

FIGURE 10.1 Who Supports Your Weight Loss Efforts? What Are Their Attitudes?

	Negative: People who disapprove, resent, or tease	Indifferent: People who neither discourage nor help	Positive: People who are encouraging or helpful
Spouse			
Significant other			
Children			
Mother			
Father			
Friends			
Employer			
Coworkers			
Other			

off-limit treats). You might put a check mark into the appropriate place in Figure 10.1 for each of the key people in your life.

It is important to realize that not everyone will be supportive—some people may tempt you to eat, tease you, or disapprove of your weight loss endeavor. These are some possible reasons for this:

- They may be uncomfortable eating in front of you and so offer you food to be polite.
- They may be jealous of your success in losing weight.
- They may not really want you to succeed. (This is their problem, not yours!)
- They think that you are starving.
- They offer you food as a sign of affection and concern. Because so many people associate food with love, they may feel that when you say no to the food they offer, you're rejecting their love and concern. So be sure to let your friends and loved ones know that you're just fine and that it is because you know they care about you (and vice versa) that you want to protect your health.

Make a list of specific things that your family, friends, or coworkers can do to support your efforts to eat healthy, be active, and lose weight. Don't hesitate to ask for their support. Here are some specific actions that you can ask your family, friends, and coworkers to take on your behalf:

Support for Healthy Eating
- Shop for, prepare, and serve low-fat, low-calorie foods and meals.
- Don't offer me second helpings.
- Encourage me to cook and taste healthy new foods.
- Eat low-fat, low-calorie foods with me.
- Don't offer me or tempt me with problem foods as a reward or a gift.

- Praise my efforts to make healthier food choices.
- Ignore my lapses and remember that lifestyle change is a process.
- Keep high-calorie, high-fat foods out of sight, and keep healthy foods handy.
- Help clear the table and put food away as soon as the meal is over.
- Remind me of my goals for healthy eating as we select places to eat out.

Support for Being Active

- Walk or exercise with me.
- Suggest social events that involve being active.
- Praise my efforts to be active.
- Ignore my lapses with activity plans.
- Help me plan and fit activity into my schedule.
- Ask me how to be helpful.

As you embark on the journey to change your lifestyle, keep in mind that you are the main traveler. While others can speed—or slow—the trip, you are primarily responsible. You should be careful that you not make the changes in lifestyle the only focus of your important relationships. We have occasionally seen couples in whom the lifestyle for one member of the couple becomes the dominant feature of the relationship, causing friction and discord. Keep your lifestyle program in perspective.

Recovering from a Lapse

Even if you have a well-developed follow-up, accountability, and support plan, if you are human you are likely to have lapses, particularly in high-risk situations. A lapse occurs when you don't follow your plans for healthy eating or increased activity. A lapse is usually a discrete event from which you can easily recover; it's part of making lifestyle changes and won't hurt your progress unless one lapse turns into a series of lapses. That's called a relapse. With a relapse, you begin to lose focus and slide into old habits and patterns. A relapse can be turned around but it will take more effort than it would to respond to the first lapse. Collapse is when relapse takes over, you have returned to all of your old habits, and you have regained all of your weight.

A common mistake is to react to a single lapse as though it were a relapse or a collapse. Lapses from healthy eating and being active are normal and to be expected; it's the way you react to lapses that is important. The truth is that no single incident of eating too much can ruin your overall progress with healthy eating and weight loss. It is critically important that you master a response to lapses so that you can resume focus as soon as possible. If you notice that a series of lapses is occurring and your weight starts to creep up (that is, if you gain more than three pounds), you'll want to take quick steps to get help and refocus. Keep a list of "clues" that help you identify when a lapse is more than just a lapse. Here are examples:

- Weight gain of more than three pounds
- More than one week without exercising
- Inability to fit into certain clothes
- Resumption of an old habit (more than one time) that you had worked hard to break

Steps in Preventing a Relapse

When you lapse from healthy eating or being active, try the following steps, used in the DPP, to make sure that your reactions to lapses don't work against you:

- **Talk back to negative self-talk or blame.** Talk positively to yourself. Rather than thinking, "I blew it," try focusing on the truth, which is, "One lapse won't ruin everything as long as I get back on track and refocus on healthy eating right away." Your positive thoughts will affect how you feel and help you refocus.

- **Ask yourself why the lapse happened, and try to learn from the experience.** A lapse is really a learning opportunity. Everyone who is trying to eat healthy, increase activity, and lose weight has a list of high-risk situations that can lead to lapses. This is your chance to learn more about what puts you at high risk for a lapse. Once you know the danger areas, you can strategize about how to avoid having a lapse in this type of situation in the future.
- **Regain focus and self-control the very next time you eat.** Don't tell yourself that you blew it for the day and that you'll start again tomorrow. Get back on track as soon as you can.
- **Talk to someone supportive.** Family, friends, coworkers, and others can be a real source of support. Talk to others about what caused you to lapse, what you've learned from the situation, and your ideas for handling this type of high-risk situation in the future. Consider regular appointments with a dietitian for more professional help.
- **Keep things in perspective.** Focus on all of the positive changes that you have made. Remember that lapses are learning opportunities and part of the process of lifestyle change—if you hadn't accomplished something, there would be no "lapse." Keep notes about what you learn from each of your lapses as they occur.

Knowing Your High-Risk Situations

High-risk situations are the circumstances most likely to disrupt your eating and activity and exercise routines and lead to a lapse. Typical high-risk situations include eating out, stress, emotional triggers (feeling bored, tired, angry, anxious, or depressed), vacations, social events, and holidays. Once you have identified your high-risk situations—which are not the same for everyone—you can use problem-solving skills to plan ahead and work around them.

For example, if you find that you overeat when you feel angry, lonely, bored, tired, stressed, or upset, make a list of other comforting things you can do in response to these feelings. Here are some ideas:

- **Share your feelings** with someone or write them in a journal rather than stuffing them down with food.
- **Take a walk** or do some other exercise that you enjoy. Exercise is a proven way to lift mood, and it may help distract you from the things on your mind.
- **Take a nap** if you are tired instead of eating to stay awake. You're likely to feel better with rest.
- **Address the problem** causing you the negative emotions, and work out a solution or a plan to deal with it. Use the problem-solving approach described in Chapter 9.
- **Don't grab food** on impulse and eat chaotically. Acknowledge how you feel and give yourself permission to choose to eat in a positive, deliberate way. If you do, then you may find that a smaller portion of food will be enough to help you feel better and still allow you to succeed in losing weight and controlling your blood sugars.

High-Risk Situations

Vacations and holidays are times when most people want to let go a little, relax, and enjoy themselves. But because they typically disrupt eating and activity and exercise routines for more than one day, it's especially important to plan ahead. As part of that, you should reassess your expectations for lifestyle changes during these times and identify reasonable eating, weight loss, and activity goals. For instance, it may be more reasonable to define success as maintaining your weight over vacation and plan to resume your focus on weight loss once the vacation or holiday is over.

If your goal is to maintain your weight, think about how you will handle food and eating in restaurants or in other people's homes. For instance, you might decide to limit the number of times that you eat out and spend the extra time and money on activities other than food. You may decide to eat some special foods but limit portions. You also might decide to set up your vacation/holiday food environment for success by bringing a variety of low-calorie food choices with you for meals and snacks that you eat on your own.

You'll also want to think ahead about how you'll stay active. Discuss your eating and activity goals with family and friends, and share ways that they can support your success. If you build in plans to keep track of your eating, your activity, and your weight, you will be more likely to meet your goals and expectations over the holidays and vacations. It may take you several vacation/holiday experiences to find the strategies that work best for you. So, don't get discouraged. Be patient, and keep learning and adjusting your strategies based on what worked (or didn't work) in the past.

Other high-risk situations that can disrupt your eating and activity and exercise routines are significant life events such as changing your job, getting married or divorced, having children, retiring, or facing the death of a spouse or partner.

Make a list of your own personal high-risk situations, identify a plan to deal with them using the problem-solving approach, and keep these strategies on hand. See Figure 10.2.

Ending the "Diet Mentality"

As we have discussed, successful lifestyle change that leads to weight loss involves more than just changing your diet. In fact, "diets" alone don't work for permanent weight loss. But you will need to learn to manage and plan your eating: how you eat, where you eat, why you eat, what you eat, and when you eat. It's a long-term commitment to your health, not a short-term test of your willpower. That means getting rid of the diet mentality. A "diet" does not sound permanent. It suggests an element inserted into your life rather than the consistent long-term change in

FIGURE 10.2 Charting Your High-Risk Situations

My High-Risk Situations	My Strategic Plan

lifestyle that is required to improve long-term health. A diet makes you feel deprived and is something that you "go on" with the idea that someday you will "go off" it.

When you truly change your lifestyle, you'll be able to eat and feel satisfied. So before you begin your effort, review the following list to make sure that you have a plan for success.

- Are you really ready and willing to change your eating habits and become more active?
- Do you have reasonable expectations for weight loss of one to two pounds per week?
- Is your living environment (home, office, car) set up for success or sabotage?
- What is your plan for eating in a toxic world?
- Is your self-talk helpful or hurtful to your goals of losing weight?

- Are you ready to eat healthier in such a way that you feel satisfied and not deprived?
- Are you willing to focus on eating to satisfy physical hunger rather than emotional hunger?
- Are you willing to use strategies other than eating to deal with your emotions?
- Are you setting effective goals?
- Are you ready to self-monitor your weight, activity, and food intake?
- Are you willing to apply problem-solving skills to deal with barriers to success?
- Do you have someone or something such as a dietitian, personal trainer, or program to which you will be accountable?
- Have you identified your personal support network?
- Have you accepted that lapses are part of the lifestyle-change process, and are you willing to work on a plan to deal with them?
- Are you willing to get rid of the diet mentality and begin to shop, cook, and eat for health?

CHAPTER 11

Popular Weight Loss Programs: Do They Work?

Everyone wants to know how to lose weight—so much so that Americans spend more than $40 billion a year on weight loss products and programs. Books selling the magic formula that people are hoping to get are always at the top of the bestseller list. And what is the magic formula? It's a diet that tastes good, is easy to follow, promises quick weight loss results without feeling hungry or deprived, and includes detailed menus of what and how much to eat.

Popular diet books such as *Dr. Atkins' New Diet Revolution*, *The South Beach Diet*, and Dr. Phil's *The Ultimate Weight Solution* imply that they have the long-awaited formula to losing weight once and for all. Each of these programs may help some people lose weight. But, like hundreds of other diet plans, they neither offer a miracle cure nor are right for everyone.

Anyone can write a diet book or devise a weight loss program. Self-styled diet gurus need not have any training in medicine, nutrition, or exercise physiology to represent themselves as weight loss experts. Even worse, they don't have to prove that the advice they offer is safe or effective. No wonder finding a safe and effective way to lose weight is so difficult!

Basic Rules

Certain basic rules about weight loss apply to all of the programs we discuss in this chapter (and in this book). Some of them probably are familiar, and some may not be:

1. **It's all about calories.** Weight loss occurs when you burn off more calories than you consume in your food. A diet works when it has helped you reduce your intake of calories. Some foods are healthy and some are unhealthy for reasons that have nothing to do with how many calories they contain. And some people may have genes that allow them to burn off calories a bit more efficiently. But at the end of the day, if you want to lose weight, it's all about calories.

2. **Choose "healthy" foods vs. "unhealthy" foods.** Certain foods are good for your health and others aren't. That is, if you eat 2,000 calories' worth of healthy foods each day, your overall health is likely to be better than if you eat 2,000 calories' worth of not-so-healthy foods. If you are trying to lose weight, making healthy food choices becomes even more important. To maintain good health, it's critical to choose foods that contain enough vitamins and other essential nutrients and avoid those that can contribute to heart disease.

3. **Exercise is good for you even if it does not lead to a healthy weight.** Exercise should be part of every weight loss program because you need to increase the calories that you burn relative to the number of calories you consume. But if you increase your activity level or exercise *and* increase the number of calories you eat, you may not lose weight despite the increased level of activity and exercise.

This causes some people to wrongly decide that exercise is not helping them. If you are exercising and not losing weight, it is usually because you are consuming too many calories.

Even if exercise doesn't immediately help you achieve a healthy weight, it is good for you in other ways. Exercise increases the levels of HDL ("good") cholesterol in your blood and can reduce your risk of many diseases (including diabetes)—even if your weight remains in the unhealthy range. So don't cut back your level of activity and don't stop exercising just because they have not yet led you to your weight goal.

4. **What matters is the long term, not the short term.** There is little scientific evidence that losing weight—even a lot of weight—for a few weeks or months and then gaining it back does you any good. In fact, some studies have indicated that "yo-yo dieting" could be harmful, although the true effect of weight cycling is still up in the air. We do know that losing weight improves health only if you can keep it off.

Almost *any* weight loss program can help almost anyone shed pounds for a few weeks or a few months. (As we will discuss, much of the very early weight loss is secondary to a loss of water rather than loss of fat or other tissue.) Very few studies have tested weight loss programs for a year or more. The limited number of studies that have been done tend to show people regaining weight by the end of one year. Long-term changes are the goal, and programs that leave you unsatisfied or feeling deprived are unlikely to be effective for very long.

In this chapter, we take a look at weight loss programs and how they work. The popular programs espoused in books, tapes, and television programs can be categorized into three basic groups: very-low-fat diets, low-carbohydrate diets, and right-food-combination diets.

Very-Low-Fat Diets

Two of the popular very-low-fat diets are Dr. Dean Ornish's *Eat More, Weigh Less* and the Pritikin program. *Eat More, Weigh Less* promises that you will "have an exciting array of foods from which to choose, creating a sense of abundance rather than deprivation" and that "the meals are so low in fat that you will get full before you consume too many calories." The Pritikin diet promises to be "the world's healthiest diet" and "a safe, sensible way to change your lifestyle, add years to your life, arresting, alleviating, and in some cases helping to reverse symptoms of heart disease, hypertension, diabetes, arthritis, hardening of the arteries, and obesity." There is more than a little hype to these claims.

How Do Very-Low-Fat Diets Work?

Very-low-fat diets recommend that you eat only 10 percent of your calories from fat. The average American consumes more than 30 percent of calories from fat, and some Americans eat as much as 40 percent or more of their calories from fat.

Very-low-fat diets can help lose weight for three reasons. First, because fat has nine calories per gram and protein and carbohydrate each have four calories per gram, reducing fat intake to only 10 percent of calories allows you to eat a greater volume of food but consume fewer calories. Second, the body burns relatively more energy in digesting and storing carbohydrates and proteins than in storing fat, and this can help weight loss. Third, very-low-fat diets tend to include more fiber, which helps the stomach feel "filled" and increases satiety.

Very-low-fat diets restrict all fats, oils, and fatty foods and either limit lean meat, poultry, and fish choices to three and a half ounces per day or eliminate them altogether. They encourage a vegetarian diet using meatless meals that incorporate legumes, tofu, egg whites, and nonfat dairy products as protein sources. The Pritikin Maximum Weight Loss Diet "allows the dieter to eat all day long and lose up to thirty pounds a month." The Pritikin diet works because it contains only about six hundred calories per day! The foods that you can eat "all day long" are mainly raw and cooked vegetables, fat-free veg-etable soups, salads, and fat-free salad dressings, which are all very low in calories and often high in fiber.

Although very-low-fat diets are touted as being simple and easy to follow, many people find them difficult to follow for the long term because of the number of food restrictions and the limited number of meal options when eating out. These diets have extensive lists of foods to avoid and restrict. You will hear claims that very-low-fat diets will reverse heart disease. Yet the research done in this area focused not on the diet alone but on the *combination* of diet, weight loss, exercise, and stress reduction. Separating the individual effects of these factors is difficult, if not impossible.

Are Very-Low-Fat Diets Healthy?

Keep in mind that there are only three food groups—carbohydrates, fats, and proteins. So restricting any one of these components means that one or both of the others will have to increase. With very-low-fat diets, the relative contribution from carbohydrates and proteins increases. Very-low-fat diets are typically very high in carbohydrates (about 70 percent carbohydrate). Such a high carbohydrate intake can increase blood-sugar levels—obviously, a major problem for people with diabetes. They also can raise the blood level of triglycerides (the main fat-carrying particle in the blood) and decrease the level of HDL (good) cholesterol, especially in people who don't exercise. For this reason, a very-low-fat diet may be a poor choice for someone who has high triglycerides and low HDL cholesterol. This includes many people with type 2 diabetes. On balance, we advise people with prediabetes or with diabetes to avoid very-low-fat diets, because they are so high in carbohydrates.

Low-Carbohydrate Diets

Given that very-low-fat diets typically are high in carbohydrates, it is interesting that in recent years, low-carbohydrate ("low-carb") diets have become extremely popular. Two of the most popular low-carbohydrate diets are the Atkins and the South Beach Diets. The books that describe these diets are currently among the bestselling books in the country.

The Atkins Diet has been through several versions, but all of them encourage eating red meat, which is rich in saturated, unhealthy fat. More recent high-fat diets have begun to emphasize foods that have healthier forms of fat. Nevertheless, the low-carb diets must include relatively higher fat and protein content. It may seem peculiar—even perverse—that these weight loss programs would recommend a high-fat-content diet, considering that most of the evidence (reviewed in Chapters 1 and 2) strongly supports high-fat diets as being part of the cause of the epidemic of obesity and diabetes. But the low-carb, high-fat programs are based on the authors' conclusions that high-carbohydrate diets have resulted in higher insulin levels, insulin resistance, increased appetites, and obesity—a controversial theory. What remains clear is that too much food—regardless of its composition—and not enough exercise/activity lead to overweight, obesity, diabetes, and heart disease.

How Do Low-Carbohydrate Diets Work?

Like all other diets, perhaps the main reason that low-carb diets work is that they are low in calories. But there are several other potential explanations for the weight loss experienced with low-carb diets.

First, low-carbohydrate diets rely, in part, on a chemical trick to cause weight loss. When you restrict your intake of carbohydrates, your body quickly uses up stored carbohydrates (glycogen stores) for energy. Glycogen is stored with water, so when you use glycogen you release water into the blood and then into the urine. For every sixteen ounces of fluid you excrete in the urine, you lose a pound of weight. Low-carb diets promise weight loss of eight to thirteen pounds in the first two weeks alone, but much of this is "water weight." The early weight loss with low-carb diets makes it easy to believe that giving up carbohydrates is the most effective way to lose weight. It is also easy to believe that carbohydrates cause weight gain and obesity because reintroducing carbohydrates into the diet causes an increase in weight, much of which is secondary to water shifts in the opposite direction.

Second, once you have used up all of your stored carbohydrates, you start to digest and use the fat stores inside fat cells. When the fatty acids are broken down, they form molecules called ketones, which accumulate in the blood. Anyone who is starving or on a low-carbohydrate diet will have an increased concentration of ketones. Such diets are therefore sometimes called "ketogenic," or ketone-producing, diets. (People with diabetes can develop a dangerous condition called ketoacidosis, which is the result of not being able to regulate the production of ketones.) High levels of ketones can cause bad breath and nausea. They also decrease your appetite. A few studies comparing low-carb/high-fat diets to low-fat/high-carb diets have shown that the low-carb/high-fat diets may more effectively suppress appetite, as we discuss a little later.

Are All Carbohydrates the Same?

Carbohydrates provide the body with energy. The National Academy of Sciences recommends we eat at least 130 grams of carbohydrates per day to provide sufficient energy for those organs—such as the brain, the rest of the nervous system, and the kidneys—that rely predominantly on glucose for their function. Virtually all of us have a lot more carbohydrate than that in our daily diets. However, the low-carb diets such as Atkins and South Beach start out with only 20 grams of carbohydrate in their initial phases.

The two main types of carbohydrates are "simple" and "complex." Simple carbohydrates are the sugars found in fruit, some vegetables, milk and milk products, sugar, honey, and syrup. Complex carbohydrates include starch and fiber and are found in grains, legumes, and starchy vegetables. Most foods contain a mixture of simple and complex carbohydrates. Simple carbohydrates and starch are digested and absorbed into the bloodstream as sugar. Fiber isn't.

Because the body can't digest fiber, it doesn't contribute calories or provide energy. That doesn't mean it is worthless. Foods that contain fiber have some important benefits. They can help you feel full on fewer calories because they contribute food volume without providing calories. They help lower cholesterol levels because fiber binds to cholesterol and reduces its absorption. Fiber-filled foods help lower blood sugar because fiber slows the absorption of sugars into the bloodstream. They also help prevent constipation.

Although all digestible carbohydrates are eventually converted into simple sugars, the rate of absorption is different for different foods. The digestion of some foods leads rapidly to relatively high levels of blood sugar, whereas other foods release sugar into the blood more slowly. Foods that release sugar rapidly are defined as having a high glycemic index, and foods that release sugar slowly have a low glycemic index.

So, all carbohydrates are not the same. And the effect of carbohydrates on your blood sugar, which is particularly important if you have diabetes, is even more complicated. Many other factors influence how different carbohydrates affect your blood sugar. These include your blood-sugar level before the meal; how the food is processed, prepared, stored, ripened, cut, and cooked; what else is eaten with the food; the portion of the food consumed; the fat and fiber content of the food or other foods eaten at the same meal or snack; your activity level; and certain medications that you may be taking.

Although consideration of the glycemic index (or "glycemic load," defined as the product of the amount of sugar in a given food and its glycemic index) may be important in fine-tuning the self-care regimen for people with type 1 diabetes, it is much less important in treating obesity and type 2 diabetes. Considering how difficult it is to address the basic concept of changing lifestyle on a consistent basis to improve energy balance and control weight, concepts such as "glycemic index" and "glycemic load" may be a distraction. In general, increasing dietary fiber content will accomplish most of the goals of the low–glycemic index diets. Don't take your eye off the main goal of decreasing calories.

Are Low-Carbohydrate Diets Healthy?

If you are overweight, long-lasting weight loss is healthy. If you can achieve long-lasting weight loss with a low-carb diet, that achievement should improve your health. Unfortunately, long-term studies with such diets have not been performed, and we don't know if they succeed in the long run. Nevertheless, there are some potential problems with low-carb diets that you should know about.

Low-carb diets, like the original Atkins Diet, encourage the use of foods that contain large amounts of saturated fats and may well be unhealthy. Strong scientific evidence suggests that diets high in saturated fats are unhealthy; in particular, they cause an increased risk of heart disease and stroke. Therefore, if you achieve long-lasting weight loss with a low-carb diet that includes relatively large amounts of saturated fat, the health benefits of the weight loss may be outweighed by the negative health effects from saturated fats.

A second potential problem with low-carb diets is that, as your body excretes the fluid stored with carbohydrates, it also flushes out potassium, sodium, calcium, and other minerals. These fluid and mineral losses can lead to light-headedness, dehydration, constipation, and leg cramps. Increased losses of the mineral calcium in the urine can cause kidney stones and bone loss. The Atkins Diet suggests that you purchase and consume a long list of nutritional supplements to replace the nutrient deficits that the diet plan creates.

For people with diabetes, an important potential benefit of low-carb diets is that they can dramatically lower blood-glucose levels and insulin requirements. However, for people who are treated with insulin or other glucose-lowering medications, such as sulfonylurea pills, the high-fat, low-carb diets require careful monitoring of blood-glucose levels and adjustments of medication to prevent potentially dangerous hypoglycemia (low blood sugar). Such individuals should consult their diabetes care team beforehand for advice and help with adjustments of medications so that the occurrence of hypoglycemia can be minimized.

A related problem with a low-carb diet is that if you don't stick with it in a consistent manner—for example, if you follow it closely one day and "cheat" another day—your blood-sugar levels can go up and down like a roller coaster. This makes it very difficult to regulate your blood sugar.

Watch out for foods and the ancillary products that are being marketed for people trying low-carb diets. They are often high in calories, are more expensive, and do not always taste very good. So, "low carb" does not necessarily mean "low calorie" or "low fat" or healthy—you need to read the nutrition facts label to be sure.

Finally, the high protein content of most low-carb diets is also of concern, especially for people with diabetes who have a higher risk for kidney disease. That's because high loads of protein can cause the kidney to overwork, adding to the damage that diabetes can do to the kidney.

Healthy and Unhealthy Fats

Whether you are considering a low-carb, high-fat diet or a more conventional higher-carb, low-fat diet, you will have fat in your diet. Are all fats the same? For many years fat in the diet has been demonized. Grocery stores are filled with foods labeled "low fat." In the past twenty years, Americans have reduced the percentage of calories that we get from fat. However, the total calories and grams of fat we consume have actually increased and remain substantially higher than in most places in the world. What have we been told is wrong with fat? We've been told that there are more calories in each gram of fat than in each gram of carbohydrate or protein, which is true. But the impression has been left that, calories aside, all fats are bad for you because they increase the chance of heart disease and other diseases. That is not true.

We need fat in our diet to provide fuel for the body's cells and to build the membranes around every cell. Not all fats are unhealthy. Some fats are good for you. In fact, they are essential for good health. If you eat more healthy fats—and stay away from unhealthy ones—you can improve your health. But don't lose sight of the main target: keeping your weight in a healthy zone.

Unhealthy Fats

There are several different types of fats in our diet. Two of them are particular problems: *saturated fats* and *trans fats*. Fats that are saturated (referring to their full saturation with, and inability to accept any more, hydrogen atoms) are abundant in meat and animal fat, dairy products, and some oils such as palm and coconut oil. They are solid rather than liquid at room temperature. Saturated fats in the diet indisputably increase the artery-clogging process known as atherosclerosis, primarily by increasing blood levels of LDL ("bad") cholesterol.

Trans fats are largely created by manufacturing, not by nature. They were created by industrial chemists who were asked to find a way of transforming liquid oils into solids, so that they would be easier to ship, and to protect the oils against becoming rancid. Trans fats have rapidly increased in our diets, finding their way into commercial baked goods, fast-food french fries, margarine, and vegetable shortenings such as Crisco. Starting in 2006, the Nutrition Facts food labels will contain the amount of trans fats in each grocery store food. Until then, look for the words *partially hydrogenated* vegetable oil or shortening on the food label; when you see it, you know there are trans fats present. The problem with trans fats is that they increase heart disease, stroke, and other diseases caused by atherosclerosis—like saturated fats.

Healthy Fats

Two types of fats in the diet that are good for you: *monounsaturated* and *polyunsaturated*. (*Unsaturated* refers to a chemical structure that can accept one or more hydrogen atoms.) The monoun-saturated fats that we use most often are found in certain oils, particularly olive, peanut, and canola oils. The polyunsaturated fats are called "essential" fats because our bodies do not make them; we must get them in our diet. The most common sources of polyunsaturated fats are plant oils such as corn and soybean oil, seeds, whole grains, and fatty fish such as salmon and tuna.

You will hear about two types of polyunsaturated fats: n–3 (also called omega-3) fats and n–6 (also called omega-6) fats. There is some controversy about whether they are equally good for you and whether the ratio of one to the other is impor-tant. In our view, the main point is that they are both healthy for you.

The healthy fats do several important things for you. First, they have the opposite effect of the saturated fats and lower your blood levels of LDL ("bad") cholesterol, reducing your risk of developing atherosclerosis. The n–3 polyunsaturated fats also reduce the chance that—if you have heart disease (including heart disease that has not caused symptoms and been diag-nosed)—you will develop life-threatening problems with the rhythm of your heart. There are also data demonstrating a ben-eficial effect on inflammation and other vascular changes that seem to underlie atherosclerosis and heart disease.

A large study called the Lyon Diet Heart Study, conducted in France, provided strong evidence that adding monounsaturated fats and polyunsaturated fats to the diet protected against ather-osclerosis and lengthened life. This randomized controlled trial assigned some people to eat a "Mediterranean" diet including more vegetables, more fruit, more fish and poultry, less red meat, and no cream. The people eating the Mediterranean diet also were given a special margarine that was low in saturated and trans fats and rich in unsaturated fats, especially the essential n–3 polyunsaturated fat known as alpha-linolenic acid. The results of the Lyon Diet Heart Study were unusually dramatic and clear: after only two and a half years, there was a 70 percent reduction in deaths from all causes.

Healthy and Unhealthy Proteins

There are not really "healthy" and "unhealthy" proteins like
there are healthy and unhealthy fats. But there are foods rich in
protein that are bad for you because they also are rich in
unhealthy fats—for example, red meats—and protein-rich foods
that are good for you because they do not contain unhealthy fats.
So picking your source of protein is very important. Keep in
mind that in general it is difficult to increase protein in your diet
without increasing fat, and vice versa.

The amount of protein you eat is important. The Recommended Dietary Allowance (RDA) for protein is forty-six to fifty
grams of protein per day for healthy adult women and fifty-eight
to sixty-three grams of protein per day for healthy adult men.
The National Academy of Sciences recommends that adults not
consume more than two times the RDA for protein. People who
eat too much protein increase their risk for kidney stones, gout,
and calcium loss from bones. High protein intakes can also stress
the liver and the kidney, the two organs that process the protein
that we eat. Some weight loss diets contain too little protein (less
than the RDA), and this can lead to feeling tired and sluggish.
Eating too little protein over a prolonged period can lead to ane-
mia, reduced muscle mass, malnutrition, hair loss, reduced organ
size, and compromised immune system.

It is not necessary to make sure that a precise percentage of
your calories come from protein, as is recommended in the Zone
Diet described later in this chapter, as long as you take in the recommended dietary allowance. The American Diabetes Association recommends that you consume 15 to 20 percent of your
calories from protein. The Institute of Medicine suggests that a
protein intake between 10 and 35 percent of your calories is
acceptable.

It is best to choose low-fat sources of protein for good health.
Vegetarians can meet their protein needs by consuming a wide
variety of grains, vegetables, legumes, and soy products. Lacto-
ovo vegetarians can add low-fat dairy products and eggs.

Right-Food-Combination Diets

The right-food-combination diets do not focus on emphasizing or avoiding one type of food, such as fat or carbohydrates. Rather, they are based on other theories. Some of the popular right-food-combination diets are the Zone Diet, the Eat Right for Your Type Diet, and Dr. Phil's Ultimate Weight Solution.

The Zone Diet

The Zone Diet promises that if you eat small meals with the correct ratio of protein, carbohydrate, and fat, then you will balance your hormones and insulin so that your body works at peak performance. According to its developer, being in the "zone" leads to decreased hunger, increased weight loss, increased energy, and the ability to burn fat and fight heart disease, diabetes, depression, and cancer (and possibly facilitate world peace).

The Zone Diet treats food as if it were a drug: "You must eat food in a controlled fashion and in the proper portions—as if it were an intravenous drip." The recommended diet is 40 percent carbohydrate, 30 percent protein (based on lean body mass), and 30 percent fat. The book aims to convince people that they need to eat foods in "blocks," with a final ratio of 1:1:1 for protein, carbohydrate, and fat blocks at each meal.

It is true that if people with diabetes eat a consistent amount of carbohydrate in each meal and snack from day to day, their blood-sugar levels will be more stable and predictable (see Chapter 4 for more details). However, asking people to follow rigid rules such as eating seven grams of protein for every nine grams of carbohydrate and one and a half grams of fat to meet this 1:1:1 ratio is cumbersome and can reduce the pleasure in planning meals and eating food.

The Zone Diet suggests that you eat a Zone breakfast within one hour of waking, have a Zone-favorable snack thirty minutes before exercise, and eat a small Zone snack before bed. Such a regimented eating plan can help you lose weight. But it can also lead to discouragement and giving up. All that is really necessary to lose weight is to lower calorie intake and increase activity level. Changing lifestyle habits is hard enough without complicating the process with unnecessary rules! Finally, the high protein intake of the Zone Diet is also of concern for people with diabetes because they are at higher risk for kidney failure.

The Eat Right for Your Type Diet

The Eat Right for Your Type Diet claims that your blood type is the key to determining what for you is the right diet, the right exercise program, and the right supplements for staying healthy, living longer, and achieving your ideal body weight. The diet implies that if you don't eat correctly according to your blood type and ancestry, you will be susceptible to certain diseases.

The truth is that eating a healthy, low-calorie diet to lose weight has nothing to do with your blood type. The Eat Right for Your Type diet may lead people to restrict certain foods and food groups unnecessarily and thus limit their enjoyment of food. What is most worrisome is that some people may use this diet to treat serious medical conditions.

Dr. Phil's Ultimate Weight Solution

Dr. Phil's Weight Solution promises, "You will learn about food in a completely different context, in a way that no diet book has ever discussed or previously put into widespread practice." Dr. Phil suggests that if you eat the right foods—he calls them "high-response cost, high-yield foods"—and minimize or avoid the wrong foods—"the low-response cost, low-yield foods"—then you will lose weight.

As Dr. Phil defines them, "high-response cost, high-yield foods" take a long time to prepare and chew and are lower in calories; allegedly, they are "hunger suppressors." "Low-response cost, low-yield foods" are easy to grab and eat, require little chewing, and provide an excess of calories for little nutritional value; allegedly, they are "hunger drivers."

There is an important measure of truth in the advice that you should eat more slowly. It takes about twenty minutes for your stomach to generate and send "stop eating"—or satiety—signals to your brain, so slowing the pace of eating is important. This is also why portion control is so important and why "supersized" meals are such a problem. If you eat a supersized meal very slowly, you might feel full by the time you are only halfway through it. But if you eat it fast, you've taken in way more calories than you need before your "stop eating" signals kick in—and then it's too late.

Another part of Dr. Phil's advice also is sound. Planning meals and snacks no more than four hours apart and including foods with more fiber in your diet will help you feel more satisfied and full with fewer calories. However, it is not true that the low-response cost, low-yield foods *drive* your hunger.

In summary, people with diabetes could benefit from Dr. Phil's plan. At the same time, however, if you have diabetes you will need to monitor your blood-sugar levels closely and work with your diabetes team to adjust medications as needed to prevent hypoglycemia. There is another reason to be careful. The high-response cost, high-yield foods and the low-response cost, low-yield foods do not reflect food choice recommendations for people with diabetes and may in fact limit food choices more than is necessary to lose weight and control blood-sugar levels.

All of these diets can produce weight loss not because of their specific macronutrient composition but because they all have one common denominator: they are each low in calories. Table 11.1 shows a sample daily menu for the low-carbohydrate diets, the right-food-combination diets, and the very-low-fat diets. Each of the diets restricts calories by restricting the consumption of specific food groups or one of the macronutrients (carbohydrate, protein, or fat). Each of the diets works because, in general, Americans eat too much food and too much of each of these macronutrients.

Table 11.1 also shows the nutritional composition of each of the diets. As you can see, the Atkins Diet is high in fat, saturated fat, and cholesterol and low in fiber. The South Beach Diet does emphasize healthier fat choices. However, the Phase 1 diet profile is more similar to an Atkins-type diet and is high in percent total fat, exceeds recommendations for percent saturated fat intake, and does not meet dietary fiber–intake recommendations. The Phase 2 diet is more moderate in percent total fat, is lower in percent saturated fat, and contains more fiber yet does not meet fiber-intake recommendations. The very-low-fat diets are very low in saturated fat and cholesterol and high in dietary fiber but may be too high in carbohydrates for people with type 2 diabetes. As you can see, just because a diet produces weight loss does not necessarily mean that it is nutritionally adequate or healthy.

How Well Do They Really Work?

Research comparing the low-carb, high-fat Atkins Diet; the high-protein, moderate-carb Zone Diet; the very-low-fat, high-carb Ornish diet; and the low-fat Weight Watchers diet has shown that each of these helps people lose weight. Why? Because each one helps people take in fewer calories.

In a one-year study conducted by researchers from Tufts University in Boston, 160 overweight men and women (average weight, 220 pounds) were randomly assigned (by chance alone) to follow one of the four diets as best as they could. Within just two months, 22 percent of the volunteers had given up. At the end of the year, 35 percent had dropped out of Weight Watchers and the Zone Diet, and 50 percent had quit the Atkins and Ornish Diets, arguably the two more radical diets—although at opposite sides of the carbohydrate/fat spectrum.

Although volunteers in each group lost weight, not surprisingly those who followed their assigned diet most closely lost the most weight—between nine and thirteen pounds, on average. (This is less than the average of fifteen pounds lost with the DPP

TABLE 11.1 One-Day Menu Comparisons of Popular Diets[1,2]

	Atkins Induction Diet	Atkins Ongoing Weight Loss	South Beach Phase 1 Diet	South Beach Phase 2 Diet
Breakfast	Smoked salmon and cream cheese rollups; 2 hard-boiled eggs	2 poached eggs over fried green tomatoes; 2 strips of nitrate-free bacon	6 ounces vegetable juice; 2 vegetable quiche cups; decaf coffee or tea	Berry smoothie (8 ounces nonfat, sugar-free flavored yogurt, ½ cup berries)
Lunch	Homemade chicken soup	Grilled turkey burger with pepper Jack cheese and green salsa; creamy red cabbage slaw	Sliced grilled chicken breast on romaine; 2 table-spoons vinaigrette; sugar-free flavored gelatin dessert	Open-faced roast beef sandwich (3 ounces lean roast beef, lettuce, tomato, onion, mustard, 1 slice whole grain bread)
Dinner	Broiled steak; oven-fried turnips; arugula and Boston lettuce salad	Cajun pork chops; sautéed kale with red pepper; spicy country cornbread	Grilled salmon; steamed asparagus; tossed salad; olive oil and vinegar; vanilla ricotta cream	Stir-fry chicken and vegetables; tossed salad (mixed greens, cucumbers, green peppers, cherry tomatoes); olive oil and vinegar to taste; ½ cup fat-free, sugar-free vanilla pudding with 3–4 sliced strawberries
Snack	Turkey, romaine lettuce, and mayonnaise rollup	Spiced pumpkin seeds	Morning snack: 1 part-skim mozzarella cheese stick; afternoon snack: celery stuffed with 1 wedge of Laughing Cow Light Cheese	Morning snack: 1 hard-boiled egg; afternoon snack: 4 ounces nonfat, sugar-free yogurt
Total Calories	1,220	1,319	1,263	1,034
Macronutrient Composition[3]	32% p 8% c 60% f	28% p 18% c 54% f	40% p 11% c 49% f	28% p 39% c 33% f
Protein	96 grams	94 grams	129 grams	74 grams
Carbohydrate	26 grams	60 grams	34 grams	102 grams
Fat	80 grams	81 grams	70 grams	39 grams
Saturated Fat	19%	17%	15.5%	6%
Cholesterol	638 milligrams	645 milligrams	300 milligrams	314 milligrams
Dietary Fiber	5 grams	4.3 grams	8.7 grams	13 grams

1. Nutrition information in this chart represents a sample one-day menu for each of the diets. Other daily menus for these diets can range from 1,000 calories to 1,700 calories per day. This range of calorie intake is sufficient to produce weight loss in most people who are overweight. The American Heart Association recommends no more than 30 percent of calories from fat, less than 10 percent of calories from saturated fat, and less than 300 milligrams of cholesterol per day. The American Dietetic Association recommends 20–35 grams of dietary fiber each day. The recommended dietary allowance (RDA) for protein is 46–50 grams of protein per day for women and 58–63 grams per day for men.
2. Abbreviations as follows: p = protein, c = carbohydrates, f = fat

Eat Right for Your Type	The Zone	Dr. Phil's Weight Solution	Pritikin Diet	Ornish Eat More Weigh Less
1 slice Ezekiel bread; all-natural low-sugar jam	4 egg whites; 1-ounce nonfat cheese; 1 cup grapes; ½ slice rye toast; ⅔ teaspoon olive oil; ½ teaspoon natural peanut butter	1 cup raspberries; 1 slice multigrain bread; 1 egg; coffee or tea	3.5 ounces cooked oatmeal; 4 ounces nonfat milk; 1 orange	Cold cereal; nonfat yogurt; fresh berries; orange juice
2–4 ounces organic roast beef; spinach salad; pineapple slices; water	4.5 ounces seafood; small salad; apple; ½ mini pita pocket; 1 tablespoon light mayo	Low-fat cottage cheese; salad vegetables; ½ cup pineapple chunks; 2 tablespoons light fruit salad dressing	8 ounces Latin Belle soup; 4 ounces bell peppers; 4 ounces raw carrots; 4 ounces cauliflower; 4 ounces cucumbers; 1 baked potato	Stuffed baked potato; broccoli, potato, and chickpea salad with lemon tarragon dressing; tossed green salad; fresh fruit
Lamb asparagus stew; steamed broccoli; steamed artichoke; mixed fresh fruit; herbal tea	Chili (4.5 ounces lean ground beef, sprinkle of nonfat cheddar cheese, ¼ cup kidney beans, 1 cup tomatoes); 1 peach; 1 teaspoon olive oil	Turkey breast; stewed tomatoes; steamed summer squash; brown rice	8 ounces tomato-rice soup; 8 ounces shredded cabbage, onions, and tomatoes; 8 ounces stuffed eggplant with tomato sauce; 4 ounces chicken; 1 slice whole wheat bread	Bruschetta with capers and sun-dried tomatoes; pasta with red peppers, greens, white beans, garlic, and lemon zest; grilled asparagus with lemon, peppers, and caper vinaigrette; tossed green salad; peaches cooked in red wine
	Afternoon snack: 1 ounce low-fat cheese and ½ orange; evening snack: 1 ounce turkey breast, 1 cup strawberries	Morning snack: low-fat milk and fresh fruit; afternoon snack: low-fat milk and orange		
987	1,330	1,112	995	1,369
22% p	32% p	30% p	25% p	18% p
40% c	41% c	54% c	63% c	75% c
38% f	27% f	17% f	12% f	5% f
57 grams	110 grams	84 grams	64 grams	65 grams
105 grams	141 grams	153 grams	165 grams	272 grams
45 grams	41 grams	21 grams	14 grams	8 grams
19%	6%	6%	3%	1%
165 milligrams	223 milligrams	323 milligrams	103 milligrams	6 milligrams
25 grams	27 grams	18.5 grams	31 grams	37 grams

program.) In this study, all of the diets lowered cholesterol levels; however, the Ornish diet reduced the LDL cholesterol (bad cholesterol) by 10 percent, whereas the Atkins Diet reduced LDL cholesterol by 2 to 3 percent.

In another study, one hundred people were randomly assigned to follow one of four diets for one year: an Atkins-type, 55 to 65 percent fat diet (high-fat); a 20 to 30 percent fat diet (low-fat); a 15 percent fat calorie-controlled diet (350- to 500-calorie deficit); or a 10 percent fat, whole foods, high-complex-carbohydrate diet (75 percent carbohydrate). Weight loss was initially one pound per week on the 10 percent fat diet and about one-half pound per week on the Atkins-type diet. After one year, those on the 10 percent fat diet had a 52 percent decrease in LDL (bad) cholesterol, whereas those on the Atkins-type diet had a 6 percent increase.

Other recent studies have compared the low-carb, high-fat Atkins Diet (20 to 30 grams carbohydrates per day) to a moderately low-fat diet (25 to 30 percent fat and 500-calorie-per-day deficit). The results may remind you of the story of the tortoise and the hare. At six months, those assigned to the Atkins Diet had lost more weight than those assigned to the low-fat diet. Yet at one year, there was no significant difference in the weight loss between those on the Atkins Diet and those on the low-fat, low-calorie diet. In another recent study comparing different popular diets, more moderate diets, such as Weight Watchers, achieved similar weight loss as more radical diets (Atkins or Ornish) over one year. Adherence to the Weight Watchers diet was superior.

The fear that high-fat diets will inevitably worsen cholesterol and other lipid levels has not proved to be the case, at least when weight loss is achieved in the short term. After one year, there was no significant difference in the reductions in total cholesterol or LDL cholesterol levels between the Atkins Diet and a low-fat diet. However, triglyceride levels decreased more and HDL (good) cholesterol levels increased more in those assigned to the Atkins Diet compared with those on the low-fat diet.

The research to date suggests that the primary reason that people on the Atkins Diet lose more weight initially is that they eat fewer calories. The diet may facilitate cutting back in calories in two ways—by the limited variety of foods to choose from and by the greater satiety and reduction in appetite that can occur with low-carbohydrate, high-fat "ketogenic" diets. The increased water loss that occurs during the first two weeks of the Atkins Diet also contributes.

The Atkins and other low-carb diets aren't for everyone. In the rigorous one-year trials conducted so far, one-third to one-half of volunteers assigned to the Atkins Diet dropped out, and others had trouble strictly sticking with the diet. This may be due in part to the requirements of the diet and the eventual lack of variation. Side effects are another reason. Constipation, headaches, bad breath, muscle cramps, diarrhea, and general weakness are reported more often by people who "do Atkins" than those who follow low-fat diets.

The research thus far suggests that the Atkins Diet may produce better short-term (six-month) weight loss than a low-fat diet, but it is difficult to maintain that pace after six months. Larger, longer studies are needed to pin down the impact of different popular diets on weight loss patterns. We also need to know more about how they affect kidney function, bone density, and cardiovascular function. This is best studied when: (1) we measure how well people stick with each of the diets; (2) weight loss and side effects are compared over time; and (3) indicators of health such as cholesterol levels or bone density are studied not only after weight loss but also once weight is stabilized, so that the acute weight loss effect is no longer trumping the effect of the macronutrient composition on health. For example, in the first six months of some clinical trials, LDL cholesterol (bad cholesterol) increased more than 10 percent in 30 percent of volunteers assigned to an Atkins Diet but in only 16 percent of low-fat dieters. Some experts believe that the reason that HDL cholesterol increases on the high-fat Atkins Diet is because the body needs to produce more HDL cholesterol so that it can remove the proportionately higher amounts of unhealthy fats being absorbed into the bloodstream. It is possible that when people following the Atkins Diet are no longer losing weight and are in the weight-maintenance phase, the higher total fat and saturated fat intakes will cause more dramatic increases in total cholesterol and LDL cholesterol levels and ultimately increase the risk for heart disease.

What About a Weight Loss Pill?

Imagine how much easier it would be if instead of following a diet you could just take a pill every day that would reduce your appetite, increase your metabolism, and not put you at any risk. That isn't a complete daydream. In the past decade there has been an explosion in the scientific understanding of the molecules in our body that control appetite and metabolism. This new research may someday lead to the creation of a "magic" pill for weight loss. But it hasn't happened yet, and past experience is sobering.

The prescription drugs that exist today are either relatively ineffective or have unacceptable side effects. These drugs— Meridia (sibutramine), Pondimin (fenfluramine), and Xenical (orlistat)—work in one of two ways. Meridia and Pondimin stimulate the nervous system, while Xenical interferes with fat absorption. The "long-term" (two-year) results of these medicines are modest at best. Compared to diet and exercise alone, they take off an extra two to eight pounds of weight. Although they may yield greater weight loss in some people, such success stories are almost always from people who have also made major changes in their diets and greatly increased their activity levels. And in some people, these drugs have no positive effect at all. The statement, "these results may not be typical," which appears with all advertising of these agents, is there for a reason: the Food and Drug Administration knows that the advertising will paint the best possible picture and that this picture may not be accurate for many people.

The modest weight loss attributable to these drugs must be viewed in light of the poor safety record for weight loss medications in general, such as amphetamines and the infamous fen-phen (fenfluramine-phentermine) combination. Amphetamines are addictive and can produce dangerous conditions such as irregular heart rhythms and high blood pressure. (Amphetamines may have a valuable role in treating some conditions, but they should not be used for weight loss.) Not long after it was approved as a new weight loss pill, fen-phen, which may have been more effective for weight loss than the currently available medications, was discovered to cause abnormalities of heart valves and related heart damage.

Still, there is reason for hope. At least in animals, new knowledge about how the chemistry of fat cells and of the brain have led to treatments that can cause marked weight loss, and many other related health benefits, in very overweight animals. It is a long way from studies in "simple" animals to results in "complex" human beings, but we think the day will come when there are weight loss pills that are both safe and effective.

There are of course dozens of nonprescription pills, sold as diet supplements, that do not fall under the watchful eye of the FDA. The pills and nostrums promise to help weight loss by stimulating your nervous system, targeting fat stores for digestion, resetting a disordered cortisol system, "balancing" your metabolism, and performing a variety of other unproven actions. None of these miracle cures, advertised in tabloids, have ever been shown to work in rigorous studies. Save your money. If it were that easy to lose weight and maintain weight loss, the epidemic of obesity and diabetes wouldn't exist.

What About Weight Loss Surgery?

The only therapy that has resulted in long-term, substantial, and sustained weight loss is gastric plication ("stomach stapling") and bypass surgery. (See Figure 11.1.) In this procedure, the stomach is sewn or stapled in such a way that food can enter only a small

FIGURE 11.1 Gastric Bypass Surgery

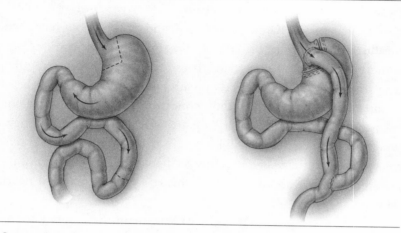

Commonly performed weight loss surgery procedures include gastric restriction where the stomach is "stapled" or sewn (dotted line) so that it will only hold a small amount of food or gastric stapling and intestinal bypass. The combined procedure, which excludes a portion of the small intestine, is more effective.

pouch. The smaller stomach causes a feeling of fullness that inhibits appetite and eating. At the same time, the small bowel is rerouted so food travels from the small pouch in the stomach to a distant point in the small intestine. This minimizes the time the body can absorb nutrients from digested food.

The procedure may reduce appetite in another way, too. It appears to alter a chemical appetite signal called ghrelin that is made by the stomach and intestine. Normally, once the stomach has been emptied several hours after a meal, the stomach and intestine release ghrelin into the blood. This hormone travels to the brain, where it turns on appetite signals. Some studies have suggested that gastric plication and bypass surgery reduce the amount of ghrelin, thereby cutting down appetite.

Gastric bypass surgery typically results in weight loss of seventy-five to one hundred pounds during the first year and maintenance of the weight loss for at least several years thereafter. (Keep in mind that patients who are considered candidates for this surgery, for reasons discussed later, are usually at least one hundred pounds over their ideal weight.) This level of weight loss has remarkable results, reinforcing the critical role that obesity plays in causing disease. Type 2 diabetes can disappear—more than 90 percent of people with diabetes or prediabetes are able to reduce or eliminate their diabetes medications and maintain normal glucose levels. Other disease states associated with severe obesity, such as sleep apnea, arthritis, and hypertension, also improve dramatically.

If this therapy is so effective, why isn't it offered to everyone who is obese? The major reason is that the surgical risks associated with the procedure (including death) the recuperation, and the other associated complications remain of great concern. Given its substantial risks, this surgery makes sense only for someone who stands to gain greatly from it, meaning someone who is very obese. National guidelines suggest that only the very obese (BMI greater than 45), or those with less profound obesity (BMI greater than 35) but with additional obesity-related complications, be considered for obesity surgery.

Finally, what about cosmetic surgery such as liposuction? This technique suctions semiliquid fat from the abdomen, thighs, and other areas and has become very popular as a means of body sculpting. Unfortunately, the studies indicate that this means of removing fat is temporary. More important, physical removal of fat stores doesn't have the same benefits for your metabolism as losing the weight the old-fashioned way: insulin resistance and other metabolic features of obesity are not reversed by these potentially dangerous procedures.

Summing Up

With all the diets that have been devised over the years, you might think that we would have some solid evidence about which ones work best in the long term. Sadly, relatively few rigorous studies have evaluated specific diets. Even fewer rigorous clinical trials have compared one against another to see which works best. And almost none have looked at long-term results. The DPP report of lifestyle changes over a period as long as almost five years, with an average follow-up of approximately three years, represents one of the longest studies available.

The little solid evidence we have to date indicates that virtually any diet that helps you take in fewer calories each day, combined with increased physical activity, will lead to weight loss over the course of a year or so. How best to keep weight off long term is still an open question.

On even the most successful diets, most people lose only modest amounts of weight and tend to regain some or all of it. For people who are overweight or obese, shedding just 5 to 10 percent of weight can yield some truly wonderful benefits. In someone with diabetes, this much weight loss can decrease, or even eliminate, the need for medications to control blood sugar. As shown in the Diabetes Prevention Program, among people without diabetes this much weight loss can decrease the chances of developing the disease by 58 percent. Weight loss of as little as five to ten pounds can lower blood pressure and decrease the development of hypertension. But these benefits can be achieved only if you keep some or all of the weight off. Our experience in the Diabetes Prevention Program—described in Chapter 3— has been that people can successfully do this.

During the 1992 presidential election, Democratic political operative James Carville kept the Clinton campaign "on message" with a simple four-word phrase: "It's the economy, stupid." A similar message applies to what makes a successful diet: "It's the calories, stupid." The source of calories, whether it is protein, carbohydrate, or fat, is almost always less important than how many calories you eat. Keep your eyes on the prize—taking in fewer calories than you burn—and you will achieve a healthier, lower weight.

Putting It All Together

If you are overweight, you don't have time to wait for the results of clinical trials to determine which diets work best. So here is what you need to know now: any diet that helps you take in fewer calories than you are used to taking in will help you lose weight, no matter whether it is high or low in carbohydrates, fat, or protein.

How do you find a weight loss program that will work for you? You have to try one that looks as if it will meet your personality and needs, not just in the short term, but as a long-term lifestyle change. If it doesn't work for you, don't consider yourself a failure. Instead, consider the program a failure and move on to another.

The reason that most popular diets succeed at first—limited food choices, many food restrictions, lack of flexibility, little decision making, and repetitive foods—are the same reasons that they ultimately fail. When evaluating popular diets, keep in mind that the people who devised them usually have little or no training in medicine, nutrition, or exercise physiology, and they certainly haven't been made to prove that their advice is safe or effective.

As you evaluate different diets, keep these things in mind:

* Be skeptical of diets that promise rapid, easy weight loss and a cure for many health problems. Remember, if it sounds too good to be true, it probably is.
* Be wary of diets that criticize the traditional medical community and then use testimonials or anecdotes instead of scientific research to support their nutrition and health recommendations.
* Look twice at diets that recommend expensive supplements or products, especially if they are sold by whoever is promoting the diet. A healthy diet plan should provide adequate nutritional balance so expensive nutritional supplements are not necessary. The weight loss industry is big business, and it is sometimes difficult to tell whether the primary motivation is to help the health of consumers or take their money.
* Question diets that limit food selections by listing forbidden foods or food groups or recommending special food combinations or rituals.

The major emphasis of this book is that "diets" and "exercise" are likely to fail if they are inserted into our lives like separate components of a home computer system. Rather, we need to identify and change those lifestyle behaviors that contribute to obesity, diabetes, and heart disease. Instead of using diets and exercise programs sporadically, jumping from one to another, we need to learn new behaviors that will improve health and incorporate them systematically into our everyday lives. Look for a weight loss plan that advocates an eating style that you can follow not just for a few weeks or months but for years.

Here are a few elements common to healthy diets that you should consider:

- **Healthy diet programs should contain a balance of protein, carbohydrate, and fat.** The American Diabetes Association recommends a diet that includes 60 to 70 percent of calories from carbohydrates and monounsaturated fats combined, 15 to 20 percent of calories from protein, about 10 percent of calories from polyunsaturated fat, less than 10 percent of calories from saturated fat, and fewer than three hundred milligrams of cholesterol.

- **Nutritional recommendations should be made by a respected professional with a proven understanding of nutrition.** His or her recommendations should be based on scientific evidence, not personal opinions or testimonials.

- **The diet should include a variety of foods that meet your needs for carbohydrate, protein, fat, vitamins, and minerals.** Supplements or pills should not be a necessary part of the diet.

- **Ideally, the diet should not exclude "forbidden foods" or categorize foods as "good" or "bad."** Instead, the plan should focus on portion control. It should let you incorporate your favorite foods so you feel satisfied with the amount of food and the types of foods you are eating.

- **The diet should fit with your lifestyle so you can follow it both at home and away from home over the long term.** Short stints relying on "willpower" do not a good diet make.
- **The plan should recommend regular physical activity as a key component to losing weight and keeping it off for better health.**
- **Lifestyle programs should also encourage you to monitor your eating habits and physical activity.** This will increase awareness of your eating and activity patterns, because they are connected to successful weight loss.

CHAPTER 12

How to Change Your Eating Behavior

Chances are you've tried to change your diet in the past and have found it difficult. It *is* difficult, and we don't mean to suggest anything otherwise. But our experience with the DPP lifestyle-change program has been that lots of people can be successful. The diet and exercise program was developed by a lifestyle-intervention committee, a multidisciplinary team of professionals including dietitians, behavioral psychologists, diabetes experts, and exercise physiologists who reviewed the evidence in nutrition, exercise, and behavioral research literature to identify the best ways to help people lose weight and keep it off. The DPP lifestyle program was then implemented in more than one thousand people from all over the country. The DPP volunteers represented a broad swath of the U.S. population, including women and men from all walks of life, and older and younger people from diverse racial and ethnic backgrounds.

People *can* lose weight and keep it off. The National Weight Control Registry has ten years of data on nearly three thousand people who have lost a minimum of thirty pounds and kept it off for more than one year. These successful weight losers consume a diet that on average has a caloric composition of approximately 21 percent from protein, 55 percent from carbohydrate, and 24 percent from fat. They also engage in regular physical activity and report participating in leisure physical activity that burns 2,500 to 3,500 calories per week (about three and one-half to five miles of brisk walking daily) to keep their weight off.

Now, here's more about the DPP lifestyle program that was introduced in Chapter 3. Some of the elements of the program such as preparing for change, preparing your environment, setting goals, and tracking progress, problem solving, and maintenance have been discussed in previous chapters.

The DPP Lifestyle Program

The DPP lifestyle program included a calorie goal that would produce a gradual weight loss of one to two pounds per week (a deficit of about 500 to 1,000 calories a day below weight-maintenance calories) with 25 percent of calories from fat. The DPP exercise goal was to achieve a minimum of 150 minutes of physical activity per week at a pace similar to that of a brisk walk. There were no forbidden foods, and there were no expensive foods or supplements to buy.

Lifestyle-intervention participants were given fat targets in grams of daily fat and calorie targets based on their starting weight. (See Table 8.1 in Chapter 8.) They were then asked to self-monitor the times of meals and snacks and the amounts and types of foods eaten each day. They learned to use their self-monitoring records to identify the sources of excess fat and calories in their diet. (See Table 8.2 in Chapter 8.) Then, they learned that they could choose one of three ways to eat less fat and reach their fat gram targets. They could choose to set goals to (1) eat high-fat foods less often, (2) eat smaller amounts of high-fat foods, or (3) eat lower-fat foods instead. The eating plan could be used by the whole family and was flexible so that participants could include a wide variety of foods in their diet within the fat and calorie guidelines. This flexibility encouraged participants to learn how they could integrate their favorite foods and cultural food preferences into their lifestyle habits and still achieve their calorie and fat gram targets and weight loss goals without feeling denied or deprived.

The program was not presented as fast and easy or as simple nutritional dos and don'ts. It was presented as a lifestyle-change process that would promote gradual, realistic changes in diet and exercise behaviors. The primary goal of the DPP was to determine whether the lifestyle program, or the drug metformin, would lead to better health and prevention of diabetes and its complications. The diet encouraged lean meat, fish and poultry, low-fat or fat-free milk and dairy products, and five or more servings of fruits and vegetables per day, and it emphasized whole grains and the healthier monounsaturated fats. Through self-monitoring of food, calorie, and fat gram intake, each participant discovered, with guidance and feedback from a lifestyle coach, the eating plan that worked best for his or her individual situation.

Participants learned how to set short-term and long-term goals that were realistic and achievable (discussed in Chapter 8) and developed and practiced problem-solving (Chapter 9) and self-management skills that helped them sustain their diet and exercise habits over time (see Chapter 10). They learned that establishing a plan of accountability and support was critical to maintaining successful lifestyle change over time. They learned that successful lifestyle change came from building upon "small wins" (small improvements in diet, exercise, and weight loss) and that focusing on "small wins" was much more important than focusing on dramatic changes in diet, exercise, and weight loss that were not sustainable. They also learned that they would encounter their own personal high-risk situations that might disrupt their eating and exercise routines and cause lapses in their progress with weight loss. However, they learned how to manage these high-risk situations because they used their goal-setting, self-monitoring, and problem-solving skills to deal with lapses in these situations (as discussed in Chapter 10).

The Sixteen-Session Diabetes Prevention Program

DPP lifestyle participants followed a sixteen-session core curriculum with their lifestyle coach. The actual content of these sessions can be accessed in English and Spanish at bsc.gwu.edu/dpp/manualsb.htmlvdoc.

DPP participants reviewed one session each week in the sequence that follows so that they could develop important skills for lifestyle change one step at a time. Not surprisingly, some people needed more attention to some lessons than others, and specific lessons could be repeated. The DPP lifestyle "curriculum" was designed to be completed over twenty-six weeks. We have modified the description of the sixteen sessions to be more accessible for people trying to change their lifestyle, rather than for health-care professionals.

Session 1: Introduction to the Lifestyle Balance Program

Focus on your own personal reasons for wanting to lose weight and become more active. Review the two lifestyle balance goals: 7 percent weight loss and 150 minutes of physical activity per week. Identify the weight you need to reach to achieve a 7 percent weight loss (see Chapter 8). Focus on the benefits to you, your family, and others in your community if you lose weight and increase your activity—prevent diabetes, look and feel better, be healthier, and set a good example for family, friends, and community. Eating too much fat is fattening and is related to heart disease and diabetes. Start self-monitoring of food intake.

Homework: The first step is to figure out how much fat you are currently eating. Write down everything that you eat and drink every day for the next week, and record the time and the amount and type of food or drink that you consume. Circle the foods that you eat or drink that you think are highest in fat.

Session 2: Keys to Becoming a "Fat Detective"

Begin to self-monitor your weight on a regular basis—at least once every week (or more often if it is helpful)—and record your weight in a booklet and on your weight graph. The DPP goals for daily fat and calorie intake, based on your weight, are summarized in Table 8.1 (in Chapter 8). Identify the kinds of foods that you eat that are high in fat by reading food labels and using a fat and calorie counter (the booklets and the fat and calorie counter that DPP participants used can be accessed at the website of the National Diabetes Education Program [NDEP]—ndep.nih.gov—or you can purchase a fat and calorie counter on your own at your local bookstore). When you read food labels, the three most important areas to look at are the serving size, the calories per serving, and the total fat grams per serving.

Homework: Continue to write down everything you eat and drink. Figure out the amount of fat in the portions of food and drinks that you consume by using your fat and calorie counter or food labels. Try to get as close as you can to your fat gram goal. Notice which food choices or portions cause you to exceed your fat gram budget. Continue to weigh yourself at least once or twice per week at the same time of day, and record your weight in your booklet and on your weight graph.

Session 3: Identifying Three Ways to Eat Less Fat

Realize that your eyes can play tricks on you. Estimate the amount of food that you think you are consuming at each meal and snack, and then weigh or measure the portion to see how accurate your eyeball estimate is. Notice how inaccurate estimates of food portions can cause incorrect estimates of the number of fat grams that you are consuming in a given day and interfere with your ability to lose weight successfully. There are three ways to eat less fat: eat high-fat food less often; eat smaller portions of high-fat foods; and substitute lower-fat foods and cooking methods.

Homework: Keep track of your weight, food intake, and fat gram intake using an eating log (Table 8.2 in Chapter 8 is a sample eating log). Write down five foods that you eat that are high in fat. Pick one of the three ways to eat less fat from one or more of these foods. Be sure it is something that you can do by setting a specific goal that is reasonable and achievable. (See Chapter 8 on setting helpful goals.) Identify any problems you have in following your plans and meeting your goals, and decide if you need to do anything differently next week.

Session 4: Keys to Healthy Eating

It is important to have a regular pattern of eating to prevent getting too hungry and losing control. If you slow down your pace of eating, then you will digest your food better, be more aware of what you are eating, and be more aware of when you are satisfied and no longer hungry. Serve yourself smaller portions so you won't have to worry about overeating if you tend to clean your plate. It is important to eat a variety of foods for nutritional balance—at least two to three servings of lean meat, fish, or poultry (each serving is two to three ounces); two to three servings of low-fat milk (a serving is one cup) or dairy products (a serving is two to three ounces); two to four servings of fruit (a serving is a small piece or one-half cup); three to five servings of vegetables (a serving is one-half cup cooked or one cup raw); up to six servings of grains (bread, cereals, rice, or pasta; a serving is one slice or one-half cup; whole grains are preferred); small amounts of fat (a serving is one teaspoon of regular fat items or one tablespoon of reduced-fat items); and limited amounts of sweets and alcohol (a serving is one beer, four ounces of wine, or one and one-half ounces of alcohol) each day. Rate your daily diet in terms of adequate variety from each of these food groups each day. Identify lower-fat alternatives in each of the food groups. Lower-fat ways of cooking such as steaming, poaching, boiling, microwaving, or stir-frying are recommended.

Homework: Keep track of your weight and eating habits. Rate your daily diet in terms of adequate variety from low-fat sources of meat, fish, poultry, vegetables, fruit, dairy, and grains (ideally whole grains). Also, tally the number of choices that you make from fats, sweets, and alcohol per day.

Session 5: Introduction to Move Those Muscles

Now, it is important to increase your physical activity, and begin to build to a goal of 150 minutes of physical activity gradually over the next four weeks. Choose activities that you like and that are of moderate intensity, similar to that of a brisk walk. Review your own personal activity history likes and dislikes—what worked and what didn't work. Remember the benefits of being more active— helps you look and feel better, lowers your blood sugar, helps you lose weight and keep it off, and lowers your risk for heart disease by lowering cholesterol, triglycerides, and blood pressure.

Homework: Be active for sixty minutes in the next week over three to four days. For example, try to do a brisk walk for twenty minutes on three different days. Plan activities that you like, and schedule activities for at least ten minutes at a time. Include a friend or family member if you like. Keep track of your weight, food intake, fat grams, and activity minutes.

Session 6: Keys to Being Active: A Way of Life

To make being active a way of life, it is important to set aside a block of time almost every day to be active. Identify when you can set aside twenty to thirty minutes to do an activity you like. Also identify when you have ten- to fifteen-minute blocks of time to make more active choices like parking the car in a more distant spot, being active while watching TV, or taking a longer walking route to or from your destination. Remember to prevent sore muscles or cramps by drinking plenty of water and including warm-up, cooldown, and stretches in your exercise routine (see Chapter 5). Be alert for signs to stop exercising and check with your doctor before changing your level of activity or exercise. (Signs of concern are chest pain or discomfort, severe nausea, shortness of breath, or feeling light-headed). If you have diabetes, and especially if you take insulin or sulfonylurea medications, you will need to discuss your exercise program with your health-care team.

Homework: Set aside a twenty- to thirty-minute block of time every day or find two or more ten- to fifteen-minute time blocks to do activities that you like. Aim for ninety minutes of activity spread out over three to five days at an intensity similar to a brisk walk. Remember to warm up, cool down, and use stretches when you are active. Keep track of your weight, activity minutes, and food intake. Continue to come as close to your fat gram goal as you can.

Session 7: Keys to Tipping the Calorie Balance

One pound of body fat stores about 3,500 calories. Therefore, to tip the calorie balance and lose one pound of weight in a week, you need to create a calorie deficit of 500 calories per day for seven days; to lose two pounds of weight in a week, you need to create a calorie deficit of 1,000 calories per day for seven days. (Chapter 2 discusses the "arithmetic" of obesity.) It is best to create this calorie deficit by eating less and being more active. One mile of brisk walking takes about fifteen to twenty minutes and burns about 100 calories. Although calories in food come from fat, starches, sugars, protein, and alcohol, fat is the highest in calories per gram with 9 calories per gram compared to carbohydrate, sugar, and protein with 4 calories per gram. Compare your starting weight to your current weight and your expected weight (based on your 7 percent weight loss graph), and then decide if you need to tip the calorie balance further. If you want to tip the calorie balance further, then add a calorie goal to your fat gram goal (see Table 8.1 in Chapter 8) or follow sample meal plans (see Appendix D).

Homework: Keep track of your weight, food intake, fat gram intake, and activity level. Aim for 120 minutes of moderate-intensity activity per week. If you want to tip the calorie balance even further, either keep track of calorie intake and stay under the calorie goal listed in Table 8.1 in Chapter 8 or follow suggested meal plans.

Session 8: How to Take Charge of What's Around You

Learn what cues make you want to eat (hunger, activities like reading or watching TV, sight or smell of food, etc.) and be less active. Try to keep high-fat, high-calorie foods out of your house and workplace (out of sight) and keep healthier, lower-fat, lower-calorie choices easy to reach and in sight. Limit your eating to one place, and do not combine eating with other activities such as TV watching or reading. (Remember that it is OK to do two things at once only if you don't need to do either of them particularly well.) To help keep unhealthy foods out of your environment, make a shopping list ahead of time, and do not go shopping when you are hungry (see Sample Shopping List in Appendix C). Add positive activity cues to your life (such as keeping workout clothes and sneakers in sight and ready to go), and get rid of cues for being inactive (try limiting TV time unless you exercise as you watch TV).

Homework: Use goal setting to identify and plan to get rid of one problem food cue and add one positive cue for being more active. Aim for 150 minutes of activity per week. Keep track of your weight, activity minutes, food intake, fat gram intake, and calorie intake if you decided to tip the calorie balance. If you decided to follow sample menus, continue this approach to tip the calorie balance.

Session 9: Keys to Problem Solving

Review the five steps to problem solving (see Chapter 9): (1) describe the problem in detail, (2) brainstorm your options, (3) pick one to try, (4) make a positive action plan, and (5) try it and see how it goes.

Homework: Use the problem-solving approach to set goals to handle eating and exercise problems. Continue with an activity goal of at least 150 minutes per week. Keep track of your weight, activity minutes, food intake, and fat gram and calorie intake if you are trying to tip the calorie balance. If you decided to follow sample menus, continue this approach to tip the calorie balance.

Session 10: Four Keys to Healthy Eating Out

There are four keys to healthy eating out: (1) plan ahead about where to eat and what to order, (2) practice assertiveness when ordering the foods you want and requesting adjustments in cooking methods or portions served, (3) take initiative to be the first to order and keep tempting food out of your reach or off of your table, and (4) choose menu items that are healthy and lower in fat by using any of the three ways to eat less fat.

Homework: Choose one of the four keys to healthy eating out, and make a positive action plan using goal-setting and problem-solving skills. Try your plan and see how it goes. Continue to keep track of your weight, activity minutes, food intake, and fat grams. Track your calorie intake or follow sample menus if you are aiming to tip the calorie balance further.

Session 11: How to Talk Back to Negative Thoughts

Learn to identify some common self-defeating negative thoughts and counter negative thoughts with positive self-talk statements. (See Chapter 7 for more information on this important lifestyle-change skill.)

Homework: Write down examples of your negative thoughts related to changing your eating and activity to lose weight. Write positive thoughts to replace the negative thoughts, and then when you hear these negative thoughts, say "stop" and replace them with your positive self-talk statements. Continue to keep track of your weight, activity minutes, food intake, and fat grams. Track your calorie intake or follow sample menus if you are aiming to tip the calorie balance further.

Session 12: Negotiating the Slippery Slope of Lifestyle Change

Learn that lapses from healthy eating and being more active are a normal part of the lifestyle-change process. The key to successful lifestyle change and weight loss is to learn to recover from lapses quickly. Identify your triggers for lapses, and learn and practice how to react to lapses and get back on track. (See Chapter 10 for more information on the critical skill of dealing with lapses.)

Homework: Describe one thing that has caused you to slip from healthy eating, and make a positive action plan using goal-setting and problem-solving skills. Describe one thing that has caused you to slip from being active, and make a positive action plan using goal-setting and problem-solving skills. Continue to keep track of your weight, activity minutes, food intake, and fat grams. Track your calorie intake or follow sample menus if you are aiming to tip the calorie balance further.

Session 13: Highlights of Jump-Start Your Activity Plan

Determine ways to prevent boredom with activity: try something new, do the same activity in a new place, make it fun, make it a way to be social, or make it a challenge. Review the basic principles of aerobic fitness, which include *frequency* of activity (ideally five to seven days per week), *intensity* (exercise at a pace so that you can talk but cannot sing), *time* (stay active for at least ten minutes and gradually increase to twenty to sixty minutes at a time), and *type* (aerobic fitness activities that strengthen your heart and large muscle groups of your arms and legs). Learn your target heart rate.

Homework: Take your pulse when you are exercising and check that you are in your target heart rate range. Exercise at a level so that you can talk but cannot sing. Keep track of your weight, activity minutes, food intake, fat grams, and calories.

Session 14: How to Make Social Cues Work for You

Identify problem social cues (sight of others eating or being inactive, being offered food to eat, or being invited to do something inactive) and helpful social cues (sight of others eating healthily, being offered healthy foods, or being invited to do something active). Aim to stay away from or change problem social cues and add helpful social cues to your life to build your new lifestyle habits. Identify people in your life who can be positive social cues for healthy eating and being active. Plan ahead for social events, parties, vacations, and so on.

Homework: Describe a social cue that is a problem for you, and use the problem-solving approach to identify a plan for changing that social cue. Make a positive action plan or goal targeted at changing the social cue. Identify a positive social cue that you would like to add to your life, and use the problem-solving approach and goal setting to select an idea to try and see how it goes. Keep track of your weight, activity minutes, food intake, fat grams, and calories.

Session 15: Keys to Managing Stress

Stress can cause people to overeat or be less active. Identify the kinds of things that make you feel stressed and ways that you can prevent or manage stress (plan ahead, practice saying "no" so you are not overwhelmed, share work with others, set realistic and achievable goals, manage your time, use problem-solving skills, exercise, use positive self-talk to counter negative self-talk, meditate).

Homework: Identify your major sources of stress. Choose one source of stress and use the problem-solving approach to select a strategy to deal with the stress and goal setting to make a plan to implement it. Keep track of your weight, activity minutes, food intake, fat grams, and calories if helpful.

Session 16: How to Stay Motivated

List the changes that you've made to be more active and to eat less fat and fewer calories. Have you reached your weight and activity goals? If not, how will you improve your progress? Remind yourself of what you have accomplished so far and the benefits that you have achieved; keep visible signs of progress (weight graphs, photos); set new goals for yourself and create rewards for yourself when you reach your goals; create friendly competition or add variety to your eating and exercise routines; continue to keep track of your weight, activity, and food intake.

Homework: Choose one way to stay motivated, and use goal-setting skills to create a positive action plan and see how it goes. Keep track of your weight, activity minutes, food intake, fat grams, and calories if helpful.

CHAPTER 13

How Study Participants Did It: Three Stories

The DPP volunteers represented a diverse group with different backgrounds and lifestyles, different starting body weights, and different barriers to losing weight and increasing activity levels. However, each shared the motivation to prevent diabetes. They all tried to integrate the DPP lessons into their own lives. Here are some of their stories.

Sandra's Story

We met Sandra, a fifty-two-year-old woman trying to prevent diabetes, in Chapter 9. Mastering the skills from Session 3 (Three Ways to Eat Less Fat, see Chapter 12) is one of the most important features of the lifestyle-change process. If you review Sandra's lifestyle logs (Tables 13.1 and 13.2) before and after Session 3, you can see how important it is to keep lifestyle logs so you can identify high-fat, high-calorie food choices and then decide how to shape your choices over time. If we use Sandra's first lifestyle log as an example, some of the high-fat foods that she typically consumed were doughnuts, cream, potato chips, and pizza. She had three options for reducing her fat and calorie

TABLE 13.1 Sandra's First Eating and Exercise Log

Time	Food	Portion	Calories	Fat (Grams)	Hunger	Location	Comments
10:00 A.M.	Glazed doughnuts	2 4-inch	798	42	3	Office	Woke up late—rushed to work, no breakfast
	Coffee	8 ounces	0	0		Office	
	Cream (half-and-half)	2 ounces	80	8		Office	
					7		Skipped lunch to make up for doughnuts
6:00 P.M.	Potato chips	3 ounces	483	33	0	Home	Tired and overhungry
7:30 P.M.	Cheese pizza (12-inch)	4 slices	1,068	48	4	Home	Split the pizza with roommate
9:00 P.M.					9		Stuffed!

Daily Totals: 2,429 calories, 131 grams of fat

Type of Physical Activity	Time
Walked	30 minutes

☐ I did no physical activity today.

intake: (1) to eat high-fat foods less often, (2) to eat smaller amounts of high-fat foods, or (3) to use lower-fat foods instead. Sandra used the guidelines in Table 13.2 to evaluate her options for reducing fat and calorie intake.

Once Sandra decided how she wanted to adjust her eating habits, she then committed to follow through on her goals. She made sure that she added English muffins, milk, fruit salad ingredients, fat-free salad dressing, and one-ounce bags of potato chips to her shopping list and that she did not keep large bags of potato chips, doughnuts, or cream in her home or office. When she tried her new plans, she found that she did not feel deprived because she was substituting foods that she enjoyed and because she was allowing herself to have a doughnut periodically. Her food log the next week looked like Table 13.3.

TABLE 13.2 The Three-Ways-to-Eat-Less-Fat Homework Assignment

My Top 5 High-Fat Foods	I Will Eat It Only This (Less) Often	I Will Eat Only This (Smaller) Amount	I Will Eat This (Lower-Fat) Food Instead
Doughnuts	Once per week	One doughnut	English muffin with jam
Cream	Never	Never	Whole milk
Potato chips	Twice per week	1-ounce individual bag	Low-fat popcorn
Pizza	Once per week	2 slices	Have salad to supplement
Regular salad dressing	Never	2 tablespoons	Fat-free dressing or vinegar

Sandra found that if she planned ahead and had the foods that she needed at home and in the office, she could dramatically reduce her fat and calorie intake and still feel satisfied with her food choices. Even if she woke up late, she could have something easy to prepare at the office instead of stopping for doughnuts on the run or being tempted to eat them when other coworkers brought them into the office. By preparing her lunch the night before, she could be sure that she had something healthy to eat. Because she did typically have a long time gap between lunch and dinner, she planned for an afternoon snack just before leaving the office so that she did not arrive home feeling overhungry. She realized that if she included salad with pizza meals, then she could fill up on the low-calorie healthy vegetables in the salad, slow down her eating speed, and then be satisfied with just two slices of pizza. She realized that she could lower her fat intake quite substantially, and once she did this with some consistency, then she was able to include more fruit and low-fat dairy choices in her diet to have better nutritional balance.

Kathy's Story

Kathy was sixty-two years old when she joined the DPP and found out that she was assigned to the lifestyle-treatment group. She had a lifelong history of being overweight and yo-yo diet-

TABLE 13.3 Sandra's Second Eating and Exercise Log

Time	Food	Portion	Calories	Fat (Grams)	Hunger	Location	Comments
9:00 A.M.	English muffin	2 halves	134	1	3	Office	Woke up late—in office breakfast
	Sugar-free jam	1 table-spoon	48	0			
	Coffee	8 ounces	0	0			
	Whole milk	2 ounces	40	2			
					6		
12:00 P.M.	Whole grain bread	2 slices	140	2	3	Office	Packed lunch night before
	Turkey	3 ounces	140	3			
	Mustard	1 table-spoon	0	0			
	Potato chips	1 ounce	161	11	7		
4:00 P.M.	Apple	1	81	0		Office	Stocked fruit at the office
7:00 P.M.	Cheese pizza (12-inch)	2 slices	534	24	4	Home	Split pizza and salad with room-mate
	Salad	2 cups	28	0			
	Fat-free salad dressing	2 table-spoons	32	0	7		Satisfied
9:00 P.M.	Sugar-free Jell-O	1 cup	0	0	4	Home	

Daily Totals: 1,338 calories, 43 grams of fat

Type of Physical Activity	Time
Walked	30 minutes

☐ I did no physical activity today.

ing. She held a sedentary desk job. She had shortness of breath walking short distances and could not walk longer than ten minutes without stopping to rest and catch her breath. She was five feet two inches and weighed 244 pounds at the start of the DPP.

Her calculated body mass index was 44, putting her into a category of severe obesity (see Table 1.4 on estimating BMI).

Kathy's motivation to lose weight was not to improve her appearance but rather to prevent getting diabetes and the health problems she learned were associated with diabetes. So for Kathy, finding out that she had impaired glucose tolerance, or prediabetes, was a strong motivator for making lifestyle changes. Based on her starting weight, her 7 percent weight loss goal would take her to 226.5 pounds. Her fat gram goal was fifty grams of fat per day. She kept the food records as requested, even though she thought it was "a pain."

As Kathy kept her records, she was surprised to see that her fat intake easily exceeded one hundred grams of fat per day. She began to make changes in her diet to lower her fat intake. She decided to pack her lunch and bring it to work three days per week and eat at the cafeteria just two days per week instead of every day. She decided on wrap sandwiches with tuna or turkey, or salads with cottage cheese—these were meals that appealed to her. Since she lived alone, she decided to use easy-to-prepare, low-calorie frozen dinners for supper on three to four days per week. For her, this was an easy way to control portions.

With these changes, Kathy found she was able to meet her fat gram targets and could even fit in a small portion of dessert. For Kathy, including a small dessert was important for her to feel satisfied and not deprived, and so she learned how to do it and still meet her fat gram goals. Her weight dropped by about one pound each week, and she plotted her weights on her weight graph and saw that she was on track for a 7 percent weight loss at her six-month check-in. She struggled with the exercise goal but attended supervised activity sessions twice per week for a total of forty-five minutes. During week 6, Kathy achieved seventy-five minutes of activity, but during weeks 7 and 8, she achieved only fifteen minutes of activity per week.

Kathy persevered, and gradually her stamina improved so that she could walk 30 minutes without stopping and then 45 minutes and then 60 minutes. She enjoyed walking outdoors in nice weather and at her best reached 250 to 300 minutes of activity per week. She felt better carrying less weight and found the steady improvements in her stamina uplifting; she participated in the American Diabetes Association annual walk on several occasions during the DPP.

Kathy did have setbacks or lapses. She loved to take vacation cruises and wanted to continue to enjoy her vacations. In order to limit the potential damage from the cruises, she planned ahead to handle her eating and activity. During previous weeklong cruises she had routinely gained five to ten pounds. Now, she walked laps around the ship decks and decided not to eat everything in sight. Instead, she reviewed the menus and made healthy choices that she enjoyed—she skipped the butter on the bread but sometimes decided to have dessert. She kept track of her activity and food intake on the cruise and was able to meet her activity goal of at least 150 minutes per week. She chose soups and salads as appetizers, which helped her to feel full, and she did not feel compelled to clean her plate at every meal. Her weight increased by only two pounds on her first cruise—a major improvement over past cruises. Kathy also knew that she could easily refocus after the cruise and lose that two pounds again, especially because she had not felt deprived on her vacation.

Kathy reached her 7 percent weight goal of 226.5 pounds by week 24 and then lost a few more pounds to reach a weight of 222 pounds. She learned that if her fat grams were over her budget of fifty grams per day, she could plan to eat fewer fat grams and calories over the next few days to make sure that her average fat gram intake for the week stayed at fifty grams per day or less. Kathy never needed or wanted to tip the calorie balance further by counting calories. For her, fat gram counting alone was sufficient.

Over the years in DPP, Kathy found that her high-risk situations were taking cruises and feeling depressed or stressed. At these times she used her problem-solving and goal-setting skills to make plans to deal with these situations. When she retired, she found it important to schedule activities and classes to keep active, stimulated, and away from boredom eating. Kathy has to this day continued to keep her weight off. She joins water aerobic classes in winter and walks outdoors in fall, spring, and summer. She has prevented diabetes and says with pride, "I have changed my lifestyle!"

Bob's Tale

Bob was forty-eight years old when he joined the Diabetes Prevention Program and was assigned to the lifestyle intervention. He weighed two hundred pounds and was five feet eleven inches (BMI of 27). He was motivated to prevent diabetes because his identical twin brother had already been diagnosed with type 2 diabetes several years earlier. Bob's doctor told him that he was highly likely to develop diabetes within five years of his brother because they had the same genes. Bob's wife was very supportive of him losing weight and decided to do the lifestyle-intervention program with him.

Bob had never tried to lose weight before, and learning about the amount of fat in his diet was new to him. Based on his starting weight, Bob's 7 percent weight loss goal would take him to 186 pounds. His fat gram goal was forty-two grams of fat per day. He found it interesting to learn about the fat content of the various foods he ate and started to make changes in his diet to include less fat. He reduced fat from butter and salad dressings by using lower-fat versions instead. His wife was Italian and cooked typical Italian dishes with liberal amounts of olive oil. Bob and his wife were initially distressed to see how much fat was in some of their favorite dishes. After some experimentation, Bob's wife was able to reduce the fat in some of the high-fat Italian recipes by using less oil and by cooking those dishes less frequently. Bob knew ahead of time when the Italian recipes were going to be served for dinner, and he would intentionally eat fewer fat grams for breakfast and lunch that day and the next day so that his average fat intake over the week would be at his target of forty-two grams of fat or less.

Bob enjoyed basketball and other activities, but he did not consistently exercise 150 minutes each week. He found that he needed to build other lifestyle activities into his weekly routine, especially if he missed his once-per-week basketball game. He decided to ride his bike to and from work and also started to jog with a friend after work several times per week. Bob lost weight gradually over the sixteen sessions but noted periodic weight gains when on vacations, after cookouts, and when lots of high-fat Italian dishes were served.

Over time, Bob developed a satisfying schedule including his favorite lower-fat Italian meals and his wife's homemade pizza with low-fat cheese and low-fat tomato sauce. Bob reached his weight goal of 186 pounds and then aimed to maintain a weight of 180 to 184 pounds so that he had a cushion below his target weight to allow for vacation meals and social events. He kept food records for one week per month after the first year. He gradually weaned from his schedule of in-person contacts. However, if his weight reached 186 pounds, Bob resumed more frequent record keeping and more frequent appointments to increase his focus and accountability.

At the end of the DPP, Bob not only had avoided getting diabetes but his blood sugars had returned to normal. His story demonstrates the power of lifestyle change to overcome a genetic predisposition, prevent diabetes, and reverse abnormal blood sugars.

Lessons from Sandra's, Kathy's, and Bob's Experiences

Sandra, Kathy, and Bob chose different ways to lower their fat and calorie intake based on their own lifestyles. Sandra changed her home and work food environment to decrease high-fat foods in her lunches and snacks. Kathy chose to buy prepackaged portioned-controlled frozen dinners and select easy-to-prepare lunches for many of her meals because she lived alone and didn't like to cook for just one person. In contrast, Bob's family typically enjoyed home-cooked meals that included many traditional Italian recipes. He and his wife therefore spent time learning how to figure out the calories and fat grams in their favorite recipes and how to use lower-fat recipe substitutions to reduce the fat and calorie content of each serving. There were no special recipes to follow in the DPP. Participants learned how to reduce the fat and calorie content of their favorite recipes and also had a list of recommended cookbooks that offered recipes for a wide variety of healthy low-fat dishes. (See Appendix B for a list of cookbooks and Appendix F for nutritious recipes.)

Fat and Calorie Goals

Like Sandra, Kathy, and Bob, you need to establish goals for the total grams of fat and total calories per day and then determine the fat and calorie content of your favorite recipes, so that you can plan meals that meet your goals. Those goals were summarized in Table 8.1 in Chapter 8.

Determining the Fat and Calorie Content of Your Favorite Recipes

To figure out the grams of fat and calories in your favorite recipes, use Table 13.4.

- List the amount and type of each ingredient on a separate line.
- Record the grams of fat and calories for each portion of each ingredient using your fat and calorie counter (see Session 2 in Chapter 12).
- Add up the total number of fat grams and calories for the whole recipe.
- Divide the total number of fat grams and calories by the number of servings that the recipe makes. This will give you the number of fat grams and calories per serving.

TABLE 13.4 Worksheet to Figure Grams of Fat and Calories in Recipes

Name of Recipe: _____ Serving Size: _____

Ingredient	Amount	Fat Grams	Calories

Totals: _____

To lower the fat and calorie content of recipes, the same three strategies for eating less fat apply.

- You can eat high-fat foods less often by cooking the usual recipe less often.
- You can consume smaller portions of high-fat foods in the recipes by omitting a high-fat food (e.g., spaghetti sauce without meat or sausage), using less of high-fat ingredients, or eating a smaller serving of the recipe.
- You can use lower-fat ingredients or cooking methods such as trimming fat from meat, using nonstick pan or nonstick vegetable sprays, steaming or microwaving, baking without adding fat, or chilling soups or stews and skimming off the fat before reheating and serving.

Once you look at the sources of fat and calories in the recipe, then you can choose to substitute lower-fat ingredients for

TABLE 13.5 Recipe Substitution Ideas

Instead of	Try
1 cup whole milk	1 cup skim or low-fat milk
1 cup heavy cream	1 cup evaporated skim milk
1 cup sour cream	1 cup nonfat plain yogurt or low-fat or nonfat sour cream or 1 cup blenderized low-fat cottage cheese
1 cup grated cheddar	1 cup low-fat grated cheddar
1 cup whole milk ricotta cheese	1 cup part-skim ricotta or 1 cup low-fat cottage cheese
1 stick (¼ pound) margarine	½ cup applesauce or low-fat margarine
8 ounces cream cheese	4 ounces skim ricotta and 4 ounces tofu or 8 ounces light Neufchâtel
2 whole eggs	4 egg whites or ½ cup frozen egg substitute
1 cup coconut	½ cup coconut
1 cup walnuts	½ cup walnuts
1 tablespoon oil	1 tablespoon wine or broth
½ cup oil	½ cup applesauce or ¼ cup applesauce and ¼ cup oil or ½ cup nonfat yogurt and 2 tablespoons oil
¼ cup brown gravy	¼ cup broth or au jus
1 ounce baking chocolate	3 tablespoons cocoa powder plus 1 tablespoon oil (or a small amount of low-fat margarine—see instructions on cocoa box label)
Regular mayonnaise or salad dressing	Nonfat or low-fat mayonnaise or salad dressing or nonfat or low-fat plain yogurt
Regular ground beef	Ground turkey breast
1 cup sugar	½ cup or ¾ cup sugar

higher-fat ones to reduce the fat and calories per serving and recalculate the total fat grams and calories in the recipe and per serving. Once you have modified your recipe so that it both tastes good and is healthier, then you are really on your way to a more satisfying and healthy lifestyle! Table 13.5 provides some common recipe substitutions that you could try.

When you remove one-quarter cup of fat or more from a recipe, it is important to add back moisture by adding the same amount of water, fruit juice, or skim milk. In baked goods, you can cut the amount of margarine or butter by one-third or one-half and replace it with an equal amount of unsweetened applesauce, pureed prunes, or skim milk.

Remember, you can also use some calorie- and fat-free strategies to add flavor. Add flavor by using wine, lemon juice, flavored vinegars or mustards, garlic, onions, hot peppers, or fresh herbs and spices.

If you would prefer to have some recipes that are already modified to be low in fat and calories, then you could try some of the recipes in this book or some of the cookbooks that are listed in Appendix B.

The following websites also are good resources for low-fat, nutritious recipe ideas:

- **American Diabetes Association (*diabetes.org*).** This site offers state-of-the-art information about diabetes prevention, treatment, research, and education, plus daily low-fat recipes.
- **Meals for You (*mealsforyou.com*).** This commercial site offers recipes, personalized meal plans, and customized shopping lists.
- **5 A Day (*5aday.org*).** The 5 A Day program endorses recipes that promote fruit and vegetables and are low in fat and cholesterol. The use of whole grains and minimal use of salt and sugar are strongly encouraged in all 5 A Day recipes. Each recipe contains at least one serving of a fruit or a vegetable per portion and contains no more than 30 percent of calories from fat, 10 percent saturated fat, 100 milligrams of cholesterol, and 480 milligrams of sodium per serving.

If you need help finding a registered dietitian to help you make these lifestyle changes, you can check with your physician for a referral. Alternatively, try the American Dietetic Association website *(eatright.org)*. This site provides hundreds of quick tips, monthly hot topics, and a searchable database to find a nutrition professional.

Participants in the DPP had homework assignments to set specific goals. One of these was to fill out the "Three Ways to Eat

Less Fat" table in which they identified the high-fat foods that they ate most often and then set a schedule for whether and how often they would eat that food.

DPP participants also learned how important it was to plan ahead for food shopping. They learned that it was crucial to not go shopping when hungry and to always go with a shopping list and stick to it. (See Appendix C for a sample shopping list.) The more fresh produce and the more whole grains that you choose, the more fiber you will consume in your diet. It is much more satisfying to consume 1,200, 1,500, or 1,800 calories per day when you include high-fiber alternatives. So, anytime you select fresh or frozen fruit and vegetables it is healthier than the canned alternatives, and anytime you choose whole grain breads, cereals, and grains it is healthier and more satiating than processed refined choices.

Appendix D includes some sample meal plans and menus similar to those provided to the DPP participants. Following menus was not the primary strategy that DPP participants used to lose weight; however, when participants wanted to get a jump start losing weight or "tip the calorie balance" (see Session 7 in Chapter 12), they followed such sample menus for several weeks at a time. Some of the menus require little food-preparation time and are good alternatives when you are busy and on the run or don't feel like cooking for one person. Other menus incorporate low-calorie, low-fat recipes for those who enjoy cooking. You'll notice that the menus focus on frequent servings of calcium-rich dairy choices. This is because some recent research suggests that including three to four servings of calcium-rich foods in your diet each day will enhance your weight loss results.

Meal Replacements

Another strategy DPP participants sometimes used to jump-start their weight loss was meal replacements. A meal replacement is a portion-controlled, prepackaged meal, soup, drink, or bar that contains approximately 150 to 300 calories and is used to replace an entire meal or snack, help you reduce your fat and calorie intake, and thus lose weight. These include nutritionally fortified shakes or meal bars that contain about 220 calories, three to nine grams of fat, ten grams of protein, and various vitamins and minerals; snack bars that usually contain 140 to 150 calories; and low-calorie frozen dinners that typically contain about 300 calories, fewer than ten grams of fat, and ten to twenty grams of protein.

Meal replacements can help you lose weight by simplifying meal planning. They are convenient, are easy to purchase, are easy to store, require little if any meal preparation, and are reasonably priced, usually costing less than the meal that they replace. Using meal replacements reduces the number of decisions that you have to make about what to eat and reduces your exposure to tempting foods that might result in overeating. Most weight loss programs that use meal replacements recommend that you use them to replace two meals and one to two snacks per day when you are trying to lose weight and then transition to one meal replacement and one snack replacement per day to maintain weight. The research that has been done on the effectiveness of such meal-replacement programs has shown that people using meal replacements achieve more weight loss in the short term and for up to four years when compared to people on self-selected diets.

If you need a jump start to lose weight, you could try substituting (remember, don't *add* meal substitutes to your meals!) a meal-replacement shake or bar for your breakfast (about 220 calories) and light meal (another 220 calories) each day and have one to two snack replacements per day (about 150 calories each) in addition to your main meal of 500 to 600 calories per day. This would total 1,240 to 1,340 calories per day, and you would definitely lose weight. A long-term weight loss study in people with type 2 diabetes called Look AHEAD (Action for Health in Diabetes) is currently under way and is using meal replacements in this manner as part of the lifestyle weight loss intervention.

Most people with diabetes notice that using meal replacements helps to lower blood-sugar levels because they help you to eat less fat, less carbohydrates, and less calories and lose weight. Although meal replacements contain limited amounts of calories and fat, the amount of carbohydrate can vary. For example, an eight-ounce can of Glucerna contains thirty grams of carbohydrate, and a low-calorie frozen dinner can contain between ten and forty-five grams of carbohydrate. If you use meal replacements with about the same amount of carbohydrate each day, your blood-sugar levels will probably be lower and more stable.

Meal replacements are not for everyone. Some people do not like the taste, and others prefer to consume home-cooked meals. If you use meal replacements incorrectly and eat them in addition to your usual meals and snacks, you will end up consuming more calories than usual, and you will gain weight. If using meal replacements makes you feel deprived or that your eating is monotonous, then they are probably not a good weight loss strategy for you.

If you have diabetes, you should check with your health-care team before trying meal replacements for weight loss. If you are at risk for hypoglycemia (low blood sugar) because of your diabetes medications, your doctor may want to adjust your dose of insulin or oral diabetes medications before you start. Your dietitian may also be able to help you with creative ideas for improving the taste, appetite satisfaction, and variety in your diet while using meal replacements.

Tips for Avoiding Dieting Pitfalls

The first tip for avoiding pitfalls is to not think about being on a diet, because being "on a diet" implies that someday you will be "off the diet." It is better to convey to yourself and others that you are working on trying to change your lifestyle to eat healthily and be more active.

Some of the best advice on how to avoid dieting pitfalls, or in other more positive words "how to change your lifestyle to lose weight *and* keep it off," comes from Helen McGrane, one of the DPP participants. She called her piece (written in diary form), "To Tell the Truth (How to Lose Weight and Keep It Off)."

> *July 1998: To my surprise, I find I am eligible for a national diabetes study for the prevention of diabetes. . . . Blame it on my genetic inheritance, the gift of increased years, and gradual weight increase.*
>
> *My mother probably had maternal diabetes with four children who had birth weights greater than nine pounds. In her sixties, she was diagnosed with diabetes and took oral medication until her death. My maternal uncle also developed diabetes in his senior years. . . .*
>
> *I've now lived longer than my mother. My weight has increased during the last ten years. Procrastination about weight loss comes to an end with the evidence of impaired glucose tolerance.*
>
> ***September 1998: "Don't view past failures as a sign that you can't succeed."*** *How many times have I shed unwanted pounds only to have them return? Past failures include the Dr. Pritikin program, the Atkins Revolutionary Diet, Weight Watchers, hypnotism. . . . Now I can succeed in the lifestyle Diabetes Prevention Program. As a bonus, I've been assigned a coach in DPP. Linda is an avid cheerleader.*
>
> *There are nagging thoughts: "Can I achieve a perception of better health or should I believe my older daughter's view of weight loss as a preliminary to the onset of dire consequences?"*
>
> ***October 1998: "No pain, no loss."*** *The Tufts Letter described research on people who had been successful with permanent weight loss. It found 60 percent had been stricter about their dietary approach, and 80 percent exercised more vigorously. The DPP gave me the guidelines about daily and weekly goals for diet and exercise. . . . I keep a food diary*

and exercise regularly; I've become a label reader; I've eliminated cookies from my shopping list; I choose substitutes and monitor my weight with the scale. Exercise has become a necessity and I love the production of endorphins. I feel good after the exercise. It's OK to be obsessive.

November 1998: Break down weight loss goals to several smaller lifestyle goals; replace "I will be" (e.g., slimmer) with "I will do" (e.g., salad dressing on the side). *Strangely, it seems to work. . . . I stay below the projected loss lines and maintain what seem to be minimum exercise targets. There are times when the [weight] loss line shows plateaus, but then follows a downward slope to boost my spirits. I think about liposuction during plateaus, but the prospect of anesthesia makes that option seem unpalatable, and besides, there is the expense.*

December 1998: Plan indulgences. *I reach my weight loss goal in DPP. Now can I maintain? . . . Christmas is too important not to celebrate. I eat less before and after indulgences. It works.*

March 1999: Exercise. *I've made exercise a pleasurable component of my daily routines with the availability of stretching and toning at the local Senior Center two to three times a week. I head for the Senior Center to be greeted by our instructor, Marlene, and fifty other seniors. Some of the exercises are done sitting down. I feel the burn as we rotate our arms. Walt plays music from the forties to distract us. It's "our" music and my thoughts deflect to early memories of ballrooms, handsome servicemen, and dancing. I recall the joy of music shared with a lifelong love. Just when I feel my arms may quit, Marlene switches to waist stretches and leg raises. We exercise muscles that seem to ask, "How come you don't use me more often?" We interrupt toning after twenty minutes for a ten-minute walk; then continue the last fifteen minutes with repetitive leg exercises. I stay for the fifteen-minute series with two-pound weights.*

I've added walks and the more vigorous exercise of ballroom dancing. There may be changes in the future, but I know exercise is here to stay.

June 1999: "Do what you want to make it work." It's been six months since I reached my exercise and weight loss goals for DPP. I continue to learn to remain motivated to prevent diabetes and stay with the lifestyle choices I've learned through the DPP program. I recall my personal experience with the potential risks from diabetes. My mother developed heart disease two years before her lingering death as a result of a disabling stroke. I'd like to avoid this, as well as an increased probability of blindness, vascular diseases, and infirmities that do occur with diabetes.

I expect my efforts to be lifelong. What will help? . . . Several small meals keep off body fat better than two large ones. Grazing may offset my temptations to binge. I keep more fruit in the house; it's handy when appetite pangs occur. . . . Strength training twice a week builds up muscle and burns fat more than any other body tissues. I'm happy at the prospect of losing flab.

July 1999: Balance. I recall the balance advocated for my emotional/social life: . . . prayer, work, love, and play. Physically, I will practice the balance of good nutrition and exercise. If I miss one or more days, I will get back on track.

June 15, 2004: Reflection. I continue to be grateful to Linda, her compatriots, and the DPP program and their effect on my health. . . . How have I stayed with the program? Much credit is due to the ongoing contacts to remind me why I joined in the first place. I feel better with the ability to pursue daily activities via the exercise and am happy with less of me, that is, less weight and the effect on my choice of clothes. I get reality checks when the weight seems to rise with a vacation cruise; there was less of a rise last time as I decided to forgo most of the desserts that were offered and to wear my pedometer. There's a pound to lose at present, but I know attention to intake and exercise will take care of that.

What Has Happened to the DPP Participants?

Now, three years after the close of the DPP study, each individual can still tell you what works for him or her. The keys to success are continuing to exercise regularly and finding an eating style that helps you meet your calorie and fat gram targets without feeling hungry or deprived.

When we ask different DPP participants how they manage their eating so that they do not feel hungry or deprived, each person gives a personal solution.

Helen says, "I continue to plan snacks between meals so that I do not go for too long without food and get overhungry."

Francine says, "I try to eat high-fiber food choices as often as I can so that I feel full with less food and calories."

John says, "I eat much less carbohydrate, and that helps me control my hunger."

They all say that they continue to monitor their weight on the scale at least once per week or more often. They also say that if they notice a few more pounds on the scale, they start to refocus right away often using food records to increase their awareness and examine their recent eating habits. They cut back on calories and fat until their weight is back down. This process has become a way of life especially after vacations, cruises, holidays, and parties.

One of our favorite personal statements was by Ronda, a woman over age sixty who has kept her weight off for many years:

> *Why did we older folks do so well? It's because we know this is just about the last chance we have to try to ensure that we stay healthy and active longer. We are already feeling some of the changes of age and we know that it is "downhill" from here.*
>
> *I often think about how this program is also helping future health concerns like osteoporosis, cardiovascular problems, simple balance problems, etc. I don't normally think about this being much easier than rehab after a stroke or after*

*amputation or blindness, but I thought about it last night.
Those thoughts make this program a simple little nothing.*

*I try to keep reminding myself about what I am really
doing long term rather than the immediate diet and exercise
program. I also know from over forty years of dieting every
couple of years that keeping track of fat intake (rather than
calories that never worked more than a few months) and
keeping track of the exercise time helps me from straying and
not realizing that I have added five or ten pounds or that I
have slipped back to doing practically no exercise. I wasn't
overly happy about walking when it was four degrees—my
eyes watered so that I had tears streaming down my face. I
had to watch my step because of icy sidewalks, and on and
on. I did not walk just going to and from work, but I did it
on Saturdays and any day I took off—like Christmas week. I
knew it was necessary to keep it up and keep the benefits
going. I also do it so that I don't have to starve myself to lose
weight or keep it off. I don't like being hungry so I would
rather eat and walk in the cold. Anyway, we old folks can
change.*

As you can see, for the participants in the DPP, learning how
to make lifestyle changes to improve their eating habits and activity levels was only part of the program. They also learned that
their thoughts and feelings had powerful influences on their
behavior with regard to food and activity choices. They learned
that it was key to learn to manage their self-talk (their cognitive
environment), to learn alternative ways to deal with stress and
negative feelings (their emotional environment), and to take
charge of social cues for eating in their living environment
(home, office, social event, restaurants, vacations). They developed skills in goal setting, self-monitoring, and problem solving
and experienced the importance of accountability and social support from their lifestyle coaches, family, and friends.

14

Conclusion

We are currently living an unparalleled "experiment" in human history, and the results are just beginning to come in. Never before has food been so plentiful, life been so easy, and life lasted so long for so many people. The early "results" of the experiment are rather frightening. Although we are living to an older age—in great part owing to our improved hygiene and the ability to conquer infectious diseases that ravaged the population in centuries past—we are developing long-term degenerative diseases that make our lives difficult as we age and are the major causes of premature death. The greatest examples of the result of our change in life and lifestyle are the worldwide epidemics of obesity, diabetes, and cardiovascular disease. These three have become the primary threats to healthy aging and are the major public health problems that we in the United States and in much of the rest of the world face for the future. A majority of the population suffers from obesity, diabetes or prediabetes, hypertension, or abnormal lipids. About 25 percent of the adult population has a constellation of these factors, called the metabolic syndrome.

Our challenge is to prevent and treat these disorders as effectively as possible. As we have outlined in the preceding chapters, the source of these problems resides in our current lifestyle (which is heavily influenced by our environment) and in our genes. We have developed powerful medications that can treat many of the underlying abnormalities that lead to heart disease and death—including effective treatments for hypertension, abnormal lipids, and diabetes. However, these therapies do not reverse the diseases. They represent a "horse-out-of-the-barn" approach. They can decrease the risk of further damage and delay death, but much of the damage has already occurred, resulting in heart failure, stroke, and other disabilities. Our goal should be to prevent disease in the first place.

Fortunately, convincing and scientifically grounded studies have now been performed to examine the effects of lifestyle change on the quadruple threats of obesity, diabetes, hypertension, and abnormal cholesterol. Although lifestyle interventions are generally not as potent as the medications available to treat hypertension or abnormal lipids, they hold the promise of correcting both of these factors with a single intervention, thus decreasing the need for numerous pharmaceuticals to treat them. In addition, lifestyle intervention may be the most effective means of reducing the risk of developing diabetes and of improving blood-sugar levels once diabetes has developed. So, for much of the population that does not yet have diabetes or has only minimal abnormalities in blood pressure and cholesterol, lifestyle changes may be just the ticket to reverse these risk factors and improve long-term health.

As we pointed out, the solutions to our lifestyle problems are not rocket science. Inactivity and overeating have set the stage—or the table—for the medical problems of the twenty-first century. Effective changes in lifestyle to increase activity and decrease weight are the solutions. The trick is to recognize how to incorporate these changes as part of your regular lifestyle. Most of the "branded" programs to address obesity and inactivity—whether they are diets with a gimmick or specialized exercise devices—ask you to "insert" them into your normal lifestyle without otherwise changing that lifestyle. These "inserts" can be effective if you stick with them consistently. Unfortunately, most of the inserted programs fall away over time. What is needed is a long-lasting change that will become part of your lifestyle and part of you. And dramatic changes are not usually necessary; rather, small steps in the right direction that are consistent will be most effective for most people.

We hope that by reading this book, you will see that lifestyle changes can prevent type 2 diabetes. The Diabetes Prevention Program has proved that losing 7 percent of your body weight and increasing your activity level by 150 minutes per week will reduce your risk of developing diabetes by 58 percent—a more powerful effect than using any medicine. If you are at risk for type 2 diabetes (if you are overweight, have a sedentary lifestyle, and have close relatives with diabetes), then the approach described in this book can help you: it can not only prevent diabetes from developing but reverse blood sugars that are in the prediabetes range back to normal levels. It takes effort, but there is proof that it can be done. Others have done it, and so can you!

If you already have type 2 diabetes, making similar lifestyle changes will minimize the amount of medication that you need to keep your blood-sugar levels as close to normal as possible. In fact, some people with type 2 diabetes have been able to manage their blood-sugar levels without medication, and others have been able to avoid insulin and control their diabetes with just lifestyle changes and pills. You won't know your personal results until you try.

If you have type 1 diabetes, your lifestyle is key to achieving stable blood-sugar levels as close to normal as possible without episodes of severe hypoglycemia. Few with type 1 diabetes need to accept a life with "brittle diabetes," with roller-coaster high and low blood sugars. If you work toward consistency in lifestyle (consistency with insulin injections by time of day, consistency in carbohydrate intake at meals and snacks from day to day, and consistency in your exercise routines), your blood sugars will be consistent and more stable, too. It is important that you find a health-care team that specializes in diabetes so that you can benefit from their years of experience in working through all the factors that contribute to erratic blood-sugar patterns and episodes of severe hypoglycemia.

Whether you have type 1 or type 2 diabetes or prediabetes, you can use your lifestyle to manage the ABCs of diabetes—A_{1c} (hemoglobin A_{1c}), **b**lood pressure, and **c**holesterol profile—so that you minimize your risk of diabetes-related complications, heart disease, and stroke—and maximize your quality of life.

You do have to learn to live with diabetes, but you don't have to let diabetes control your quality of life. Now is the time to make lifestyle choices to beat diabetes so it doesn't beat you!

Appendix A

Explaining Scientific Studies of Nutrition and Weight Loss

The advancement of science and, in particular, medical science in the past two centuries has occurred largely owing to experimentation. Prior to that, science relied predominantly on empiricism, or pure observations, to provide knowledge.

In the nineteenth century, however, scientists increasingly turned to experimentation, having recognized the limitations and fallibility of pure empiricism. In the experimental method, the scientist causes a change (an intervention), observes the result, and repeats this process several times. The experiment is performed with and without the intervention. If the same result occurs repeatedly after the same intervention, then the intervention is proved to cause the result. Such experiments or controlled clinical trials allow a scientist to see the direct effects of a selected intervention. They also reduce the potential for bias—the tendency for subjective influences to interfere with results and the interpretation of those results.

Modern medicine has become much more scientifically based because of controlled clinical trials. While careful observational studies help to determine what interventions should be studied, clinical trials are needed to demonstrate definitively whether an intervention works. More often than not, the conclusions from good observational studies are proved by subsequent clinical trials. However, there are enough important exceptions to this rule to underline the critical role of clinical trials. We will discuss both observational studies and clinical trials in more detail.

Observational Studies: The Difference Between Association and Causation

In an observational study, a group of people is examined either once (cross-sectional study) or over time (longitudinal study). In a study of lifestyle or medications, for example, the scientists measure two things:

- "Exposures": lifestyle practices or medications used over time
- Health outcomes, such as diseases that develop

The goal of observational studies is to identify associations between exposures and outcomes. For example, is smoking associated with lung cancer? If the measurements of the exposures and the health outcomes are careful and accurate, and if large numbers of people are studied, valuable new health information can emerge.

One of the most famous observational (or epidemiologic) studies, the Framingham Heart Study, examined a population of approximately five thousand residents of Framingham, Massachusetts, a small town west of Boston, beginning in 1948. Over the next fifty years, the investigators documented the occurrence of a variety of conditions, including diabetes, elevated cholesterol, hypertension, and heart disease. The Framingham Study showed that the risk of developing heart disease was greater in people with high blood pressure, increased cholesterol, and diabetes. This, in turn, led to randomized controlled clinical trials that proved that lowering blood pressure and cholesterol protected people against heart disease. These findings encouraged the development of more potent drugs to lower blood pressure and cholesterol. The observational studies showed an association between having high blood pressure or high cholesterol levels and having an increased risk of getting heart disease. The controlled clinical trials proved that lowering blood pressure and cholesterol levels reduced heart disease. In this case, the observational studies turned out to be right, and millions of people have been protected from heart disease as a result. But it required randomized controlled clinical trials to prove the causality that the observational studies could only suggest.

There have been other associations that have not been shown to be causal in clinical trials. Probably the most famous recent example is the role of estrogens in heart disease in women. Numerous observational studies had demonstrated an association of estrogen replacement therapy with lower rates of osteoporosis and hip fracture. In addition, the risk of heart disease was lower in women who had been treated with estrogen. Therefore, estrogen therapy was recommended for most postmenopausal women. However, when estrogen therapy was put to the more rigorous scientific test, a controlled clinical trial, a very different answer emerged. Not only did estrogen therapy not protect women against heart disease, compared with placebo therapy, it appeared to increase the risk. The lessons of the observational studies were proved wrong by the controlled clinical trial.

Clinical Trials: The Basis of Modern-Day Medical Care

Clinical trials—the application of experimental methods to clinical medicine—came rather late in medical history. The first controlled clinical trial of a medical intervention in the modern era (the treatment of tuberculosis with antibiotics) occurred in the late 1940s. The most common types of clinical trials involve testing a particular medication. Such clinical trials usually have the following features:

- An experimental (or intervention) group and a control (or comparison) group are created, using a random process in which the investigator cannot influence which individuals enter the intervention and control groups. Indeed, most of the time the investigator does not even know which people are in the intervention and control groups until the study has been completed. Random assignment makes it likely that the two study groups will be similar at baseline, so that any differences between them over time will be due to their assigned intervention.

- Detailed information is collected on all of the subjects in the study about their past health or health status at baseline and their subsequent health during the study.
- The subjects in the "active" or experimental intervention group are given the medicine being tested—or the surgical procedure or lifestyle intervention—while the subjects in the control group are given a placebo ("sugar pill") that looks like the real medicine. Sometimes the subjects in the control group are given a different (usually an older) drug or therapy, for comparison to the experimental intervention. Ideally, neither the doctors nor the participants know which subjects are taking the real medicine.
- The outcome of the subjects in the intervention group is compared to that of the subjects in the control group using standardized methods of data collection that are applied identically in both groups. The scientists evaluate whether there were health benefits or side effects in those who received the experimental intervention compared with the control group.
- Statistical techniques are used to estimate whether any apparent differences in the health of the people in the intervention and control groups are likely to be related to the intervention (rather than just being a chance event).

It would not be an exaggeration to say that in the past fifty years controlled clinical trials have done more than any other advance to increase our understanding of the effectiveness and safety of medical care, including the use of medications, devices, and procedures. The U.S. Food and Drug Administration (FDA) and similar regulatory agencies from other countries require controlled clinical trial data to demonstrate effectiveness and examine safety prior to approving any medication and many medical devices.

Controlled clinical trials have provided the objective, trustworthy results that guide modern medicine. More than ten thousand clinical trials are performed each year in the United States. "Evidence-based medicine" has replaced the mystery and witchcraft of previous centuries when leeching, cupping, and other unproven therapies were accepted tools of medicine. In the place of guessing what therapy might benefit a given condition, we have evidence provided from controlled clinical trials. Such evidence-based medicine serves as the basis of our teaching in medical schools and teaching hospitals, directs our choices of therapy, and often determines whether medical insurance will pay for specific procedures or medications. Although there are limitations to the controlled clinical trial, it remains the most trusted experimental method to determine cause and effect and direct modern-day therapy.

Clinical Trials of Lifestyle to Prevent Disease

Most clinical trials involve using medicines, and most involve treating a disease that has already developed in a person. But clinical trials can also test changes in lifestyle rather than medicines, and the prevention of disease rather than its treatment.

Unfortunately, the application of clinical trial methodology to dietary and other lifestyle interventions has lagged behind the study of medications. There are several reasons. First, the study of lifestyle interventions, whether it involves manipulation of diet or of activity, is much more difficult to design and implement than the study of an active drug versus a placebo. For example, it is much easier to ask someone to take a pill each day and to count the number of pills that have been taken, than to ask someone to follow a particular lifestyle and to be confident about what they have eaten or what activities have been performed.

Second, one of the principal elements of a controlled clinical trial is to mask the interventions so that neither the participant nor the investigator knows which therapy is being used until the end of the study. The reason for masking is to decrease the potential for any bias being introduced into either treatment arm. Masking is relatively easy when a drug is being studied: one group is given the drug under study, and an identical appearing placebo is given to the control group. However, with a lifestyle intervention, such as a diet intervention, it is difficult, if not impossible, to mask the therapies. Everyone knows who is getting which therapy. This barrier has sometimes discouraged investigators from studying lifestyle interventions.

The third reason for the dearth of clinical trials that study lifestyle interventions is that there are no federal regulations governing lifestyle interventions. Diets, supplements, and exercise programs require no government stamp of approval and no incontrovertible scientific data to support them before they can be marketed. This has resulted in the proliferation of popular diet books, lifestyle programs, dietary supplements, and specialized vitamin preparations that can all claim spectacular results without providing evidence to back up the claims. Clinical trials are expensive to perform, and in the absence of a requirement to do them, the diet book, exercise tape, diet supplement, and vitamin industries have not provided the funding to conduct them.

In recent years, with more support from governmental agencies, such as the National Institutes of Health, and foundations, an increasing number of clinical trials has been directed at the role of lifestyle interventions in the treatment of obesity, hypertension, diabetes, heart disease, and cancer—all of the diseases in which our lifestyle has been implicated as a cause. Reliable scientific data are finally becoming available to support or refute the role of specific lifestyle changes in preventing or ameliorating the chronic diseases that have become the major public health problems of the twentieth and twenty-first centuries.

Appendix B

Lower-Calorie, Lower-Fat Cookbook Suggestions

American Diabetes Association. Month of Meals series. Alexandria: VA: American Diabetes Association (for a free catalog call 1-800-232-6733).

Bays Avis, Jen, and Kathy F. Ward. *Southern but Lite*. West Monroe, LA: Avis and Ward Nutrition, Inc., 1990.

Bohannon, Richard, Kathy Weinstock, and Terri P. Wuerthmer. *Food for Life: The Cancer Prevention Cookbook*. Chicago: Contemporary Books, Inc., 1986.

Brody, Jane E. *Jane Brody's Good Food Gourmet Cookbook: Recipes and Menus for Delicious and Healthful Entertaining*. New York: Bantam Books, 1990.

Cooking Light Cookbook. Birmingham, AL: Oxmoor House (published annually).

Down Home Healthy Cooking. National Cancer Institute, 1995.

Hinman, Bobbie, and Millie Snyder. *Lean and Luscious*. Rocklin, CA: Prima Publishing, 1992.

Johnson, Carlean. *Six Ingredients or Less: Cooking Light & Healthy*. Gig Harbor, WA: C.J. Books, 1992.

Jortberg, Bonnie, M.S., R.W. *Que Bueno: Five a DAY Cookbook*. Denver: Colorado Department of Public Health and Environment.

Kerr, Graham. *Graham Kerr's Creative Choices Cookbook*. New York: G. P. Putnam and Sons, 1993.

Kerr, Graham. *Graham Kerr's Smart Cooking*. New York: Doubleday, 1991.

Langholz, Edna, Betsy Manis, Sandra Nissenberg, Jane Tougas, and Audrey Wright. *Over 50 and Still Cooking: Recipes for Good Health and Long Life*. San Leandro, CA: Bristol Publishing, Inc., 1990.

Parker, Valerie. *A Lowfat Lifeline for the 1990s*. Lake Oswego, OR: Lowfat Publications, 1990.

Piscatella, Joseph C. *Controlling Your Fat Tooth*. New York: Workman Publishing, 1991.

Ponichtera, Brenda J. *Quick and Healthy Recipes and Ideas*. Dalles, OR: The ScaleDown, 1994.

Smith, M. J. *All-American Low-Fat Meals in Minutes*. Minneapolis: DCI Publishing, Inc., 1990.

Spear, Ruth. *Low Fat and Loving It*. New York: Warner Books, Inc., 1991.

Stanley, Kathleen, and Connie Crawley. *Quick and Easy Diabetic Recipes for One*. Alexandria, VA: American Diabetes Association, 1997 (for a free catalog call 1-800-232-6733).

Appendix C

Sample Shopping List

(Check only the food items you need to follow your eating plan.)

Fruits

☐ Apples
☐ Apricots
☐ Bananas
☐ Blueberries
☐ Cantaloupe
☐ Cherries
☐ Grapefruit
☐ Grapes
☐ Honeydew melon
☐ Kiwis
☐ Mangos
☐ Nectarines
☐ Oranges
☐ Papayas
☐ Peaches
☐ Pears
☐ Plums
☐ Raspberries
☐ Strawberries
☐ Tangerines
☐ Watermelon
☐ _____
☐ _____

Lean Proteins

☐ Chicken
☐ Cottage cheese
☐ Dried beans and peas
   (kidney, navy, split, etc.)
☐ Egg substitute
☐ Halibut
☐ Ham

☐ Lean ground meat
☐ Lentils
☐ Lima beans
☐ Low-fat cheese
☐ Low-fat peanut butter
☐ Low-fat yogurt
☐ Pork (tenderloin, loin)
☐ Salmon
☐ Shrimp
☐ Tofu
☐ Tuna
☐ Turkey
☐ _____
☐ _____

Vegetables

☐ Artichoke
☐ Asparagus
☐ Beans (green, wax)
☐ Beets
☐ Broccoli
☐ Brussels sprouts
☐ Cabbage
☐ Carrots
☐ Cauliflower
☐ Celery
☐ Cucumber
☐ Eggplant
☐ Green onions or
   scallions
☐ Greens (collard, kale,
   turnip)
☐ Kohlrabi

☐ Leeks
☐ Mushrooms
☐ Okra
☐ Onions
☐ Peapods
☐ Peppers
☐ Radishes
☐ Salad greens

Frozen Dinners

(≤ 300 calories,
 ≤ 10 grams of fat)
☐ Budget Gourmet
☐ Healthy Choice
☐ Lean Cuisine
☐ Light and Healthy
☐ Weight Watchers
   Smart Ones
☐ _____

**Salad Dressings/
Condiments**

☐ Fat-free salad dressing
☐ Fat-free mayonnaise
☐ Horseradish
☐ Ketchup
☐ Lemon
☐ Mustard
☐ Nonstick pan spray
☐ Spices _____
☐ Taco or picante sauce
☐ Vegetable oil
☐ Vinegar

Cereals and Grains

☐ Bran flakes
☐ Bulgur
☐ Cheerios
☐ Cornflakes
☐ Couscous
☐ Grits
☐ Kasha
☐ Low-fat granola
☐ Oatmeal
☐ Pasta (whole wheat, white)
☐ Rice (brown, white, or wild)
☐ Shredded wheat
☐ _____
☐ _____

Breads

☐ Bagel
☐ Bread (whole wheat, white)
☐ Bread sticks
☐ Crackers (whole wheat)
☐ English muffin
☐ Hot dog or hamburger bun
☐ Low-calorie bread
☐ Low-fat popcorn
☐ Pita bread
☐ Tortilla
☐ Waffle
☐ _____
☐ _____

Starchy Vegetables

☐ Baked beans
☐ Corn
☐ Peas
☐ Plantain
☐ Potato
☐ Winter squash
☐ Yams, sweet potato

Beverages

☐ Diet drinks
☐ Juices_____
☐ Milk (skim or 1 percent)
☐ Sugar-free hot cocoa
☐ _____

Adapted from the Diabetes Prevention Program.

Appendix D

Sample Meal Plans for 1,200, 1,500, 1,800, and 2,000 Calories

Daily Averages	1,200-Calorie Plan (33 Grams Fat)	1,500-Calorie Plan (42 Grams Fat)	1,800-Calorie Plan (50 Grams Fat)	2,000-Calorie Plan (55 Grams Fat)
Breakfast	250 calories 6 grams fat	300 calories 6 grams fat	350 calories 8 grams fat	400 calories 8 grams fat
Light Meal	350 calories 10 grams fat	400 calories 12 grams fat	450 calories 15 grams fat	500 calories 15 grams fat
Main Meal	500 calories 15 grams fat	600 calories 22 grams fat	700 calories 25 grams fat	800 calories 30 grams fat
Snacks	100 calories 2 grams fat	200 calories 2 grams fat	300 calories 2 grams fat	300 calories 2 grams fat

Adapted from the DPP Lifestyle Intervention Manual, available at bsc.gwu.edu/dpp/manualsb .htmlvdoc and the Diabetes Prevention Program (DPP) Research Group, "The Diabetes Prevention Program (DPP). Description of Lifestyle Intervention," *Diabetes Care 2002*; 25(12): 2165–71.

2,000-Calorie Meal Plans

Mix-and-Match Menus for Breakfast, a Light Meal, a Main Meal, and a Snack

Breakfast 350–400 Calories	¾ cup hot cereal **or** 1 cup unsweetened cold cereal 1 cup low-fat milk **or** yogurt ½ cup fruit juice **or** 1 small fruit 1 slice toast **or** ½ English muffin 1 tablespoon low-fat margarine **or** 1 teaspoon regular margarine	2 slices whole grain toast **or** 1 English muffin **or** 2-ounce bagel 2 teaspoons sugar-free jam or jelly ½ cup fruit juice **or** 1 small fruit 1 egg **or** 2 egg whites **or** 1 tablespoon low-fat peanut butter 1 tablespoon low-fat margarine **or** 1 teaspoon regular margarine	2 waffles **or** ½ cup low-fat granola **or** 2 slices toast 2 teaspoons sugar-free jam or jelly **or** 2 tablespoons sugar-free syrup 1 cup nonfat yogurt ½ cup mixed fruit **or** 1 small fruit **or** ½ cup fruit juice	1 egg **or** 1 egg substitute 2 slices toast **or** 1 pita bread **or** 1 English muffin 2 teaspoons sugar-free jam or jelly ½ cup fruit juice **or** 1 small fruit 1 tablespoon low-fat margarine **or** 1 teaspoon regular margarine
Light Meal 400–500 Calories	2 slices whole grain bread 3 ounces lean protein (chicken, ham, turkey, tuna, **or** 1 tablespoon peanut butter and 2 teaspoons sugar-free jelly) Fat-free mayonnaise or mustard 1 small fruit **or** ½ cup fruit 1 cup low-fat milk or fat-free yogurt	Salad of colorful vegetables 3 ounces turkey, chicken, tuna, ham, or low-fat cheese 2 tablespoons fat-free salad dressing 1 small whole wheat pita **or** 1 tortilla **or** 2 breadsticks **or** 1 cup Chilled Couscous Salad (see Appendix F) 1 cup low-fat milk or fat-free yogurt 1 small fruit **or** ½ cup fruit	Chicken and vegetable stir-fry (3 ounces chicken, 1 cup vegetable, 1 teaspoon peanut oil) ⅔ cup brown rice **or** ½ cup Fiesta Rice (see Appendix F) **or** 1 whole wheat pita 1 cup low-fat milk or fat-free yogurt 1 small fruit **or** ½ cup fruit	Low-calorie frozen entrée (≤ 300 calories, ≤ 10 grams fat) Salad with fat-free dressing or balsamic vinegar 1 dinner roll **or** 1 slice whole grain bread 1 small fruit 1 cup low-fat milk or fat-free yogurt

Main Meal **750–800 Calories**	6 ounces chicken, turkey, fish, or lean red meat 1 cup pasta or rice or 1 baked potato 1½ cups nonstarchy vegetables 1 teaspoon regular margarine or 1 tablespoon low-fat margarine 1 small fruit or ½ cup fruit or Strawberries with Orange-Ricotta Cream (see Appendix F) 1 cup low-fat milk or fat-free yogurt	2 low-calorie frozen entrées (≤ 600 calories, ≤ 20 grams fat) Salad with fat-free dressing or balsamic vinegar 1 dinner roll or 1 slice whole grain bread 1 teaspoon regular margarine or 1 tablespoon low-fat margarine 1 cup low-fat milk or nonfat yogurt 1 small fruit or ½ cup fruit or ½ cup nonfat frozen dessert	2 servings Cheesy Lasagna (see Appendix F) Salad with fat-free dressing or balsamic vinaigrette 1 cup Fresh Vegetable Mélange (see Appendix F) 1 cup fresh fruit ½ cup nonfat frozen dessert 1 cup low-fat milk or nonfat yogurt	1½ servings Grilled Halibut Steak with Pineapple-Lime Salsa (see Appendix F) ⅔ cup brown rice or ½ cup Fiesta Rice (see Appendix F) ½ cup Chilled Multi-Melon Summertime Soup (see Appendix F) or ½ cup fruit or 1 small fruit 1 cup low-fat milk or nonfat yogurt
Snacks **300 Calories**	Choose from snack recipes in Appendix F or create your own	Choose from snack recipes in Appendix F or create your own	Choose from snack recipes in Appendix F or create your own	Choose from snack recipes in Appendix F or create your own

1,800-Calorie Meal Plans

Mix-and-Match Menus for Breakfast, a Light Meal, a Main Meal, and a Snack

Breakfast 350–400 Calories	¾ cup hot cereal **or** 1 cup unsweetened cold cereal; 1 cup low-fat milk or yogurt; ½ cup fruit juice **or** 1 small fruit; 1 slice toast **or** ½ English muffin; 1 tablespoon low-fat margarine **or** 1 teaspoon regular margarine	2 slices whole grain toast **or** 1 English muffin **or** 2-ounce bagel; 2 teaspoons sugar-free jam or jelly; ½ cup fruit juice **or** 1 small fruit; 1 egg **or** 2 egg whites **or** 1 tablespoon low-fat peanut butter; 1 tablespoon low-fat margarine **or** 1 teaspoon regular margarine	2 waffles **or** ½ cup low-fat granola **or** 2 slices toast; 2 teaspoons sugar-free jam or jelly **or** 2 tablespoons sugar-free syrup; 1 cup nonfat yogurt; ½ cup mixed fruit **or** 1 small fruit **or** ½ cup fruit juice	1 egg **or** 1 egg substitute; 2 slices toast **or** 1 pita bread **or** 1 English muffin; 2 teaspoons sugar-free jam or jelly; ½ cup fruit juice **or** 1 small fruit; 1 tablespoon low-fat margarine **or** 1 teaspoon regular margarine
Light Meal 400–500 Calories	2 slices whole grain bread; 3 ounces lean protein (chicken, ham, turkey, tuna, **or** 1 tablespoon peanut butter and 2 teaspoons sugar-free jelly); fat-free mayonnaise or mustard; 1 small fruit **or** ½ cup fruit; 1 cup low-fat milk or fat-free yogurt	Salad of colorful vegetables; 3 ounces turkey, chicken, tuna, ham, or low-fat cheese; 2 tablespoons fat-free salad dressing; 1 small whole wheat pita **or** 1 tortilla **or** 2 breadsticks **or** 1 cup Chilled Couscous Salad (see Appendix F); 1 cup low-fat milk or fat-free yogurt; 1 small fruit **or** ½ cup fruit	Chicken and vegetable stir-fry (3 ounces chicken, 1 cup vegetable, 1 teaspoon peanut oil); ⅔ cup brown rice **or** ½ cup Fiesta Rice (see Appendix F) **or** 1 whole wheat pita; 1 cup low-fat milk or fat-free yogurt; 1 small fruit **or** ½ cup fruit	Low-calorie frozen entrée (≤ 300 calories, ≤ 10 grams fat); Salad with fat-free dressing or balsamic vinegar; 1 dinner roll **or** 1 slice whole grain bread; 1 small fruit; 1 cup low-fat milk or fat-free yogurt

Main Meal 600–700 Calories	5 ounces chicken, turkey, fish, or lean red meat ⅔ cup pasta or rice **or** 1 cup potato **or** 1 cup peas or corn 1½ cups nonstarchy vegetables 1 teaspoon regular margarine **or** 1 tablespoon low-fat margarine 1 small fruit **or** ½ cup fruit **or** Strawberries with Orange-Ricotta Cream (see Appendix F) 1 cup low-fat milk or fat-free yogurt	Low-calorie frozen entrée (≤ 300 calories, ≤ 10 grams fat) Salad with fat-free dressing or balsamic vinegar 1 dinner roll **or** 1 slice whole grain bread 1 teaspoon regular margarine **or** 1 tablespoon low-fat margarine 1 cup low-fat milk or nonfat yogurt 1 small fruit **or** ½ cup fruit ¾ cup nonfat frozen dessert	Cheesy Lasagna (see Appendix F) Salad with fat-free dressing or balsamic vinaigrette 1 cup Fresh Vegetable Mélange (see Appendix F) 1 cup fresh fruit ½ cup nonfat frozen dessert 1 cup low-fat milk or nonfat yogurt	1 serving Grilled Halibut Steak with Pineapple-Lime Salsa (see Appendix F) ⅔ cup brown rice **or** ½ cup Fiesta Rice (see Appendix F) ½ cup Chilled Multi-Melon Summertime Soup (see Appendix F) **or** ½ cup fruit **or** 1 small fruit 1 cup low-fat milk or nonfat yogurt
Snacks 200–300 Calories	Choose from snack recipes in Appendix F or create your own	Choose from snack recipes in Appendix F or create your own	Choose from snack recipes in Appendix F or create your own	Choose from snack recipes in Appendix F or create your own

1,500-Calorie Meal Plans

Mix-and-Match Menus for Breakfast, a Light Meal, a Main Meal, and a Snack

Breakfast 200–250 Calories	¾ cup hot cereal **or** 1 cup unsweetened cold cereal 1 cup low-fat milk ½ cup fruit juice **or** 1 small fruit	2 slices whole grain toast **or** 1 English muffin **or** 2-ounce bagel 2 teaspoons low-fat margarine **or** 2 teaspoons sugar-free jam or jelly ½ cup fruit juice **or** 1 small fruit	1 cup nonfat yogurt ½ cup fruit **or** 1 small fruit 1 waffle 1 tablespoon sugar-free syrup	1 egg **or** 1 serving egg substitute cooked with nonfat spray 1 toast **or** ½ pita bread **or** ½ English muffin 2 teaspoons sugar-free jam or jelly ½ cup fruit juice **or** 1 small fruit
Light Meal 300–400 Calories	2 slices whole grain bread 2 ounces lean protein (chicken, turkey, tuna, ham, **or** 1 tablespoon low-fat peanut butter and 2 teaspoons sugar-free jelly) fat-free mayonnaise or mustard 1 small fruit **or** ½ cup fruit 1 cup low-fat milk or fat-free yogurt	Salad of colorful vegetables 2 ounces turkey, chicken, tuna, ham, or crabmeat ½ whole wheat pita **or** 1 tortilla **or** 2 breadsticks **or** 1 cup Chilled Couscous Salad (see Appendix F) 1 cup low-fat milk or fat-free yogurt	Chicken and vegetable stir-fry (2 ounces chicken, 1 cup vegetable, 1 teaspoon peanut oil) ⅓ cup brown rice **or** ⅓ cup Fiesta Rice (see Appendix F) **or** ½ whole wheat pita 1 cup low-fat milk or fat-free yogurt 1 small fruit **or** ½ cup fruit	Low-calorie frozen entrée (≤ 300 calories, ≤ 10 grams fat) Salad with fat-free dressing or balsamic vinegar 1 dinner roll **or** 1 slice whole grain bread **or** 1 small fruit 1 cup low-fat milk or fat-free yogurt

Main Meal 600–700 Calories	5 ounces chicken, turkey, fish, or lean red meat ⅔ cup pasta or rice **or** 1 cup potato **or** 1 cup peas or corn 1½ cups nonstarchy vegetables 1 teaspoon regular margarine **or** 1 tablespoon low-fat margarine 1 small fruit **or** ½ cup fruit **or** Strawberries with Orange-Ricotta Cream (see Appendix F) 1 cup low-fat milk **or** fat-free yogurt	Low-calorie frozen entrée (≤ 300 calories, ≤ 10 grams fat) Salad with fat-free dressing or balsamic vinegar 1 dinner roll **or** 1 slice whole grain bread 1 teaspoon regular margarine **or** 1 tablespoon low-fat margarine 1 cup low-fat milk or nonfat yogurt 1 small fruit **or** ½ cup fruit ¾ cup nonfat frozen dessert	Cheesy Lasagna (see Appendix F) Salad with fat-free dressing or balsamic vinaigrette 1 cup Fresh Vegetable Mélange (see Appendix F) 1 cup fresh fruit ½ cup nonfat frozen dessert 1 cup low-fat milk or nonfat yogurt	Grilled Halibut Steak with Pineapple-Lime Salsa (see Appendix F) ⅔ cup brown rice **or** ½ cup Fiesta Rice (see Appendix F) ½ cup Chilled Multi-Melon Summertime Soup (see Appendix F) **or** ½ cup fruit **or** 1 small fruit 1 cup low-fat milk or nonfat yogurt
Snacks 200 Calories	Choose from snack recipes in Appendix F or create your own	Choose from snack recipes in Appendix F or create your own	Choose from snack recipes in Appendix F or create your own	Choose from snack recipes in Appendix F or create your own

1,200-Calorie Meal Plans

Mix-and-Match Menus for Breakfast, a Light Meal, a Main Meal, and a Snack

Breakfast 200–250 Calories	¾ cup hot cereal **or** 1 cup unsweetened cold cereal 1 cup low-fat milk ½ cup fruit juice **or** 1 small fruit	2 slices whole grain toast **or** 1 English muffin **or** 2-ounce bagel 2 teaspoons low-fat margarine **or** 2 teaspoons sugar-free jam or jelly ½ cup fruit juice **or** 1 small fruit	1 cup nonfat yogurt ½ cup fruit **or** 1 small fruit 1 waffle 1 tablespoon sugar-free syrup	1 egg **or** 1 egg substitute cooked with nonfat spray 1 slice toast **or** ½ pita bread **or** ½ English muffin 2 teaspoons sugar-free jam or jelly ½ cup fruit juice **or** 1 small fruit
Light Meal 300–400 Calories	2 slices whole grain bread 2 ounces lean protein (chicken, turkey, tuna, ham, or 1 tablespoon low-fat peanut butter and 2 teaspoons sugar-free jelly) fat-free mayonnaise or mustard 1 small fruit **or** ½ cup fruit 1 cup low-fat milk or fat-free yogurt	Salad of colorful vegetables 2 ounces turkey, chicken, tuna, ham, or crabmeat ½ whole wheat pita **or** 1 tortilla **or** 2 breadsticks **or** 1 cup Chilled Couscous Salad (see Appendix F) 1 cup low-fat milk or fat-free yogurt	½ cup cottage cheese 1 cup fresh fruit ½ whole wheat pita **or** 2 breadsticks **or** 6 whole grain crackers 1 cup low-fat milk or fat-free yogurt	Low-calorie frozen entrée (≤ 300 calories, ≤ 10 grams fat) Salad with fat-free dressing or balsamic vinegar 1 small fruit

Main Meal 500–550 Calories	3 ounces chicken, turkey, fish, or lean red meat ½ cup pasta or rice or potato 1½ cups nonstarchy vegetables 1 teaspoon regular margarine **or** 1 tablespoon low-fat margarine 1 small fruit **or** ½ cup fruit **or** Strawberries with Orange-Ricotta Cream (see Appendix F) 1 cup low-fat milk or fat-free yogurt	Low-calorie frozen entrée (≤ 300 calories, ≤ 10 grams fat) Salad with fat-free dressing or balsamic vinegar 1 small fruit **or** ½ cup fruit 1 cup low-fat milk or nonfat yogurt ½ cup nonfat frozen dessert	Chicken and vegetable stir-fry (3 ounces chicken, 1½ cups vegetables, 1 teaspoon peanut oil) ½ cup brown rice ½ cup fruit **or** 1 small fruit **or** ½ cup Chilled Multi-Melon Summertime Soup (see Appendix F) 1 cup low-fat milk or nonfat yogurt	Cheesy Lasagna (see Appendix F) Salad with fat-free dressing or balsamic vinaigrette 1 cup Fresh Vegetable Mélange (see Appendix F) ½ cup fresh fruit 1 cup low-fat milk or nonfat yogurt
Snacks 100 Calories	2 servings Pico de Gallo Salsa with Garlic Pita Triangles (see Appendix F) **or** ½ cup nonfat frozen yogurt **or** choose from snack recipes in Appendix F	1 Mini Mexican-Style Pizza (see Appendix F) **or** 3 cups nonfat popcorn **or** choose from snack recipes in Appendix F	½ cup Zesty Pumpkin Custard (see Appendix F) **or** ½ cup sugar-free pudding **or** choose from snack recipes in Appendix F	⅔ cup Sweet Potato Pudding (see Appendix F) **or** 1 slice cinnamon toast with 1 teaspoon low-fat margarine **or** choose from snack recipes in Appendix F

Appendix E

Healthy Snack Choices and Ideas

Options	Calories	Fat (Grams)
1 small fruit	60	0
1 medium fresh fruit	100	0
¾ cup berries	60	0
½ cup mixed fruit with cinnamon	60	0
1 cup melon	60	0
½ cup applesauce sprinkled with nutmeg	52	0
1 ounce pretzels	108	1
3 cups air-popped popcorn	92	1
1 cup baked tortilla chips	78	1
2 breadsticks (5 inches long)	128	2
8 crackers (saltine type)	101	3
20 oyster crackers	84	3
30 Goldfish crackers	82	2
2 rice cakes with 2 teaspoons fruit spread	102	1
1 slice cinnamon toast with nonfat butter spray	80	1
1 cup broth-based soup	83	3
1 cup nonfat yogurt	137	0
½ cup nonfat yogurt and ½ cup fruit	100	0
¼ cup cottage cheese and 4 crackers	92	2
½ cup sugar-free pudding with skim milk	116	1
½ cup nonfat frozen yogurt	100	0

Free Foods (Fewer than 20 Calories, Fewer than 5 Grams of Carbohydrate)

Raw vegetables (up to 1 cup)
Bouillon
Club soda or sugar-free carbonated beverages
Pickles, dill unsweetened
Sugar-free gelatin
Sugar-free Popsicle
Coffee/tea

See recipes in Appendix F for other snack ideas.

Appendix F

Nutritious Recipes

The following recipes for appetizers, soups, salads, main dishes, desserts, and snacks can be used to create menus that fit into your calorie and fat-gram targets for your snacks, light meal, or main meal of the day (see Appendix D). All of the main dish recipes contain less than 300 calories and fewer than 10 grams of fat per serving. Some of these recipes are already incorporated into the sample menus in Appendix D.

Appetizers

Creamy Guacamole

Makes 4 servings (4 tortilla wedges and 2 tablespoons dip per serving)

   2 (6-inch) flour tortillas, each cut into 8 wedges
   ½ cup peeled, cubed avocado
   ¼ cup nonfat ricotta cheese
   1/3 cup coarsely chopped onion
   2 tablespoons coarsely chopped fresh cilantro
   2 tablespoons fresh lime juice
   1 tablespoon coarsely chopped jalapeño pepper
   ½ teaspoon salt (omit if on a low-sodium diet)

Heat oven to 350°F. Place tortilla wedges on a baking sheet; bake for 10 minutes or until crisp. Set aside. Place avocado and next six ingredients in a food processor. Process until smooth. Spoon mixture into a bowl; cover and chill. Serve with toasted tortilla wedges.

Nutrition information per serving: calories: 24, fat: .93 gram, saturated fat: .15 gram, monounsaturated fat: .5 gram, polyunsaturated fat: .2 gram, carbohydrates: 3 grams, fiber: .4 gram, cholesterol: .75 milligram, sodium: 49 milligrams, protein: 1 gram

Gorgonzola Bruschetta with Crisp Apples

Makes 4 servings (1 bruschetta and 2 apple wedges per serving)

Cooking spray
⅓ cup crumbled Gorgonzola (or another type of blue cheese)
1½ teaspoons butter, softened
1 teaspoon brandy or cognac
¼ teaspoon black pepper
4 (1-inch-thick) diagonally cut slices French bread (about
    1 ounce each)
2 garlic cloves, halved
1 medium Granny Smith apple, cut into 8 wedges

Prepare grill (or a grill pan) by coating it with cooking spray. Combine the Gorgonzola, butter, brandy or cognac, and black pepper in a small bowl, stirring until blended. Place the bread slices on the grill rack; cook for 2 minutes on each side or until slightly brown. Remove bread from the grill or the pan. Rub the cut sides of the garlic over one side of each bread slice. Spread 2 teaspoons of the cheese mixture over each bread slice. Serve with the apple wedges.

Nutrition information per serving: calories: 48, fat: 2 grams, saturated fat: .85 gram, monounsaturated fat: .3 gram, polyunsaturated fat: .1 gram, carbohydrates: 7 grams, fiber: .7 gram, cholesterol: 4 milligrams, sodium: 87 milligrams, protein: 1.5 grams

Stuffed Clams

Makes 4 servings (2 stuffed shells per serving)

8 clams in shells, scrubbed (1 pound)
2½ cups cold water
½ tablespoon cornmeal
½ teaspoon olive oil
¼ cup finely chopped onion
⅓ cup finely chopped shallots
¼ cup finely chopped celery
2 cloves garlic, crushed
⅛ cup finely chopped fresh parsley
½ teaspoon grated lemon rind
¼ teaspoon dried oregano
¼ teaspoon dried thyme
¼ cup fresh bread crumbs, toasted
¼ teaspoon salt
⅛ teaspoon black pepper
Dash of ground red pepper
Fresh parsley leaves (optional for garnish)

Place clams in a large bowl, and cover with ½ cup cold water. Sprinkle with cornmeal, and let stand for 30 minutes. Drain and rinse. Bring 2 cups water to a boil in a large dutch oven. Add the clams; cover and cook for 4 minutes or until shells open. Remove the clams from pan, reserving 1 cup of cooking liquid; discard any unopened shells. Let clams cool. Remove meat from shells; chop and set aside.

Reserve eight large shell halves; set aside. Heat oil in a large nonstick skillet over medium–high heat. Add onion, shallots, celery, and garlic; sauté 3 minutes. Add chopped clam meat, parsley, lemon rind, oregano, and thyme; sauté 1 minute. Remove from heat. Stir in bread crumbs, salt, black pepper, and red pepper. Add the reserved cooking liquid, stirring until dry ingredients are moistened.

Heat oven to 350°F. Divide the bread crumb mixture evenly among reserved clam shell halves, pressing mixture gently into shells. Place stuffed shells on a baking sheet; bake for 20 minutes. Garnish with fresh parsley, if desired and serve hot.

Nutrition information per serving: calories: 47, fat: .86 gram, saturated fat: .16 gram, monounsaturated fat: .43 gram, polyunsaturated fat: .13 gram, carbohydrates: 7 grams, fiber: .53 gram, cholesterol: 3.3 milligrams, sodium: 80 milligrams, protein: 2.4 grams

Large Shrimp with Creamy Blue Cheese Dip

Makes 4 servings (6 shrimp and 2 tablespoons dip per serving)

24 large fresh unpeeled shrimp (1 pound)
1 tablespoon dark brown sugar
3 tablespoons chopped onion
1½ tablespoons cider vinegar
1 tablespoon water
1 tablespoon ketchup
½ tablespoon Worcestershire sauce
1 teaspoon hot sauce
⅛ teaspoon pepper
1 clove garlic, chopped
⅓ cup nonfat cottage cheese
1½ tablespoons skim milk
1 tablespoon crumbled blue cheese or Gorgonzola
⅛ teaspoon pepper
Cooking spray

Peel and devein shrimp, leaving tails intact. Place shrimp in a shallow dish; cover and chill. Combine sugar and next eight ingredients in a blender. Cover and process until smooth. Pour sugar mixture into a small saucepan; place over medium–low heat and cook 10 minutes, stirring occasionally. Let mixture cool, and pour over shrimp. Cover and marinate in refrigerator for about 30 minutes, turning the shrimp occasionally.

Combine cottage cheese, skim milk, blue cheese, and pepper in a blender. Cover and process until mixture is smooth. Spoon into a bowl; cover and chill.

Remove shrimp from marinade, reserving marinade. Arrange shrimp in a single layer on a rack coated with cooking spray, and place rack in a shallow roasting pan. Broil three inches from heat for 3 minutes. Turn shrimp over; baste with reserved marinade. Broil for an additional 3 minutes or until shrimp are bright pink. Serve with cheese dip.

Nutrition information per serving: calories: 120, fat: 2.2 grams, saturated fat: .7 gram, monounsaturated fat: .4 gram, polyunsaturated fat: .6 gram, carbohydrates: .2 gram, fiber: .2 gram, cholesterol: 120 milligrams, sodium: 220 milligrams, protein: 20 grams

Snack Wedges of Sweet Potato with Savory Hummus

Makes 4 servings (2 wedges and ½ tablespoon hummus per serving)

For the potato wedges:

2 medium-size sweet potatoes

2 tablespoons olive oil

½ teaspoon salt (omit if on a low-sodium diet)

¼ teaspoon garlic powder

½ teaspoon paprika

¼ teaspoon ground cumin

Cooking spray

For the hummus:

2 tablespoons tahini (sesame seed paste)

1½ teaspoons lemon juice

½ teaspoon ground coriander

½ teaspoon cayenne pepper

5 ounces garbanzo beans, drained

1 clove garlic

¼ teaspoon ground cumin

2 tablespoons water

To prepare the potato wedges, preheat oven to 450°F. Cut each potato lengthwise twice, so that you have eight wedges; place in a large bowl. Drizzle the olive oil over the potato wedges, tossing well to coat. In a separate bowl, combine the salt, garlic powder, paprika, and cumin. Sprinkle over potatoes and toss well to coat. Arrange wedges in a single layer on a baking sheet that's been coated with cooking spray. Bake for 20 minutes or until tender.

To prepare the hummus, place the remaining ingredients in a food processor. Process 4 minutes or until mixture is smooth. Serve the wedges with the hummus.

Nutrition information per serving: calories: 71, fat: 2 grams, saturated fat: .20 gram, monounsaturated fat: .90 gram, polyunsaturated fat: .60 gram, carbohydrates: 11 grams, fiber: 2.5 grams, cholesterol: 0 milligrams, sodium: 30 milligrams, protein: 2.5 grams

Soups

Chilled Multi-Melon Summertime Soup

Makes 4 ½-cup servings

3 cups peeled, cubed honeydew melon
3 cups peeled, cubed cantaloupe
¼ cup vodka
¼ cup firmly packed brown sugar
4 teaspoons fresh lime juice
¾ cup sliced strawberries

Place honeydew in blender, and process until smooth; pour into a bowl. Place cantaloupe in blender, and process until smooth; pour into another bowl. To each bowl of pureed melon, add 2 tablespoons of the vodka, 2 tablespoons of the brown sugar, and 2 teaspoons of the lime juice; stir well. Cover and chill. Place strawberries in blender; process until smooth. Pour into a bowl; cover and chill.

To serve, evenly divide the cantaloupe mixture into each of four individual bowls. In each bowl, pour ½ cup of the honey-dew mixture into the center of cantaloupe mixture. Dollop each serving with 2 tablespoons pureed strawberries, and swirl decoratively with a wooden pick.

Nutrition information per serving: calories: 70, fat: .3 gram, saturated fat: 0 grams, monounsaturated fat: 0 grams, polyunsaturated fat: .1 gram, carbohydrates: 17 grams, fiber: 1.5 grams, cholesterol: 0 milligrams, sodium: 17 milligrams, protein: 1 gram

Creamy New England Clam Chowder

Makes 4 1-cup servings

2½ pounds steamer clams in shells
Cooking spray
2 cups chopped onion
1 cup cubed red potato
¼ cup diced celery
1 slice turkey bacon, chopped
1 cup bottled clam juice
1⅛ cups water
¼ teaspoon salt (omit if on a low-sodium diet)
½ teaspoon dried thyme
¼ teaspoon coarsely ground pepper
2 fresh parsley sprigs
2 bay leaves
1½ tablespoons all-purpose flour
1 cup low-fat (2 percent) milk

Drain clams. Remove the clams from shells and discard shells. Slip the black skin off the foot of each clam and discard. Set clams aside.

Coat a dutch oven with cooking spray; place over medium-high heat until hot. Add onion, potato, celery, and bacon, and sauté for 7 minutes. Add clam juice, water, salt, thyme, pepper, parsley, and bay leaves; bring to a boil. Cover, reduce heat, and simmer for 20 minutes or until potato is tender. Discard parsley and bay leaves.

Place flour in a bowl. Gradually add milk, blending with a whisk; add to pan. Cook over medium heat for 10 minutes or until thickened, stirring frequently. Stir in clams; cook 2 minutes or until heated.

Nutrition information per serving: calories: 140, fat: 2 grams, saturated fat: .45 gram, monounsaturated fat: .35 gram, polyunsaturated fat: .40 gram, carbohydrates: 12 grams, fiber: .95 gram, cholesterol: 44 milligrams, sodium: 150 milligrams, protein: 17.5 grams

Slightly Piquant Squash Soup

Makes 4 1-cup servings

1¾ cups low-salt chicken broth
¾ cup chopped onion
⅛ teaspoon crushed red pepper
1¾ cups peeled, cubed acorn squash
⅛ teaspoon salt (omit if on a low-sodium diet)
1¾ cups water
⅛ cup uncooked long-grain rice
⅛ cup chunky peanut butter
Chopped fresh parsley (for garnish)

Place ¼ cup of the chicken broth in a large saucepan; bring to a boil. Add onion and crushed red pepper; cook 5 minutes over high heat until tender. Add remaining chicken broth, squash, salt, and water. Bring to a boil. Cover, reduce heat, and simmer for 20 minutes. Add rice; cover and simmer another 20 minutes or until squash and rice are tender. Place peanut butter and half of soup in a blender; cover and process until smooth. Pour puree into a bowl. Puree the remaining soup, and add to the same bowl, stirring well. Return mixture to stove top and heat for 2 minutes. Divide the soup among four individual bowls. Garnish with parsley, if desired.

Nutrition information per serving: calories: 73, fat: 2.5 grams, saturated fat: .51 gram, monounsaturated fat: 1.3 grams, polyunsaturated fat: .80 gram, carbohydrates: 11 grams, fiber: .70 gram, cholesterol: 40 milligrams, sodium: 243 milligrams, protein: 0 grams

Salads

Mixed Mesclun Greens and Apple Salad

Makes 4 servings (1 cup apple mixture and 1 cup greens per serving)

For the dressing:
¼ cup fresh lemon juice
3 tablespoons honey
1 teaspoon olive oil
Dash of salt
Dash of freshly ground pepper

For the salad:
¼ cup crumbled blue cheese
2 cups chopped Granny Smith apple
1 cup chopped Braeburn apple
1 cup chopped McIntosh apple
2 slices turkey bacon, cooked in a pan or on a panini grill and
    chopped
4 cups mixed salad greens (a mesclun mix works well)

Combine all the dressing ingredients in a small bowl and stir well with a whisk. Combine cheese, apples, and bacon in a separate bowl. Drizzle the dressing over the apple mixture and toss gently to coat. Divide the greens among four salad plates, and top each with about 1 cup apple mixture.

Nutrition information per serving: calories: 153, fat: 4 grams, saturated fat: 1.5 grams, monounsaturated fat: 2 grams, polyunsaturated fat: .5 gram, carbohydrates: 28.5 grams, fiber: 4 grams, cholesterol: 7 milligrams, sodium: 190 milligrams, protein: 3.5 grams

Mesclun Mix with Grilled Apple and Onion and Grated Gruyère Cheese

Makes 4 servings (1½ cups salad and 2 onion slices per serving)

Cooking spray
8 ¼-inch-thick onion slices
1 teaspoon sugar
6 cups salad greens
2 cups sliced Fuji or Gala apple
¼ cup (about 1 ounce) grated Gruyère cheese
1 tablespoon water
1 tablespoon white wine vinegar
1 teaspoon olive oil
¼ teaspoon salt (omit if on a low-sodium diet)
¼ teaspoon black pepper

Coat a large nonstick skillet with cooking spray and heat it over medium heat. Carefully arrange four onion slices in the skillet and sprinkle with ½ teaspoon of the sugar. Sauté 4 minutes on each side or until golden brown. Wipe skillet; repeat procedure with remaining onion slices and ½ teaspoon sugar. Combine salad greens, apple, and cheese in a bowl. Set aside. In a small bowl, combine water with the vinegar, oil, salt, and pepper. Pour vinegar mixture over salad greens; toss to coat. Divide the salad evenly among four plates, and top each plate with two onion slices.

Nutrition information per serving: calories: 86, fat: 3.5 grams, saturated fat: 1.5 grams, monounsaturated fat: 1.5 grams, polyunsaturated fat: .4 gram, carbohydrates: 9.5 grams, fiber: 2.5 grams, cholesterol: 8 milligrams, sodium: 178 milligrams, protein: 3.5 grams

Side Dishes

Cheese-Filled Potatoes

Makes 4 servings (1 potato per serving)

4 medium baking potatoes (about 2½ pounds)
½ cup shredded, reduced-fat cheddar cheese
1 cup nonfat sour cream
⅓ cup finely chopped green onions
¼ teaspoon salt (omit if on a low-sodium diet)
Paprika

Preheat oven to 400°F. Bake potatoes for 1 hour or until done (when fork pierces potatoes with no resistance); let cool slightly. Place each potato on a flat surface, and cut a ¼-inch-thick slice from the top; carefully scoop pulp into a bowl, leaving the shells intact. Add cheese and sour cream to pulp, and mash. Stir in green onions and salt. Preheat oven to 450°F. Stuff shells with potato mixture, and sprinkle with paprika. Place on a baking sheet, and bake for 15 minutes or until thoroughly heated.

Microwave directions: pierce potatoes with a fork, and arrange in a circle on paper towels in the microwave oven. Microwave on high for 16 minutes or until done, turning and rearranging potatoes halfway through cooking time. Let stand for 5 minutes. Cut a ¼-inch-thick slice from the top of each baked potato; carefully scoop pulp into a bowl, leaving the shells intact. Add cheese and sour cream to pulp, and mash. Stir in green onions and salt. Stuff shells with potato mixture and sprinkle with paprika. Microwave on high for 5 minutes or until thoroughly heated.

Nutrition information per serving: calories: 130, fat: .85 gram, saturated fat: .50 gram, monounsaturated fat: .25 gram, polyunsaturated fat: .07 gram, carbohydrates: 20 grams, fiber: 1 gram, cholesterol: 9 milligrams, sodium: 186 milligrams, protein: 5.5 grams

Chilled Couscous Salad

Makes 4 servings (1 cup per serving)

1½ cups no-salt-added chicken broth
½ cup uncooked couscous
½ cup seeded, chopped unpeeled tomato
¾ cup chopped red bell pepper
⅓ cup chopped celery
⅓ cup seeded, chopped unpeeled cucumber
¼ cup chopped green onions
¼ cup chopped fresh parsley
2 tablespoons balsamic vinegar
1 tablespoon olive oil
1 tablespoon Dijon mustard
½ teaspoon grated lemon rind
¼ teaspoon black pepper

In a medium saucepan over high heat, bring broth to a boil. Stir in couscous. Remove from heat. Let stand, covered, for 5 minutes; fluff with a fork. Uncover and let cool for 10 minutes. Combine cooked couscous, tomato, bell pepper, celery, cucumber, green onions, and parsley in a large bowl, and toss gently. In a small bowl, combine vinegar, oil, mustard, lemon rind, and pepper. Stir with a wire whisk. Add to couscous mixture; toss to coat. Serve chilled or at room temperature.

Nutrition information per serving: calories: 89, fat: 1.5 grams, saturated fat: .25 gram, monounsaturated fat: 1 gram, polyunsaturated fat: .25 gram, carbohydrates: 15.5 grams, fiber: 1.5 grams, cholesterol: 0 milligrams, sodium: 98.5 milligrams, protein: 4 grams

Fiesta Rice

Makes 4 servings (½ cup per serving)

    1 teaspoon olive oil
    1 cup chopped onion
    4 cloves garlic, minced
    ½ cup uncooked long-grain rice
    1 cup water
    10 ounces canned diced tomatoes with green chilies, undrained
    ½ cup chopped fresh cilantro

In a large saucepan over medium heat, heat olive oil. Add onion and garlic; sauté for 4 minutes. Add rice, water, and tomatoes with chilies. Bring to a boil. Cover, reduce heat, and simmer 20 minutes or until the liquid is absorbed. Remove from heat; stir in cilantro and serve.

Nutrition information per serving: calories: 173, fat: 1.4 grams, saturated fat: .2 gram, monounsaturated fat: .8 gram, polyunsaturated fat: .2 gram, carbohydrates: 28 grams, fiber: 1.5 grams, cholesterol: 0 milligrams, sodium: 11 milligrams, protein: 1.5 grams

Fresh Vegetable Mélange

Makes 4 servings (1 cup per serving)

    1½ teaspoons vegetable oil
    1½ cups sliced onion, separated into rings
    1 cup red bell pepper strips
    2 cloves garlic, minced
    1¾ cups sliced yellow squash
    1¾ cups sliced zucchini
    1 cup chopped unpeeled plum tomatoes
    1 tablespoon julienne-cut fresh basil
    ½ teaspoon lemon pepper
    ¼ teaspoon salt (omit if on a low-sodium diet)
    1 tablespoon grated Parmesan cheese

Heat oil in a large nonstick skillet over medium–high heat. Add onion, bell pepper, and garlic; stir-fry for 2 minutes. Add squash and zucchini; stir-fry 3 more minutes or until the vegetables are crisp-tender. Add tomatoes, basil, lemon pepper, and salt; cook 1 minute or until thoroughly heated. Remove from heat; sprinkle with cheese.

Nutrition information per serving: calories: 67, fat: 2.8 grams, saturated fat: .7 gram, monounsaturated fat: 1.3 grams, polyunsaturated fat: .5 gram, carbohydrates: 9 grams, fiber: 2.5 grams, cholesterol: 2 milligrams, sodium: 184 milligrams, protein: 2.5 grams

Golden Beet and Yukon Gold Gratin

Makes 4 servings (1 cup per serving)

Cooking spray
2 cloves garlic, minced
1 cup sliced (¼-inch) Yukon gold potatoes (about ½ pound)
½ golden beet, cut into ¼-inch slices
1½ tablespoons salt (omit if on a low-sodium diet)
1½ tablespoons black pepper
1¼ cups evaporated skim milk
½ cup grated Asiago cheese

Preheat the oven to 350°F. Spray a 6″ × 8″ × 2″ baking pan generously with cooking spray and then sprinkle the minced garlic on the bottom of the pan. Alternate layers of potatoes and beets, seasoning each layer with salt and pepper and pouring a few ounces of evaporated skim milk over each layer (enough to slightly cover the beets and potatoes). Bake, covered, for 40 minutes or until beets and potatoes are tender. Put a layer of the grated Asiago cheese on top, and bake uncovered for an additional 10 minutes or until cheese is melted and golden brown.

Nutrition information per serving: calories: 68, fat: 2 grams, saturated fat: .85 gram, monounsaturated fat: .3 gram, polyunsaturated fat: .1 gram, carbohydrates: 2.5 grams, fiber: 2 grams, cholesterol: 6.5 milligrams, sodium: 119 milligrams, protein: 4 grams

Lentils with Garlic and Rosemary

Makes 4 servings (1 cup per serving)

1½ cups water
¾ cup chopped onion
½ cup diced cooked ham
⅓ cup diced carrot
1 teaspoon crushed dried rosemary
¾ teaspoon dried sage
¼ teaspoon pepper
⅓ pound dried lentils
4 ounces fat-free beef broth
2 cloves garlic, chopped
1 bay leaf
Chopped fresh parsley (optional)

In an electric slow cooker (Crock-Pot) combine all the ingredients except the parsley. Cover and cook on high-heat setting for 3 hours or until lentils are tender. Discard bay leaf, garnish with parsley, and serve.

Nutrition information per serving: calories: 76, fat: 1.5 grams, saturated fat: .30 gram, monounsaturated fat: .45 gram, polyunsaturated fat: .15 gram, carbohydrates: 4 grams, fiber: 1.5 grams, cholesterol: 5 milligrams, sodium: 152 milligrams, protein: 6.5 grams

Main Dishes

Asian-Style Chicken-Peanut Pasta

Makes 4 servings (about 1¼ cups per serving)

1 teaspoon sugar

1 teaspoon cornstarch

1 teaspoon peeled, minced gingerroot

2 tablespoons plus 1 teaspoon low-sodium soy sauce

1 teaspoon white vinegar

⅛ teaspoon hot sauce

½ cup water

2–3 cloves garlic, minced

½ pound skinless, boneless chicken breast, cut into thin strips

1 teaspoon vegetable oil

1 cup minced green onions

1 cup fresh snow peas, halved

2½ cups hot cooked fusilli (corkscrew pasta), cooked without salt or fat

1 teaspoon dark sesame oil

¼ cup unsalted dry-roasted peanuts

Combine sugar, cornstarch, gingerroot, 2 tablespoons of the soy sauce, vinegar, hot sauce, water, and garlic in a large bowl; stir well. Add chicken, and toss gently to coat. Cover and chill 1 hour.

Remove chicken from marinade and reserve marinade. Heat vegetable oil in a large skillet over medium–high heat. Add chicken; stir-fry for about 5 minutes, until chicken is cooked through. Add reserved marinade, green onions, and snow peas; stir-fry 2 minutes or until slightly thickened. Remove from heat. Combine fusilli, sesame oil, and remaining 1 teaspoon of soy sauce in a large bowl; toss gently to coat. Add chicken mixture and top with peanuts, tossing gently.

Nutrition information per serving: calories: 284, fat: 5 grams, saturated fat: .80 gram, monounsaturated fat: 2 grams, polyunsaturated fat: 1.5 grams, carbohydrates: 41 grams, fiber: 2.5 grams, cholesterol: 23 milligrams, sodium: 272 milligrams, protein: 18 grams

Cheesy Lasagna

Makes 4 servings (1¾ cups per serving)

12 lasagna noodles
⅓ pound ground round
Cooking spray
½ cup chopped onion
3 cloves garlic, minced
¼ cup chopped fresh parsley
12 ounces whole canned tomatoes, undrained
6 ounces Italian-style canned stewed tomatoes, undrained
3½ ounces no-salt-added tomato sauce
2½ ounces tomato paste
2 teaspoons dried oregano
1 teaspoon dried basil
¼ teaspoon pepper
1 cup nonfat cottage cheese
½ cup finely grated fresh Parmesan cheese
6½ ounces nonfat ricotta cheese
1 egg white, lightly beaten

Prepare lasagna noodles according to directions on box. Set aside in cool water so noodles don't stick together. Cook meat in a large saucepan over medium heat until browned, stirring to crumble; drain and set aside. Wipe pan with a paper towel. Coat pan with cooking spray; add the onion and garlic, and sauté 5 minutes. Return meat to pan. Add 2 tablespoons of the parsley, the whole tomatoes, stewed tomatoes, tomato sauce, tomato paste, oregano, basil, and pepper; bring to a boil. Cover, reduce heat, and simmer 15 minutes. Uncover; simmer 20 more minutes. Remove from heat.

In a bowl, combine the remaining parsley with the cottage cheese, Parmesan cheese, ricotta cheese, and egg white. Stir well, and set aside.

Spread ¾ cup of the tomato/meat mixture on bottom of a 13″ × 9″ baking dish coated with cooking spray. Arrange three noodles on top of the tomato mixture. Top with half of cheese mixture and 2¼ cups tomato/meat mixture. Repeat layers, ending with noodles. Spread the remaining tomato mixture over noodles.

Cover; bake at 350°F for 1 hour. Let stand 10 minutes before serving.

Nutrition information per serving: calories: 234, fat: 6.5 grams, saturated fat: 3 grams, monounsaturated fat: 2 grams, polyunsaturated fat: .45 gram, carbohydrates: 26 grams, fiber: 1.5 grams, cholesterol: 24 milligrams, sodium: 260 milligrams, protein: 17.5 grams

Chicken Thighs with Roasted Apples and Garlic

Makes 4 servings (2 thighs and about ⅔ cup apple mixture per serving)

4½ cups chopped, peeled Braeburn apples (about 1½ pounds)
1 teaspoon chopped fresh sage
½ teaspoon ground cinnamon
½ teaspoon ground nutmeg
4 garlic cloves, chopped
½ teaspoon salt (omit if on a low-sodium diet)
Cooking spray
8 chicken thighs (about 2 pounds), skinned
¼ teaspoon black pepper

Preheat oven to 475°F. Combine the apples, sage, cinnamon, nutmeg, and garlic in a large bowl. Add ¼ teaspoon of the salt and mix well. Spread the apple mixture on a jelly-roll pan that's been coated with cooking spray. Sprinkle the chicken with ¼ teaspoon salt and the pepper, and arrange on top of the apple mixture. Bake for 25 minutes or until chicken is cooked through and apple is tender. Remove chicken from pan; keep warm. Partially mash apple mixture with a potato masher and serve with chicken.

Nutrition information per serving: calories: 257, fat: 5.5 grams, saturated fat: 1 gram, monounsaturated fat: 1.5 grams, polyunsaturated fat: 1 gram, carbohydrates: 26.5 grams, fiber: 3.5 grams, cholesterol: 107 milligrams, sodium: 405 milligrams, protein: 25.5 grams

Chicken with Mushroom and Almond Cream Sauce

Makes 4 servings (⅔ cup noodles, 1 chicken breast half, ⅓ cup sauce per serving)

- ½ cup coarsely chopped almonds, toasted
- ½ cup water
- 1 teaspoon salt (omit if on a low-sodium diet)
- 4 (4-ounce) skinless, boneless chicken breast halves
- 1 teaspoon freshly ground black pepper
- Cooking spray
- ¼ cup finely chopped garlic
- 8 ounces mushrooms, sliced
- 3 cups cooked egg noodles
- Chopped parsley (for garnish)

Place the almonds in a food processor and process until smooth (about 1 minute), scraping the sides of the bowl at least once. With the processor on, add water and ¾ teaspoon of the salt. Process until smooth, continuing to scrape the sides of the bowl.

Sprinkle the chicken with the remaining ¼ teaspoon salt and the black pepper. Coat a large nonstick pan with cooking spray, and heat over medium heat. Add chicken; sauté 3 minutes on each side or until cooked through. Remove chicken from pan; keep warm. Add garlic and mushrooms to pan; sauté 3 minutes or until mushrooms are tender. Stir in almond mixture; bring to boil. Cook 1½ minutes.

Place ⅔ cup noodles on each of four plates. Top each serving with one chicken breast half and ¼ cup sauce. Garnish with parsley.

Nutrition information per serving: calories: 255, fat: 8.5 grams, saturated fat: 1 gram, monounsaturated fat: 4.5 grams, polyunsaturated fat: 2.5

grams, carbohydrates: 21 grams, fiber: 2.5 grams, cholesterol: 67.5 milligrams, sodium: 385 milligrams, protein: 22.5 grams

Ginger-Infused Beef and Pineapple Stir-Fry

Makes 4 servings (1 cup steak mixture and 1 cup noodles per serving)

½ pound lean flank steak
1 tablespoon peeled, minced gingerroot
2 teaspoons sugar
1½ tablespoons low-sodium soy sauce
1½ tablespoons sherry
2 cloves garlic, minced
2 teaspoons cornstarch
4 teaspoons rice vinegar
Cooking spray
2 teaspoons dark sesame oil
1½ cups cubed fresh pineapple
½ cup diagonally sliced (3-inch) green onions
½ cup thinly sliced fresh mushrooms
½ cup fresh snow peas (¼ pound)
½ cup julienne-cut (3-inch) red bell pepper strips
4 cups hot cooked somen noodles or angel hair pasta, cooked
    without salt or fat

Trim fat from the steak and cut it lengthwise with the grain into ¼-inch-thick slices. Cut these slices in half crosswise. Combine steak, gingerroot, sugar, soy sauce, sherry, and garlic in a large zip-top heavy-duty plastic bag. Seal bag, and marinate in refrigerator for 2 hours, turning the bag occasionally. Remove steak from bag, and discard the marinade.

In a small bowl, combine the cornstarch and vinegar. Stir well and set aside. Coat a large nonstick skillet with cooking spray. Add the sesame oil and place over medium-high heat until hot. Add the steak; stir-fry for 4 minutes. Add the cornstarch mixture, pineapple, green onions, mushrooms, snow peas, and red pepper strips to the skillet; stir-fry for 3 minutes or until vegetables are crisp/tender. Serve over noodles.

Nutrition information per serving: calories: 272, fat: 6.5 grams, saturated fat: 2.5 grams, monounsaturated fat: 2.5 grams, polyunsaturated fat: .87 gram, carbohydrates: 36 grams, fiber: 3 grams, cholesterol: 36 milligrams, sodium: 780 milligrams, protein: 15 grams

Grilled Halibut Steak with Pineapple-Lime Salsa

Makes 4 servings (1 halibut steak and ¼ cup salsa per serving)

For the salsa:
- ⅓ cup pineapple preserves
- ¼ cup finely chopped red bell pepper
- 2 tablespoons finely chopped red onion
- 1 tablespoon seeded, finely chopped jalapeño pepper
- 1 teaspoon dried mint flakes
- ⅛ teaspoon salt (omit if on a low-sodium diet)
- 2 tablespoons fresh lime juice
- 8 ounces canned unsweetened pineapple tidbits, drained

For the fish:
- 1 teaspoon vegetable oil
- 1 large garlic clove, minced
- 4 (4-ounce) uncooked halibut steaks (about ¾-inch thick)
- ¼ teaspoon salt (omit if on a low-sodium diet)
- Cooking spray
- Lime wedges (optional)
- Cilantro sprigs (optional)

Combine the salsa ingredients in a bowl. Stir well. Set salsa aside. In a small bowl, combine oil and garlic; brush over fish. Sprinkle salt over fish; set aside. Heat grill, broiler, or grill pan; coat the grill rack or broiler pan with cooking spray, and place fish on it. Cook 3 minutes on each side or until fish flakes easily when tested with a fork. Spoon the salsa over the fish. Serve with lime wedges and garnish with cilantro sprigs, if desired.

Nutrition information per serving: calories: 283, fat: 5 grams, saturated fat: .7 gram, monounsaturated fat: 1.8 grams, polyunsaturated fat: 1.7 grams, carbohydrates: 22.5 grams, fiber: 9 grams, cholesterol: 0 milligrams, sodium: 303 milligrams, protein: 35.5 grams

Lemon-Infused Pistachio Sliced Chicken over Mixed Greens

Makes 4 servings (1½ cups salad and 4 ounces chicken per serving)

¾ cup cornflakes

2 tablespoons pistachios, toasted

2 teaspoons grated lemon rind

½ teaspoon salt (omit if on a low-sodium diet)

½ teaspoon black pepper

4 (4-ounce) skinless, boneless chicken breast halves

1 tablespoon honey

Cooking spray

6 cups salad greens

1 tablespoon fresh lemon juice

1 teaspoon olive oil

Lemon wedges (optional for garnish)

Combine cornflakes, pistachios, lemon rind, ¼ teaspoon of the salt, and ¼ teaspoon of the pepper in a food processor; pulse until coarsely ground. Place crumb mixture in a shallow dish.

Place each chicken breast half between two sheets of heavy-duty plastic wrap. Using a meat mallet or rolling pin to pound the chicken, flatten to ¼-inch thickness. Brush the chicken with honey, and then dredge the chicken in the crumb mixture.

Heat a large nonstick skillet coated with cooking spray over medium heat. Add the chicken and sauté 5 minutes on each side or until cooked through. Cut chicken into ½-inch strips; set aside.

Place the salad greens in a large bowl. In a small bowl, combine the remaining ¼ teaspoon salt, the remaining ¼ teaspoon pepper, lemon juice, and olive oil. Just before serving, drizzle this dressing over the salad greens, tossing gently to coat. Divide the salad greens and chicken evenly among four plates. Garnish with the lemon wedges, if desired.

Nutrition information per serving: calories: 217, fat: 5.5 grams, saturated fat: .9 gram, monounsaturated fat: 3 grams, polyunsaturated fat: .9 gram, carbohydrates: 12 grams, fiber: 2 grams, cholesterol: 66 milligrams, sodium: 427 milligrams, protein: 29 grams

Tuna Steaks on Mediterranean Salad

Makes 4 servings (4 ounces tuna and 1⅓ cups salad mixture per serving)

⅓ cup finely chopped green bell pepper
⅓ cup finely chopped red bell pepper
½ cup finely chopped red onion
1 tablespoon minced fennel leaves
2 tablespoons plus 1 teaspoon red wine vinegar
1 tablespoon extra-virgin olive oil
⅓ teaspoon sugar
¼ teaspoon salt (omit if on a low-sodium diet)
⅓ pound fresh green beans
1 cup peeled, cubed (½-inch) baking potato
¾ cup thinly sliced fennel bulb
2 large ripe tomatoes, each cut into 12 wedges
4 (4-ounce) tuna steaks (about ¾-inch thick)
12 kalamata olives

Combine the first eight ingredients in a bowl. Stir well, and set aside. Wash green beans; trim ends and remove strings. Set aside. Arrange potato in a vegetable steamer over boiling water; cover and steam for 8 minutes. Add beans to steamer; cover and steam for 8 more minutes. Combine potato, beans, fennel, and tomato wedges in a large bowl. Add the bell pepper mixture; stir well. Place a large nonstick skillet over medium-high heat until hot. If desired, spray pan with nonstick cooking spray and then add tuna; cook for 4 minutes on each side or until medium-rare.

To serve, arrange 1⅓ cups vegetable mixture, 1 tuna steak, and 3 olives on each of four plates.

Nutrition information per serving: calories: 233, fat: 8 grams, saturated fat: 1.5 grams, monounsaturated fat: 3 grams, polyunsaturated fat: 2 grams, carbohydrates: 11 grams, fiber: 2 grams, cholesterol: 44 milligrams, sodium: 191 milligrams, protein: 28 grams

Turkey, Beef, and Pork Bolognese with Fettuccine

Makes 4 servings (1½ cups per serving)

½ tablespoon olive oil
¾ cup coarsely chopped onion
½ cup coarsely chopped celery
½ cup coarsely chopped carrot
¼ cup ground pork (about 2 ounces)
¼ cup ground turkey (about 2 ounces)
¼ cup lean ground beef (about 2 ounces)
½ cup dry white wine
¼ teaspoon salt (omit if on a low-sodium diet)
¼ teaspoon black pepper
1 bay leaf
¼ teaspoon ground nutmeg
½ (14½-ounce) can fat-free, low-sodium chicken broth
½ (10¾-ounce) can tomato puree
½ cup 2 percent milk
1 tablespoon minced fresh flat-leaf parsley (also called Italian
     parsley)
1 9-ounce package fresh fettuccine, cooked and drained
1 tablespoon grated fresh Parmesan cheese

Heat olive oil in a large dutch oven over medium heat. Chop the onion, celery, and carrot in a food processor or blender for 15 seconds or until a chunky consistency is achieved. Add the onion mixture to the dutch oven; cover and cook for 8 minutes, stirring occasionally. Remove onion mixture from pan and set aside.

Add pork, turkey, and beef to pan; cook over medium heat until browned, stirring to crumble. Remove pan from stove, add white wine, and then put the pan back on the stove. Add the salt, pepper, bay leaf, and nutmeg; bring to a boil. Cook for 5 minutes. Add the onion mixture, chicken broth, and tomato puree. Bring to a simmer. Cook for 1 hour, stirring occasionally. Stir in milk and minced parsley; bring to boil. Reduce heat and simmer for 40 minutes. Discard the bay leaf. Add the pasta and toss to coat. Sprinkle evenly with cheese.

Nutrition information per serving: calories: 175, fat: 4.5 grams, saturated fat: 1.5 grams, monounsaturated fat: 2.5 grams, polyunsaturated fat: .7 gram, carbohydrates: 21.5 grams, fiber: 2.0 grams, cholesterol: 41 milligrams, sodium: 275 milligrams, protein: 10.5 grams

Desserts

Honey-Glazed Pineapple

Makes 4 servings (3 pineapple spears per serving)

1 (2½-pound) fresh pineapple, peeled and cored
1 tablespoon plus 1 teaspoon honey
1½ teaspoons trans-fat-free margarine
Fresh mint, minced (optional)

Cut pineapple lengthwise into 12 spears. Arrange spears on a broiler pan, and set aside. Combine honey and margarine in a small saucepan; place over low heat, and cook until margarine melts. Divide the honey mixture in half. Brush one portion of the honey mixture evenly over one side of each spear. Broil the pineapple about 3 inches from heat for 7 minutes. Turn spears over; brush evenly with remaining honey mixture. Broil for an additional 7 minutes. To garnish, sprinkle with minced mint.

Nutrition information per serving: calories: 70, fat: 1.5 grams, saturated fat: .27 gram, monounsaturated fat: .67 gram, polyunsaturated fat: .54 gram, carbohydrates: 15 grams, fiber: 1 gram, cholesterol: 0 milligrams, sodium: 16 milligrams, protein: .40 gram

Strawberries with Orange-Ricotta Cream

Makes 4 servings (½ cup strawberries with 4 tablespoons cheese mixture per serving)

- ½ cup part-skim ricotta cheese
- ½ cup vanilla low-fat yogurt
- 1 tablespoon sugar
- 1 teaspoon grated orange rind
- 1 teaspoon vanilla extract
- 2 cups quartered strawberries

Combine the first five ingredients in a blender; process until smooth. Spoon the cheese mixture into a small bowl; cover and chill for 3 hours. Spoon ½ cup of the strawberries into each of four small bowls. Top each with 4 tablespoons of the cheese mixture.

Nutrition information per serving: calories: 76, fat: 2 grams, saturated fat: 1 gram, monounsaturated fat: .6 gram, polyunsaturated fat: .2 gram, carbohydrates: 11 grams, fiber: 1.5 grams, cholesterol: 7 milligrams, sodium: 39 milligrams, protein: 3.5 grams

Sweet Potato Pudding

Makes 4 servings (⅔ cup pudding per serving)

- 1⅓ cups mashed cooked sweet potato
- ½ cup sugar
- 2 teaspoons ground cinnamon
- 2 teaspoons grated orange rind
- 1 teaspoon salt (omit if on a low-sodium diet)
- 1 teaspoon ground ginger
- ½ teaspoon ground cloves
- ⅓ cup egg substitute
- 16 ounces evaporated skim milk
- Cooking spray

Combine sweet potato and the next seven ingredients in a large bowl. Beat at medium speed with a mixer until smooth. Add milk; mix well. Pour mixture into a 2-quart casserole coated with cooking spray. Bake at 375°F for 1 hour or until a knife inserted near the center comes out clean. (For individual servings, pour ⅔ cup potato mixture into each of 4 custard cups. Bake at 375°F for 40 minutes or until a knife inserted near center comes out clean.) Let pudding cool. Cover and chill for 2 hours.

Nutrition information per serving: calories: 83, fat: .86 gram, saturated fat: .20 gram, monounsaturated fat: .20 gram, polyunsaturated fat: .43 gram, carbohydrates: 15 grams, fiber: .40 gram, cholesterol: 1 milligram, sodium: 116 milligrams, protein: 3.5 grams

Tropical Crisp

Makes 4 servings (½ cup per serving)

⅓ cup flaked sweetened coconut

1 tablespoon all-purpose flour

¼ teaspoon vanilla extract

Dash of salt

1 egg white

8 teaspoons sugar

Cooking spray

1 half small graham cracker, crumbled

1 tablespoon plus 1 teaspoon trans-fat-free margarine, melted

10 ounces unsweetened canned crushed pineapple, with juice

⅛ cup thinly sliced dried apricot halves

½ cup peeled, chopped mango

2 tablespoons cornstarch

2 tablespoons water

Heat oven to 325°F. Combine coconut, flour, vanilla, salt, egg white, and 4 teaspoons of the sugar in a bowl; stir well. Spread coconut mixture evenly onto a baking sheet coated with cooking spray. Bake for 20 minutes or until edges are lightly browned. Let cool completely.

Break coconut mixture into small pieces. Place the coconut pieces and graham cracker crumbs in a food processor, and process until blended. With the processor running, slowly add the margarine; process until blended. Set aside.

Heat oven to 350°F. Drain pineapple, reserving ½ cup of the juice (or use a separate can of pineapple juice). Combine ¼ cup of the pineapple juice and apricots in a 1-cup glass measuring cup. Cover with heavy-duty plastic wrap, and vent. Microwave on high for 2½ minutes. Let stand, covered, 15 minutes. Drain. Combine apricot mixture, remaining pineapple juice, and the remaining 4 teaspoons sugar with the pineapple, mango, cornstarch, and water in a bowl. Stir well. Spoon the fruit mixture into a 1-quart baking dish; sprinkle with coconut and graham cracker mixture. Bake for 35 minutes or until golden.

Nutrition information per serving: calories: 113, fat: 4 grams, saturated fat: 1.5 grams, monounsaturated fat: 1 gram, polyunsaturated fat: .80 gram, carbohydrates: 15 grams, fiber: 1.14 grams, cholesterol: 0 milligrams, sodium: 84 milligrams, protein: 1.14 grams

Zesty Pumpkin Custard

Makes 4 servings (½ cup per serving)

⅛ cup sugar
1 tablespoon honey
¾ teaspoon ground cinnamon
½ teaspoon ground allspice
1 egg
6 ounces canned evaporated skim milk
8 ounces canned cooked pumpkin
¼ cup reduced-calorie frozen whipped topping, thawed

Preheat oven to 325°F. Combine first seven ingredients in a large bowl. Using an electric mixer, beat at low speed until smooth.

Spoon ½ cup of the pumpkin mixture into each of four 6–ounce ramekins or custard cups. Place four ramekins in a 9–inch square baking pan; add hot water to the pan to a depth of 1 inch. Bake for 1 hour or until set. Remove ramekins from pans; let cool. Top each serving with 1 tablespoon whipped topping.

Nutrition information per serving: calories: 77, fat: 2.5 grams, saturated fat: 1.5 grams, monounsaturated fat: .9 gram, polyunsaturated fat: .15 gram, carbohydrates: 11 grams, fiber: .5 gram, cholesterol: 32 milligrams, sodium: 34 milligrams, protein: 2.5 grams

Snacks

Apple-Infused Muffins with Pecans

Makes 12 servings (1 muffin per serving)

For the filling:
- 1 cup peeled and finely chopped Rome apple
- 1¾ cups chopped pecans, toasted
- 2 tablespoons sugar
- ¾ teaspoon ground nutmeg
- 1 tablespoon trans-fat-free margarine, melted

For the batter:
- 1½ cups all-purpose flour
- 1 cup wheat bran flakes cereal with raisins
- ⅔ cup sugar
- ⅓ cup graham cracker crumbs
- 1¼ teaspoons baking soda
- ¼ teaspoon salt (omit if on a low-sodium diet)
- 1 cup nonfat buttermilk
- 2 tablespoons trans-fat-free margarine, melted
- 1 egg (or 2 ounces egg substitute, if preferred)
- Cooking spray

For the topping:
- 1 tablespoon sugar

For the filling, combine filling ingredients in a bowl. Stir well, and set aside.

To make the batter, combine the flour, cereal, sugar, graham cracker crumbs, baking soda, and salt in a separate bowl and make a well in the center of the mixture. Combine buttermilk, melted margarine, and egg; stir well. Add the buttermilk mixture into the well of the flour mixture, stirring just until moistened.

Spoon 2 tablespoons batter into each of 12 muffin cups coated with cooking spray. Divide apple mixture evenly among muffin cups. Top apple mixture with remaining batter, dividing evenly. (The second layer of batter will not cover the apple–nut mixture completely, but this gives the muffins a wonderful textured appearance after they're baked.) Sprinkle 1 tablespoon sugar evenly over muffins. Bake at 350°F for 25 minutes. Remove from pan immediately.

Nutrition information per serving: calories: 90, fat: 2 grams, saturated fat: .25 gram, monounsaturated fat: .75 gram, polyunsaturated fat: .40 gram, carbohydrates: 15 grams, fiber: .30 gram, cholesterol: 5 milligrams, sodium: 85 milligrams, protein: 1 gram (*If using egg substitute, levels of cholesterol, saturated fat, and total fat content will be slightly lower.)

Chilled Fruit Salad

Makes 4 servings (¾ cup per serving)

¾ cup halved seedless red grapes
¾ cup sliced ripe banana (1½ medium)
¾ cup grapefruit sections (1 large)
¾ cup cubed fresh pineapple
¾ cup unsweetened pineapple juice
⅛ cup frozen orange juice concentrate, thawed and undiluted
⅛ cup water

Combine all ingredients in a large bowl. Pour into a 13″ × 9″ × 2″ baking dish. Cover and freeze 8 hours or until firm. Let stand at room temperature 1 hour before serving or until slightly thawed.

Nutrition information per serving: calories: 55, fat: .2 gram, saturated fat: .05 gram, monounsaturated fat: 0 grams, polyunsaturated fat: .05 gram, carbohydrates: 14 grams, fiber: .9 gram, cholesterol: 0 milligrams, sodium: 1 milligram, protein: .6 gram

Mini Mexican-Style Pizzas

Makes 4 servings (1 tortilla per serving)

- 1⅓ cups seeded, diced unpeeled tomatoes
- 1½ teaspoons minced fresh cilantro
- 1½ teaspoons finely chopped green onions
- ½ teaspoon ground cumin
- ⅛ teaspoon garlic powder
- 1 tablespoon fresh lime juice
- 4 (8-inch) flour tortillas
- 1 cup fat-free refried beans
- ½ cup shredded reduced-fat Monterey Jack cheese

Preheat oven to 400°F. Combine first six ingredients in a bowl; stir well, and set aside. Arrange tortillas on baking sheets, and bake for 2 minutes. Turn over tortillas, and bake an additional minute. Spread ¼ cup beans over each tortilla; top with ⅓ cup tomato mixture and 2 tablespoons cheese. Bake at 400°F for 6 minutes or until the tortillas are crisp and the cheese melts; cut into wedges.

Nutrition information per serving: calories: 120, fat: 4.5 grams, saturated fat: 2 grams, monounsaturated fat: 1.5 grams, polyunsaturated fat: .80 gram, carbohydrates: 17 grams, fiber: 3 grams, cholesterol: 6.5 milligrams, sodium: 166 milligrams, protein: 8 grams

Pico de Gallo Salsa with Garlic Pita Triangles

Makes 4 servings (3 pita wedges and 4 tablespoons salsa per serving)

For the salsa:
  1½ cups seeded, chopped tomato
  ¼ cup chopped onion
  2 tablespoons chopped fresh cilantro
  1 tablespoon finely chopped serrano pepper

For the pita triangles:
  ½ tablespoon trans-fat-free margarine
  1 clove garlic, minced
  1 6-inch pita bread
  1½ teaspoons grated Parmesan cheese
  ½ teaspoon paprika

Preheat the broiler. Combine all the salsa ingredients in a bowl; stir well. Set aside. To make the triangles, begin by combining the margarine and garlic in a small microwave–safe bowl. Microwave on high for 30 seconds or until margarine melts. Split pita bread into two rounds, and brush margarine mixture evenly over the pita halves. Cut each half into six wedges, and sprinkle with cheese and paprika. Arrange pita triangles in a single layer on a baking sheet, and broil 1 minute or until golden. Serve with salsa while the triangles are still warm.

Nutrition information per serving: calories: 44, fat: .57 gram, saturated fat: .15 gram, monounsaturated fat: .15 gram, polyunsaturated fat: .3 gram, carbohydrates: 8 grams, fiber: 3.5 grams, cholesterol: 0 milligrams, sodium: 61 milligrams, protein: 1.5 grams

Index

Exercise, 11, 72, 177
  activity vs., 67–68
  aerobic, 66, 72–74, 177
  anaerobic, 72, 74
  benefits of, 71, 138–39
  for cardiovascular conditioning, 72
  determining safety of, 76–77
  for diabetics, 75–78
  and diary, 196–98
  fad programs for, 66–67
  and hypoglycemia, 77
  increasing, 64–78
  and insulin adjustment, 49
  intensity of, 73–74, 75, 77–78, 177
  log for, 117
  and medication, 77
  pros and cons of, 68
  regular, 71, 199
  and safety, 74–75, 78
  first scientific studies of, 30–32
  and stages of change, 79–81
  and type 2 diabetes, 51
  without weight loss, 138–39
Exercise log, 182, 184
Exercise mode, 73
Exercise-related injuries, 66
Exercise-tolerance test, 76, 77
Expectations, realistic, 101
Experiments, 32, 205
Eyes, 76

Fads, 66–67, 81
Farmers and farming, 10, 11, 12, 16, 30, 36, 71
Fast food, 15
Fast-acting carbohydrates, 46, 47
Fasting blood-sugar test, 50
Fasting plasma glucose, 5
Fat and calorie counter, 171
Fat cells, 7
Fat(s)
  absorption of, 158
  animal, 147
  in Atkins Diet, 142, 153
  beneficial, 60
  body, 26
  breakdown of, 4
  calories in, 146–47, 174
  in DASH diet, 56, 57
  in digestion, 22
  in DPP study, 34
  in fast food, 15
  as fuel, 22
  goals for, 168, 169, 189

healthy vs. unhealthy, 146–48
hydrogenated, 63
intake of, 61, 170, 172, 185, 190–91
  as main nutrient group, 2
monounsaturated, 60, 61, 147, 148, 164
partially hydrogenated, 63
polyunsaturated, 60, 61, 147, 148, 164
in processed foods, 14
in recipes, 189–91
reducing intake of, 35, 172, 182, 183, 190–91
saturated, 59, 60, 147
in South Beach Diet, 153
substituting for, 190–91
trans, 14, 59, 60, 63, 147
unsaturated, 147–48
in "value" meals, 96
in very-low-fat diets, 140–41, 141
in Zone Diet, 150
Fatty acids, 2, 4, 22
Fatty fish, 148
FDA See Food and Drug Administration
Federal regulation and lifestyle intervention, 210
Feelings, 98–99, 99, 122, 133
Feet, 6, 75–76
Fenfluramine, 158
Fen-phen (fenfluramine-phentermine), 159
Fiber, 54, 61, 63, 119, 140, 144
Fiesta Rice (recipe), 239
1,500-calorie a day meal plan, 215, 220–21
Filtering, 102
Finland, study of lifestyle changes in, 36–37
Fish
  fatty, 148
  Grilled Halibut Steak with Pineapple-Lime Salsa (recipe), 247–48
  and heart attacks, 39
  Tuna Steaks on Mediterranean Salad (recipe), 249–50
Fish oil, 39
5 A Day program, 192
Flavor, adding, 192
Flexibility, in eating plan, 168–69
Focus, regaining, 132
Follow-up, 125–26
Food and Drug Administration (FDA), 209
Food intake
  adjustment of insulin dosage with, 47–48

changes in, from 1971 to 2000, 13
in DPP, 170
increasing, 11–14
insulin adjustments for, 49
log for, 116, 119, 120
and lowering fat intake, 59, 60
self-monitoring of, 115–16, 118–20
underestimation of, 25
Food labels, reading, 171
Food(s)
and blood glucose, 47
choices in, 92–98
and digestion, 22
forbidden, 163, 164
free, 226
as fuel, 22
"healthy" vs. "unhealthy," 138
high-fiber, 199
high-sodium, 56, 57
and nutritional balance, 172
processed, 14
as reward, 98
tempting, 92
unhealthy, 93
variety of, 164, 172
wasting, 91–92
Foot ulcers, 6
Forbidden foods, 163, 164
Framingham Heart Study, 206
Free foods, 226
French fries, 94, 95
Fruit juice, 53–54
Fruit(s), 54
and blood pressure, 38
and blood-sugar, 119
daily servings of, 63
Chilled Fruit Salad (recipe), 256–57
increasing, 54

Garlic Pita Triangles, Pico de Gallo Salsa with (recipe), 258
Gastric bypass surgery, 159, 160–61
Gastric plication, 159, 160
Ghrelin, 160
Ginger-Infused Beef and Pineapple Stir-Fry (recipe), 246–47
Glimepiride (Amaryl), 85
Glucerna, 195
Glucophage. See Metformin
Glucose, 2, 4, 5. See also Blood glucose and blood-glucose levels
Glucose intolerance, 1. See also Prediabetes
Glucose-tolerance test (stress test), 5, 50

Glycemic index, 144–45
Glycogen, 2, 4, 22, 142
Goals
commitment to, 182
and dealing with problems, 123, 124
in DPP, 33–34, 168–69, 171, 172
focus on, 114–15
in high-risk situations, 134
for nutrition, 111–14
for physical activity, 111
setting, 107–8, 169, 186, 187
for weight loss, 108–10, 127
Golden Beet and Yukon Gold Gratin (recipe), 240
Gorgonzola Bruschetta with Crisp Apples (recipe), 228–29
Gout, 149
Gravy substitutes, 191
Grazing, 97–98, 197
Grilled Halibut Steak with Pineapple-Lime Salsa (recipe), 247–48
Guacamole, Creamy (recipe), 227–28
Gym, 67

Habit(s)
adjusting, 182
changing, 79–81, 87, 104
eating, 104–6, 127
forming, 85
and positive self-talk, 107
and relapses, 82
self-monitoring of, 165
Hair loss, 149
Half-size portions, 97
Halibut Steak, Grilled, with Pineapple-Lime Salsa (recipe), 247–48
Hamburger, 94
HDL cholesterol ("good" cholesterol)
affecting, 60
and Atkins Diet, 156–57
and lifestyle change, 60
and low-fat diets, 156
in metabolic syndrome, 8
in people with diabetes, 58
raising, 61
and very-low-fat diets, 141
Health Behavior Change: A Guide for Practitioners (S. Rollnick, P. Matson, and C. Butler), 82–84
Health risks (for weight loss programs), 127
"Healthy" foods, 138
Heart, 2, 76–77, 159
Heart attack, 39, 58, 74, 76, 78